D1272732

SCRATCH A SURVEYOR...

SCRATCH A SURVEYOR ...

The nearest anyone will ever get
to telling the story of Drivers Jonas,
traced through the diaries, letters, memos,
reports which might have been written
– and some that were –
between 1725 and 1975

by

Hugh Barty-King

HEINEMANN : LONDON

William Heinemann Ltd
15 Queen St, Mayfair, London W1X 8BE
LONDON MELBOURNE TORONTO
JOHANNESBURG AUCKLAND

© Drivers Jonas 1975

First published 1975

434 04900 x

Printed in Great Britain
by Richard Clay (The Chaucer Press), Ltd.,
Bungay, Suffolk

FOREWORD

by SIR DESMOND HEAP, LL.M., Hon.LL.D.

*Past President, the Law Society; Past President, the Royal Town Planning Institute;
Associate Member, the Royal Institution of Chartered Surveyors.*

I am a lawyer and in this year of grace, 1975, the Law Society has just celebrated its Sesquicentenary which means (I mention this only to show that I understand it myself – the reader, I know, has the matter at his fingertips) that the Law Society, this year, is 150 years old. But what is all that compared with the 250th Anniversary of Drivers Jonas which also falls in 1975? This book tells the story of this famous firm of Surveyors and happily – very happily indeed for the reader – it tells it in factual, fanciful and imaginative manner against the background of events of the time. I am honoured by the invitation to write this Foreword.

1725–1975; it is a long time but not too long for Drivers Jonas; it is the span of their continuous (and continuing) performance – two and a half centuries; twenty-five decades; in the words of that great English comedian (whom many of my generation remember with affection), Mr Syd Field, '*What a performance!*' It is indeed an astonishing performance by any standard of approach – an unchallenged record in the World of Surveying.

It is difficult to take the mind back to the times of 1725. The population of the United Kingdom in that year was $7\frac{1}{4}$ millions; today it is 56 millions. In 1725 it would still be 64 years before the Fall of the Bastille and at least 45 years before William Wordsworth – 'we must be free or die who speak the tongue that Shakespeare spake' – was to be born and, later, to be so affected by the 1789 Wind of Change blowing from the Continent of Europe.

The canals were waiting in the wings ready to take the stage (the Duke of Bridgewater was first onto the boards with his own historic 'cut') when all the 'measuring-up' by the surveyors had first been done, but the railways (the next major preoccupation of surveyors) were still in the far future. It would be another hundred years before 'Locomotion' would draw (by steam) the first '*train* of wagons' from Stockton to Darlington and the first train out of London (from 'Euston Grove' towards Birmingham) would not be leaving for another hundred and fourteen years. As for the Great Western Railway, there was (in 1725) more than a century yet to elapse before Mr Brunel would be laying-out (with the assistance of Drivers Jonas) his famous line from London to Bristol. Any firm that could accept (and survive) Instructions from the mighty Isambard Kingdom Brunel (seven-foot gauge and all) must be an Institution in its own right and worthy of a place in anybody's Hall of Fame.

And it all started in a market garden – 'We Drivers are country people, used to the land and the ways of cultivating it' – around the year 1725 when Samuel Driver (of Wandsworth) was to be found talking to his brother Charles Driver (of Rotherhithe) about 'inclosures' and about land not giving its full return and being, thereby, 'ripe for development'. Baking and market gardening (the Drivers did both) were all very well in their way but in 1725 Charles Driver, moving from tilling the land to measuring it (for in 1725 'Rotherhite, Sir, is a fast developing area' – the South Sea Company was at work thereabouts!) – Charles Driver was already 'set on the path of becoming a land-surveyor – indeed I would regard this year of 1725 as the beginning of an activity which I can see being associated with this family for many years to come'.

How right he was! A second generation of nurserymen-surveyors came along with Samuel Driver 2. There followed three further generations of Drivers, their surveying work developing and multiplying as the years went by. A redoubtable combination was that of Edward Driver and his nephew Robert Driver. These were the gentlemen – 'the Messrs. Driver' was the appellation by this time – who were Stewards to royalty, particularly in the matter of the New Processional Highway (Regent Street) from Carlton House to Regent's Park. Robert Driver was present at the Westminster Palace Hotel in 1868 at the creation of the 'Institution of Surveyors' (John Clutton in the Chair) and then began to look around for permanent headquarters 'somewhere near the Houses of Parliament if possible – Great George Street, for instance, would be ideal'. And so it proved.

The next generation of Drivers (the sixth) came with the birth of Charles Driver in 1853. His twenty-first birthday party in 1874 was an occasion big with fate for the partnership – a positive hinge on which a very great deal was to turn. It was a grand party and a gay evening. A good time was clearly had by all and not least by one Henry Jonas, a guest and a surveyor, who not only danced a quadrille with Mrs

Singleton (whoever that lady might have been) but then went on to do the lancers with Miss Maria Driver, sister of Charles. This was 'Cissie' (as she was affectionately known) and she was the point of no return for Drivers Jonas. In 1878 Henry Jonas married 'Cissie' Driver, the new dynasty being launched at Holy Trinity, Brompton, 'and afterwards at Melrose House, Cromwell Road'.

The partnership (like others) experienced the impact of Lloyd George's Land Tax of 1910 (seeing it come and seeing it go) and sustained itself through the First World War. In 1925 it celebrated its 200th Anniversary (who was it who seems to have forgotten the 100th Anniversary?) and in 1928 Henry Jonas died after the remarkable span of 50 years as partner. But by then another generation of Drivers and Jonases was already functioning including Harold Driver Jonas who also knocked up half a century as partner.

At the end of World War II a new figure takes the stage in the person of William Bishop – in 220 years only the second partner who had *not* been a member of the Driver family. A firm which had dealt (successfully) with Instructions from I. K. Brunel could well be expected to deal with the equally imperative requirements of the Corporation of Trinity House – the Lighthouse People – as embodied (for example) in the admonition of Sir Arthur Morrell, Deputy Master, when he declared (in delivering the formal instructions of the Corporation), 'Mr Bishop, we will not often give you a directive, but if we do please remember that we are seamen and have been used to giving orders from the bridge and having them carried out with alacrity'. And so it proved to be and in due time (in 1963) William Bishop was made a Younger Brother of Trinity House.

The eighth generation of Drivers and Jonases in the firm concluded with the retirement last year of Philip Jonas. But the line prevails and the ninth generation is today represented by Christopher Jonas, the recently retired Chairman of the Chartered Surveyors Junior Organisation.

Thus the eventful history of this famous firm persists and continues. Two and a half centuries of professional life are marked with this collection of glimpses into their past, seen through the everyday lives of the partners – while the reader is left the fascination of separating fact from fiction as Mr Barty-King's story unfolds. . . .

DESMOND HEAP

The Law Society,
  London.

CONTENTS

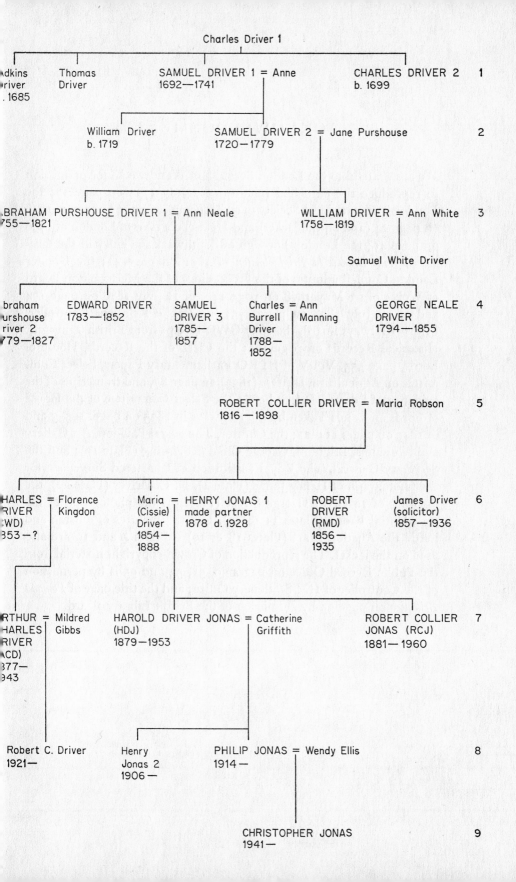

Charles Driver 1

1 | adkins river . 1685 | Thomas Driver | SAMUEL DRIVER 1 = Anne 1692—1741 | CHARLES DRIVER 2 b. 1699

2 | William Driver b. 1719 | SAMUEL DRIVER 2 = Jane Purshouse 1720—1779

3 | BRAHAM PURSHOUSE DRIVER 1 = Ann Neale 755—1821 | WILLIAM DRIVER = Ann White 1758—1819

Samuel White Driver

4 | braham urshouse river 2 779—1827 | EDWARD DRIVER 1783—1852 | SAMUEL DRIVER 3 1785— 1857 | Charles = Ann Burrell Manning Driver 1788— 1852 | GEORGE NEALE DRIVER 1794—1855

5 | ROBERT COLLIER DRIVER = Maria Robson 1816 — 1898

6 | HARLES RIVER WD) 353—? = Florence Kingdon | Maria (Cissie) Driver 1854— 1888 = HENRY JONAS 1 made partner 1878 d. 1928 | ROBERT DRIVER (RMD) 1856— 1935 | James Driver (solicitor) 1857—1936

7 | RTHUR HARLES RIVER CD) 377— 943 = Mildred Gibbs | HAROLD DRIVER JONAS (HDJ) 1879—1953 = Catherine Griffith | ROBERT COLLIER JONAS (RCJ) 1881— 1960

8 | Robert C. Driver 1921— | Henry Jonas 2 1906— | PHILIP JONAS = Wendy Ellis 1914—

9 | CHRISTOPHER JONAS 1941—

ACKNOWLEDGEMENTS

We are grateful to the London Borough of Wandsworth for permission to reproduce the parochial minutes of 7 July 1734 on page 17; the London Topographical Society part of Rocque's map of London of 1746 on page 24 (and on the jacket) and Horwood's map of London of 1799 on page 41; the London Borough of Southwark the entry in the *Companion from London to Brightelmston* of 1801 on page 41; the Greater London Council minutes of the Proceedings of the Metropolitan Board of Works of 23 May 1878 on page 149, of 12 July 1878 on page 174 and of 26 July 1878 on page 175; the Public Relations Controller, British Railways Board, the 1837 GWR receipt from British Transport Historical Records on page 105; the Clerk of the Records, House of Lords, page 555, Vol V of HLRO Parliamentary Papers, Select Committee on Agricultural Distress (1833) on page 87, and transcripts of the evidence of Edward Driver before the Select Committee of the House of Lords on Lands Taken by the Railways in 1835 on pages 100–3 and in 1845 on pages 114–21; the Curator, The Royal Pavilion, Art Gallery and Museums, Brighton, George Childs's drawing (Plate 13); and the Secretary-General, The Royal Institution of Chartered Surveyors, for the photograph of Henry Jonas (Plate 4), R. C. Driver (Plate 22), the drawing of 12 Great George Street (Plate 9), the photograph of the presidential badge (Plates 11 & 12), and the pictures of outside and inside the Auction Mart (Plates 18 & 19) – Plates 4 and 19 are also used on the jacket. The reproduction of Crown-copyright material from the Public Record Office on pages 39, 51, 53 and 95 is by permission of the Controller of HM Stationery Office; and the title page of *Pomona Britanica* on page 35 by permission of the British Library Board.

ILLUSTRATIONS

PLATES

The Eighteenth Century Drivers

———◆———

A 'NURSERY BUSINESS' TOO

The Abraham and William Partnership

1725–1802

Journal of Samuel Driver 1

October 15th, 1725

'Scratch a baker, a tailor, an undertaker, in Wandsworth these days, and you will find a market gardener.'

My remark was by way of explaining to the elderly gentleman about twice my age who had joined me and my brother Charles at our table in the garden of the Falcon Inn, how I, a thirty-three year old master baker, in this year of grace 1725 came to be concerned with garden-stuff. We were escorting him through the cauliflowers and turnips I grew on the land at Creek's Mouth I had been renting from the parish these last three years, with the intention of taking him for an excursion on the river Thames.

'I do not aspire to the feats of my Battersea neighbour with his forty acres of natural asparagus, and none of us here beside the Wandle have the reputation of Battersea for early cabbage. It is virtually one big market garden from the Piggery to Sheepgut Lane and Marsh Lane – some three hundred acres at least, I should say, within a mile of the parish church. There are ten thousand acres under cultivation for vegetables within four miles of Charing Cross and three thousand planted with fruit; and we in Wandsworth have our share. My acre here for which I might say I pay £9 6s a year makes its due contribution. I have seen Richard Chandler's camellias at Vauxhall, and very fine they are; but exotics are not for me.'

Our companion's questioning of our mode of life as we sat at the Falcon had been more than casual. He had dismissed with little more than a polite smirk the customary jokes with which one regales every newcomer to the inn touching the name of mine host, John Death – the one about drinking at Death's door and the one about those who neglected to pay their bills having Death staring them in the face. He returned at once to his searching enquiries. He was engaged, he said, in

3

a Tour Through The Whole Island of Great Britain, a report of which he was committing to paper and the first part of which was to be published within the month. In his tour, he said, he had covered most of the country, but had never seen the villages on the banks of the Thames except from the seat of a boat as it passed them by. He was now repairing that omission, though he was not at all sure that he would be able to include what he had seen in his book.

I caught the eye of brother Charles, and it was obvious that we were both of the same mind as to the identity of the man we were entertaining. 'From Richmond to London' said Mr Defoe – for assuredly it was he – 'the river sides are full of villages and those villages so full of beautiful buildings, charming gardens and rich habitations of gentlemen of quality, that nothing in the world can imitate it; no, not the country for twenty miles round Paris, though that indeed is a kind of prodigy. It is only since the Revolution that our English gentlemen began so universally to adorn their gardens with evergreens and led to the strange passion for fine gardens which has so commendably possessed the English gentlemen of late years.'

'Gentlemen may have their gardeners build them gardens to beautify their estates' I said, without I hope a hint of disapprobation, 'but we tradesmen have been making them with our own hands long before the events of 1688'.

By now we had walked from the Falcon and reached my market garden at Creek's Mouth.

'You are correct, of course,' he said, 'to distinguish what I might call pure gardening from the applied form which is a trade, an animadversion of a particular relevance at the present time as I am in the course of preparing a volume which I propose to call *The Complete English Tradesman*. The growing of herbs for medicinal purposes and the production of tinctures and essences, together with the supply of fruit and vegetables for the great markets of Westminster and London at the Stocks and Covent Garden to feed the ever increasing inhabitants of these congested areas, is a public service and the business of professionals.'

'We Drivers are country people, used to the land and the ways of cultivating it. We were yeomen farmers in Burstow and Nutfield in Sussex. We were forced from our smallholdings by a land grabbing landlord who threatened and intimidated, and when his blustering and ignorance was of little avail, began stealthily erecting fences over our land in pursuit of what was alleged to give authority, if not respectability, to his predatory activities – Inclosure.'

4

'A necessary step along the path of progress, but one which today we take in a more civilised manner.'

'If we were not to be allowed to use our traditional skills in sowing and reaping, we could take the wheat at a further stage in its processing and make loaves of it. My father Charles Driver was a baker, and I, the third of his four sons, am a baker too. I myself married six years ago and am the father of two sons and a daughter. My father came to this village before the Revolution and took a tenancy of a cottage here on land belonging to Mr John Symball, a brewer. There were five plots, but only three were built on. In 1686 Mr Symball fell into debt and raised a loan from a City gentleman, a Mr Laurence Wood of Holborn, by mortgaging the land to him. That two-fifths of the site should lie idle was of little consequence to Brewer Symball –'

'Until he was out of pocket.'

'– when it was too late. But to Mr Wood, whose mind was more attuned to commercial ways and making the best of what to him had become an investment, it was evident that land which did not give its full return was ripe for improvement.'

'Happy word! The key, Mr Driver, is it not, to all advancement? Where would we be in this enlightened age without our improvers?'

'My father being of similar way of thinking undertook to build tenantable cottages on the vacant messuages.'

'A pupil no doubt of Mr William Leyburn and the imbiber of the wisdom he distilled in that excellent publication of his, brought out for the edification of the public in 1685, if I recollect correctly, entitled *A Platform for Purchasers*.'

'My father was not, as you infer, a builder. He did not construct the cottages, but he did all else besides.'

'By way of a land-surveyor, you might say?'

'In a manner of speaking. He was not a plotter and measurer. He learnt from Mr Wood who had familiarised himself with the niceties of leases and agreements, covenants and distraints. The management of estates was Mr Wood's business. My father milked him of his experience, if you will excuse a farmyard analogy.'

'And he passed what he had learnt on to us.'

It was the first intervention into the conversation of my brother Charles, seven years my junior, who had finally thrown off the awe which had overcome him on realising that our chance acquaintance at the Falcon was the notorious – no, the renowned – Mr Daniel Defoe,

5

author of *Moll Flanders* and the *Shortest Way With Dissenters* the satire of which had backfired and landed him in gaol.

'To you at any rate' I said, laying my hands on Charles's shoulder. 'You are the man of property.'

'And so young?' smiled Mr Defoe.

'I came to Battersea to-day to meet my brother Samuel to discuss the implications of the will which I was advised to make in order to secure the continued benefit within the family of that part of the property I own in Wandsworth –'

'Which you have deserted for Rotherhithe' I said.

'You own property in Rotherhithe too?' Mr Defoe was visibly impressed.

'Rotherhithe, sir, is a fast developing area. A wet dock – the Great Dock as it was called – was built there in 1700, and the South Sea Company have taken a lease of it this year with a view of reviving the Greenland Fishery. They have re-named it the Greenland Dock. I have been assisting them. I am already set on the path of becoming a land-surveyor – indeed I would regard this year of 1725 as the beginning of an activity which I can see being associated with this family for many years to come. I can see the demand for the skills such as I have acquired never lagging, rather increasing. I would never aspire to be an estate steward; I have neither the education nor the family connections. It is a position for an attorney, younger son of the gentry. I am neither. The role of my kind is organising the essential part of buying and selling land which is the evaluation of its worth, and relying not on gossip and hearsay, but on what someone untouched by social taboos can give, sound commercial judgement.'

'A laudable Puritan sentiment' cried Mr Defoe. 'You are right, sir. The closed circuit of the feudal mode of life which is only just losing its grip on this country is opening up opportunities of service to the Crown and participation in the affairs of the country by the likes of you in a way that will transform society and bring you a prosperity hitherto undreamt of. The landed aristocracy who have been running this country for so long without let or hindrance are beginning to lose their domination, and not a moment too soon!'

'The services of the valuer' hazarded Charles, 'will be in demand as the population grows, as husbandry improves, manufacture develops, new forms of transport and means of construction evolve; as for us in our station of life, there is more learning and less warring.'

'If the Whigs and the middling class of which you and I, sir, and your

6

brother, are representative are allowed to inherit the earth, so be it,' said Mr Defoe. He welcomed the dismissal of the Stuarts and their time-wasting obsession with religion, as he termed it, as unhitching this country from a peg on which it could ill afford to remain suspended from reality for very much longer.

And then to my surprise he turned to Charles and said 'I trust the Jacobite cause has never held any attraction for you?' I knew that many suspected Mr Defoe of being a Government spy and I hastened to assure him in as light a manner as I could muster, that Charles might be the romantic member of the family but that high treason was an adventure of a kind no Driver would ever contemplate. 'Leave that to the Tories!' I said with a laugh designed to dispel any suggestion that I had taken his remark with any gravity or that it was in need of serious refutation.

'That the St John family' I continued 'have been lords of the manor of Wandsworth and Battersea these last hundred years – the father of the attainted Lord Bolingbroke still resides there – is no reason for thinking that the Jacobite sympathies of that iniquitous son of a noble house have rubbed off on us humbler folk, unconcerned with the great affairs of state and the intrigues of the court. Young Henry St John was born in the family mansion here nearly 60 years ago, but in the days of his youth he was more of a Whig than a Tory. Since then Wandsworth has seen little of him.'

'And for good reason!' sneered Mr Defoe. 'The court of Versailles and the 'court' of the Chevalier de St George at Comercy have had prior claim on his time. But only last month, as you will have read in your news sheets, he successfully petitioned Parliament to be able to inherit the family estate in spite of the attainder of ten years ago, and, no doubt against Mr Walpole's better judgement, an Act of Parliament has been passed to suspend the law by which his estates were forfeited. So Bolingbroke will be returning to these parts.'

'When his father dies.'

'He is 73.'

'You are well informed, sir.'

'It is my concern to be.'

'It is no concern, I can assure you, of Samuel Driver, master baker and market gardener, as loyal a subject of King George as any you will find in Wandsworth.'

The danger, if it ever existed, passed with Mr Defoe extolling Charles as, it seemed to him, a man of vision with an eye for the main chance and a head for business. 'At twenty five, twenty six? – with property to dispose of, partitioning it to your elder brother –?'

Charles was glad of the opportunity to explain, as much for my benefit as for Mr Defoe's.

'To all my brothers and sisters – in the absence of a family of my own' he said. 'I am yet a bachelor. Brother Samuel may consider me a romancer but for romances of the heart my time is too occupied to give serious consideration. Besides I have no wish to "settle down" – as yet. My next of kin are my brothers and sisters, and I wish them to share, so there should be no uncertainty and no dispute, the fruits of my good fortune and my industry. As you have said, it may be trite to say so, but these *are* unsettled times, and the hazards of cheating death are apparent to all. Life is cheap in 1725. It is nothing more than an act of business prudence to ensure that in the event of my career being cut short at the outset, those whom I love should benefit. Samuel here, who though not the eldest of my brothers has showed himself possessed of a commercial sense displayed by none of the others, I have made my sole executor.'

By way of explanation I told Mr Defoe that for some years now I had concerned myself in the parish affairs of Wandsworth and that Mr Edgley, the minister, and the churchwardens, were accustomed to turn to me when any matter arose involving the disposition of land and the drawing up of leases and the like. As a case which I happened to remember I instanced the occasion in March 1723 when Mr Acworth one of the churchwardens had been ordered at the Vestry meeting to warn me that the house wherein Mrs Moldham dwelt might be quitted and let to Mr Street, the sexton of the parish, according to an agreement for that purpose annexed to the lease of the house. There was also the occasion last October when the Vestry agreed that parish money standing out be called in and the South Sea Stock sold, and that the produce from it together with the outstanding monies be invested in the purchase of freehold land for the benefit of the parish. Here too I was consulted and asked to make the necessary arrangements.

Our conversation having thus reverted to the particular matter which Charles had come from Rotherhithe to discuss with me, and the fact not escaping the wit of our distinguished and sympathetic acquaintance, I invited him to accompany us for an excursion on the river, but he politely excused himself by saying that if we would permit him he would return to the Falcon, untether his horse and return to London by road.

Dusk was upon us, and on the point of Mr Defoe's departure there came the sound of men's voices from the river. A swaying lantern revealed a broad boat, well down in the water, slowly approaching our pier. Mr D. took fright, but I was able to assure him they were not the smugglers he took them for, though he was right in his assumption that the Wandsworth Creek was a favourite off-loading point for their contraband. It was Jack Salter and his men bringing me my regular load of horse manure from the London stables with the aid of which my ground became so fertile. Jack had come the five miles from Westminster on the tide with enough dung to supply most of the 220 acres of market garden beside the Thames at Wandsworth, and many of his customers on the 300 acres at Battersea. The naturally alluvial soil of the southern bank of the Thames supplied food for our plants indeed, I told Mr Defoe, and manifested a degree of fertility rarely surpassed in other parts of England, but my ration of Jack's steaming load gave my fruits and vegetables, and my young tree shoots, an added quality I could not do without.

July 30th, 1727

My unofficial assistance to the parish of Wandsworth in such matters as the rebuilding of the church steeple last year, advising them on leases and the management of their property, led to my being appointed two weeks ago, much to my gratification, an Overseer of the Poor in the place of Mr John Barker. At a meeting of the Vestry today I became closely involved in the discussion on plans for structural alterations to the church including taking down entirely the south west corner and staircase, and putting a diagonal beam or needle of oak across the belfry floor and shoring up the corner.

Letter from Charles Driver to his brother Samuel

Rotherhithe,
March 4th, 1728

Dr Samuel,

You were telling me that Wandsworth Vestry had charged you, as the parishioner acquainted with gardening matters and wood plantations, with the procuring of the timber required for the repairs to the church. Knowing that in fact you are little versed in the ways of buying and selling timber, I believe you would welcome an account of a conversation I recently had with Mr Batty Langley of Twickenham who has exposed the cheating and fraudulent methods adopted by many dealers in his book, publish'd last month, entitled *A Sure Method of Improving Estates by Plantations of Oak, Elm, Ash, Beech and Other Timber-trees, whereby Estates may be greatly improv'd.*

Awareness of such deceitful practices is of great benefit to me in my position, now well consolidated, of land-surveyor, whose business is so much concerned, as my own experience confirms, with advising ignorant stewards and agents about the timber on their master's estates – when to cut, how to cut in order to achieve the highest price, when to sell, where to sell, what is their true value in the market. Timber is an important and valuable part of any estate these days, and knowledge of it is essential to anyone who, like myself, seeks to advance, not so much as a measurer but in that branch of the surveyor's business which it seems to me will lead by greater fulfilment, greater respect and greater reward, namely that of the valuer.

It is as well that anyone who claims to give authoritative and professional advice as I do, on the improvement of an estate, knows, for instance, that on all timber trees of upwards of 20 years growth no tithes are payable, but if they are cut down before this time they become liable. To a steward of a large estate in Essex I met only last week this information came as somewhat of a shock, for he had just completed the extensive felling of a screen of elms to which he had taken some aesthetic objection. He had managed to persuade his master to concur and permit the felling – which he is unlikely to have done if he had known that the youth of the trees reduced the amount he would receive from their sale by the extent of the tithes due on them to the local vicar.

I must confess I am fast becoming fully knowledgeable with the aid of persons like Batty Langley on such matters as the suitability of old Roman Plane Trees for planting in walks and groves, the Portugal chestnut and lime tree for avenues, and the improvement which can be effected with aquaticks like poplars, oziers and willows. Such knowledge is all part of the surveyor's stock-in-trade, as I know you are well aware.

Your affectionate brother,
Charles

Journal of Samuel Driver 1

June 12th, 1727
The news sheets report the death at Osnabruck of King George I,

having been seized with a paralytic fit while riding in his carriage on the road to Hanover.

November 14th, 1727

At today's Vestry meeting we discussed a proposal for empowering the minister, churchwardens and overseers – I am one of two such – to join with the governors of Christ's Hospital in making a lease of the farm at Wilsdon to Daniel Hunt. We decided to ask the governors of Christ's Hospital to lay before the parish the proposed lease and an account of the security proposed to be given by Daniel Hunt. I undertook to do this on behalf of the Vestry, as well as to advise them on the present state of the trust concerning the farm at Wilsdon, to inspect the last lease of the property and Sir Francis Willington's will.

Letter from Revd. Samuel Edgley, MA, to Samuel Driver 1

The Vicarage, Wandsworth,
August 13th, 1728

Dʳ Mr Driver,

It ill behoves me to reproach a parishioner as faithful in his attendance and dutiful in the services he performs in behalf of the parish as you, but I confess I was sorely vexed when I saw you not only allow Mr Everard Falkener's unwelcome guest to pat your little Samuel's head while he stood beside you to watch Joe Comlyn taking the punishment he deserved in the stocks yesterday morning, but also to engage him, it seemed, in conversation. Mr Falkener's visitor – I cannot bring myself to mention his infamous name – rarely shows himself in public in Wandsworth, and for this we who live here and profess the Christian faith should be grateful. He is, I know, spending his time in our village with the worthy silk merchant at his house beside the common, whom he met in Paris, in order to learn our language which at present he speaks imperfectly. By thus doing he seeks to equip himself to converse with the merchants and men of letters and politics whom he will meet when he goes to the metropolis, in the hope no doubt of seeking to incline them towards the hateful doctrine which he unctuously calls 'Deism'. I cannot believe you would contaminate yourself willingly by contact with a man who reputedly speaks against Our Saviour and openly derides, so they say, the account given by the evangelists of

11

His birth and miracles. The only explanation I can give myself is that you did not know to whom you were talking.

Yours etc.

Sam¹ Edgley

P.S. Though I hope neither you nor any of your family will ever come to dissent from the Church of England, I would be able to tolerate that well enough, though all dissenters in my view are sorrowfully mistaken. But to deny Christ as the Son of God as do these so-called Deists (Lord St John is another) is an abomination I cannot recognise.

Letter from Samuel Driver 1 to Revd. Samuel Edgley

Wandsworth,

August 18th, 1728

Dʳ Mr Edgley,

The circumstances of my solicitation beside the pillory in the market place last Wednesday by the person who for some time now has been staying with Mr Falkener in Wandsworth, and we both know to be Monsieur Francois Arouet de Voltaire, was, I can assure you, altogether innocent and uncontrived. In talking to a distinguished Frenchman whose name will be remembered when yours and mine are long forgotten and whose lack of English did not prevent him from making the friendly gesture towards my son, I was only according to him the customary civilities.

It happened that my companion on this occasion, apart from young Samuel, was a fellow market gardener, Mr Thomas Fairchild, whom I was showing something of the life of village, as I presume Mr Falkener was doing for M. de Voltaire. Mr Fairchild has a renowned nursery in Hoxton whence he had come that afternoon to see me and my garden. He of course was unaware of the stranger's identity, and I was unable, I regret, to prevent him prounouncing at length, as is his wont to any whom he has not previously encountered, on his intention to leave the sum of £25 in his will for an annual Fairchild Lecture every Whit Tuesday in St Leonards Church, Shoreditch, on 'the Certainty of the Resurrection of the Dead Proved by the Certain Changes of the Animal and Vegetable Parts of the Creation'.

M. de Voltaire was not, I am pleased to say, able to understand one word of this declaration, or else there would have occurred, I feel sure, a public altercation of an unseemly nature which would have given your reverence just cause to reprimand

Yours very truly,
Samuel Driver

P.S. I am not a necromancer, but I have no reason at this time for believing that I, or Samuel, or any other of my children would dissent; but if Providence so decrees when I am no longer here to affect the decisions of those I have left behind, so be it.

Journal of Samuel Driver 1

March 20th, 1730

I have to-day been informed by Mr Lambrecht the Vestry clerk that I am one of three bakers in Wandsworth, along with John Stanford and Abraham Cross, appointed to serve the workhouse with the second sort of bread at 9 and the half peck loaf, each of us alternately a month at a time. Those that serve the bread, he says, are to bake the puddings gratis.

May 17th, 1732

At Rotherhithe yesterday, Charles introduced me to Mr John Warner – 'a gentleman of great curiosity' he said – who made a pipe of wine from a hundred and twenty vines in his Rotherhithe vineyard the first year of their bearing.

'I am becoming an authority of this particular mode of estate improvement' he said. 'I have raised the value of many an estate by recommending the planting of vines in parts of it hitherto neglected, the careful management of which can produce a valuable crop. More and more too, I am being asked to advise on the best way of making use of common land after enclosure. This of course is the worst kind of land imaginable; it is the land no one has wanted. That is why it has become common. It generally contains a variety of soils good and bad. Often as not it is a question of cutting away heath with a breast plow, turning up the turf and digging until you find marle. If the soil is too dry, you must devise a reservoir; if too wet, drainage. If it is sufficiently dry you can plough it and plant with liquorish, and then in March sow lettuce to stand for seed which would raise 40s an acre. If you lift the liquorish the third year, your acre will be worth £50. Plant another parcel with carrots, another with red rin'd turnip, and French yellow turnips;

another with buck wheat. It is a long drawn out process taming the wilderness, but so long as you know what you are doing – and this I make my business – Gold can come from Dirt.'

But there were many objectors, I said, and instanced John Cowper.

'Improvement will necessarily be accompanied by a degree of hardship,' said Charles. 'Enclosure means more tillage and less pasturage; that is the nub of most objections, and I am sure it is of John Cowper's. The small man is deprived of room to graze his cow, and the pleasure he derives from doing so. It was what our forebears suffered; our progress, such as it is, has come from their regression. The civilising process – call it what you will – can never stand still, and we surveyors are trying to guide it along the course that leads to the greatest happiness not only for the high, but the low, of the land.'

November 20th, 1733

To-day I submitted to the Vestry my application for a new lease of the property my father and, since his death, I, have been renting from the parish of Wandsworth and been occupying with my wife Ann these 15 years. I have asked for it to be renewed for a further thirty one years from Michaelmas last at a yearly rent of £15 10s according to the covenant of the former lease. I understand the churchwardens will soon be coming to oversee the house and the buttings (the bounds, that is), before agreeing to this.

Letter from Samuel Driver 1 to Revd. Samuel Edgley

Wandsworth,
February 11th, 1734

Dʳ Mr Edgley,

Cognisant as I am of your views on dissent, and not wishing that you should hear the news I am about to impart to you from sources other than myself, I thought it right to inform you that I am apprenticing my third son Samuel, who has shown an early aptitude in this direction, and has now reached the age of 14, to a distant relative of mine, Thomas Bincks by name, who hails from Southgate (Edmonton), is a member of the Clothworkers Company (by what token I know not for he had nothing to do with cloth), has been happily married since the year 1710 and – here comes the burden of my information – been a lifetime member of the Society of Friends. That Samuel whom you

14

christened at the font of All Saints in the rites of the established church is in no danger of allying himself with the Quaker connection, I can assert without fear of contradiction. These fine people do not seek now to gain new recruits; the tradition is handed from Quaker family to Quaker family. I mean no offence when I say that I greatly respect them. That they should show higher regard for Christian qualities than Christian dogma is something perhaps we can all admire without abandoning in any way our allegiance to the Church of which, you, sir, are so worthy a pillar.

My eldest son William is, as you know, taking over my bakery business. Samuel will be indoctrinated in what has always been my second love, the art and science of gardening, the production of fruit and vegetables and in particular the growing of trees and shrubs for planting out in estates for their improvement. In this he will have the benefit of the experience of his Uncle Charles at Rotherhithe who since 1725 has been fully established as a land surveyor and valuer. His services are already in demand, I understand, by the nobility and gentry in the home counties and beyond, whose confidence he has gained by his thoroughness and professional deportment. He has too, I understand, carried out a number of auctions of land in behalf of many such clients.

In recent years, as you will be aware, there has been a further bout of investment to improve rivers in order to make them suitable for inland navigation. Since 1720 surveyors have had the right to take levels and make a survey on the banks of rivers in preparation for a private Parliamentary bill, and in the last five years Charles has been engaged quite extensively on work of this kind.

In all these matters he will be anxious to share his knowledge with his nephew – he has remained a bachelor and Samuel will be to him as a son.

Mr Bincks's father had a nursery in Bermondsey, and Tom has a very much larger garden in Kent Street Road, a district I recollect being told by the celebrated Mr Daniel Defoe some years ago was beggarly and ruinous, but I trust is now, true to the spirit of the age, vastly improv'd. However that may be, here will Samuel Driver 2 enter upon his apprenticeship – the second generation of nurseryman-surveyors, a race for whom in these quickly changing times I foresee a great future.

Finely equipped as he will be with all he has learnt from Mr Bincks on emerging as a journeyman seven years from now, his talents will be much in demand. I trust you will join me in wishing him good fortune in his new venture and give him your blessing – if only to save him from too swift a surrender to the blandishments of the Quaker form of Dissent.

I am, sir, yours truly
Samuel Driver

Journal of Samuel Driver 1

July 7th, 1734

Malachi Hawtayne, I see, is in the ascendant. He has claimed, and the Vestry have agreed, that he and his family be allowed to sit in the pew in church which Mrs Moncks sits in. I see too that in the minutes which Mr Lambrecht the clerk was kind enough to show me in relation to another matter, that he is now styled 'Malachi Hawtayne *Esquire*', and that along with *Mr* Nicholas Constable has been appointed an Overseer of the Poor. I trust his elevation to the ranks of the gentry is not unassociated with the lowering of the Poor Rate to the sixpence in the pound which raises £86 – an event on which we are all to be congratulated. I would merely add without further comment that it has coincided with the appointment as a churchwarden along with Mr Buckler Young, the vintner, of *Mr* Samuel Driver, the baker.

I esteem this an honour and it is a parochial duty I am proud to perform. I am not unmindful either of the fine of £15 imposed on Mr Edward Applegarth who in 1728, if I remember, declined service as a churchwarden.

At the parishioners meeting to-day Malachi Hawtayne Esq announced that he had had the honour of seeing the Right Honourable Lord Viscount St John, Lord of the Manor of Battersea and Wandsworth, and that his lordship had wondered that we parishioners did not see to the getting of the grant he had formerly given to us for enlarging our burying ground on the hill. The matter was then discussed by all present and it was resolved earnestly to recommend the churchwardens – Buckler Young and myself – to wait upon Mr Osborn, Lord St John's steward, to know the compass of the ground which his lordship was pleased to give the parish and to execute what deed his lordship pleased. We were enjoined to make a report of our visit at the next Vestry meeting so that the proper workmen could be employed to do whatever was necessary.

At a meeting of the Parishoners in
Free & open Vestry the 7th July 1734, —

Present.

Mr. Buck: Young } Church Wardens
Mr. Sam: Driver

Mr. Nich: Constable. Overseer

Mab: Hawtayne Esqr

Mr. Tho: Smith	Mr. Tho: Skinner
Mr. Richd Stables	Mr. John Hoanes —
Mr. John Barker	Mr. Jno. Stanford
Mr. Jas: Stocker	Mr. Hugh Cumlyn
Mr. John Winter	Mr. Daven: Hamond

Mab: Hawtayne Esqr being present acquainted the parishoners then in Vestry that he had the
Honour of seeing the Right Honourable Lord
Viscount St John and that His Lordship wondered
that the parishoners of this Parish did not see
to the setling of the Grant He had formerly given
to them for to Enlarge their Burying ground on
the Hill. — — —

Wherefore it is Ordered and earnestly recommended to the present Church Wardens to wait
upon Mr. Osborn (His Lordships Steward) to —
know the Compass of the ground His Lordship is
pleased to give to this parish to enlarge the said burying ground and forthwith to Execute what —
Deed His Lordship pleases for the same and to
make report thereof to the next Vestry to the Intent
that proper Workmen might be employed to do the
same. — — —

Wandsworth Parochial Minutes of July 7th, 1734

February 8th, 1735

Talk which followed the termination of the business part of the visit of churchwardens to Mr Osborn was admittedly not on any high intellectual level, but that was not to say that, accelerated by the latter's claret it was not convivial.

The professional verdict of Mr Young the vintner was that the wine was of a rare quality, and he followed this assertion, which was based on lengthy tasting, by querying whether in Mr Osborn's considered opinion the use of part of his master's estate as burying ground could strictly be referred to as improvement.

'Within the meaning of the Act' I said, looking Mr Osborn in the face and taking my cue from Buckler's serio-comic demeanour.

'What Act?' said Mr Osborn in a tone which demonstrated that he was not yet in accord with our mood.

'As used in common parlance' said Buckler, gesturing with his hand in the French manner.

'Parliaments?' expostulated our host. I had not thought Buckler's speech was that slurred.

'Parlance.'

'Oh.'

'Planting carrots one day' said Buckler eyeing his glass as if on the verge of enunciating a philosophical observation of great moment, 'and corpses the next. Improvement?'

'The benefit' said Mr Osborn drawing himself up in his chair, 'is to the parish, not his lordship.'

'If improvement is to be achieved by digging' pursued Buckler not to be deterred, 'a more pertinent use of their spades in my opinion would have been the creation of an ornamental water in which carp and tench could be allowed to breed and, if they survived the frost, greatly multiply – particularly, if cattle have access to it for the fish will thrive, am I not right Mr Driver, on account of the nutriture in the dung.'

Mr Osborn, who prided himself on being a gentleman, was not entirely prepared for a discourse of this nature to take place in his room in milord St John's mansion, and to hide his confusion he buried his nose firmly in his glass. But with the subject thrown so deftly in my direction I felt it my duty to support my fellow-churchwarden by contributing information to which as a market gardener I had special access. Indeed I had been consulted on numerous occasions by gentlemen wishing to improve their estates by the addition of ponds and lakes, and was glad of the opportunity of impressing on Mr Osborn my competence in this regard in the event of Lord St John contemplating such a project.

'Not only frost but frogs antagonise fish' I asserted with an authoritative air. 'I recollect on occasion when my advice had been sought on this very matter by Lord Mulworthy when I was able to indicate to his lordship several frogs chasing tench. To the astonishment of both of us we then observed a frog with its paw in a tench's eye, which rendered it motionless on the surface of the water. As soon as the fish was disengaged from its enemy, however, it soon recovered. Though frogs only tease and chase tench in this way, they destroy carp.'

When I had finished, Mr Osborn came over to fill our glasses, a welcome gesture which to me indicated he had taken my observations on frogs in good part. Did he concur, I asked him as he poured the wine, with the advice given by Mr Edward Laurence in his *Office and Duty of a Land-Steward* published as recently as 1727 that the efficient steward should have a map drawn out of the estate he managed in the most perfect method, which might serve to show not only the quantity but also the true figure of the parts as well as the whole; which represented the bends in the hedges and other boundaries so clearly that any fraud in alienating even the least part might be quickly detected?

He said there were few stewards in England who had not had Mr Laurence's book called to their attention. He agreed with his remarks about the map and had already had a surveyor make one for him before he had read what he could only describe as a thoroughly offensive attack on the work of stewards and agents. In his preface Laurence said he had learnt of the ignorance and slothfulness of some stewards and the knavery and wickedness of others. These were not attributes which could be laid at his door, he hoped; and Buckler and I were quick in nodding our heads in assent.

'If we fail in our stewardship,' he said, 'there are many others in these times ready to take over. I have taken to heart the observation of Mr Addison which is probably well known to you and I have copied out so it should look me in the face whenever I sit down to this desk.'

He took a sheet of paper in his hand and read to us.

' "It is the misfortune of many other gentlemen to turn out of the seats of their ancestors, to make way for such new masters as have been more exact in their accounts than themselves; and certainly he deserves the estate a great deal better who has got it by his industry, than he who has lost it by his negligence." '

19

April 13th, 1735

The churchwardens reported that the Rt Hon. Lord Viscount St John had executed a lease bearing date 7 April for 31 years at a yearly rent of two shillings p'annum. The parishioners of Wandsworth having ordered and directed Mr Young and Mr Driver to apply to and entreat Lord Viscount St John to grant them a piece of waste ground adjoining the burying ground belonging to the parish as an addition to the burying ground in July 1734, the indenture of the lease dated 7 April 1735 is presented between Viscount St John, Baron of Battersea, Lord of the Manor of Battersea and Wandsworth of the one part, and Buckler Young, vintner, and Samuel Driver, baker, churchwardens of the other part. So Lord St John did demise to Mr Young and Mr Driver all that piece of waste ground lying at the East end of the town of Wandsworth – 117 ft in breadth to the East, 94 ft to the West and 56 ft long – to be enclosed with a brick wall to be used as a burying ground and nothing else for 31 years from Lady day last at a yearly rent of two shillings.

William Porter and Mrs Loat did the work of enlarging the burying ground for £33 7s and were paid 2s for cutting down docks and thistles.

Letter of Samuel Driver 2 to his 42-year-old Uncle Charles

Kent Street Road,
September 17th, 1741

Dʳ Uncle Charles,

The coincidence of my father's death – I hear he was well enough to attend a Vestry meeting on the 13th – and the completion of my apprenticeship in the market garden here of Mr Bincks both falling in the same month has been a double milestone pointing two ways, giving cause for reflection on a happy past under the guidance of a wise and resourceful Parent and a peering into a future released from the tutelage of a knowledgeable Master. I am comforted in the knowledge that the family bakery will continue in the capable hands of my brother William, as eldest son and heir, who will maintain the estate in Wandsworth as Samuel Driver 1 would have wished. I have set a new path for myself, away from Wandsworth, away from traditional family skills, as befits a younger son. The talents I have now acquired from Mr Bincks encourages me to establish myself as a market gardener, nurseryman and seedsman, and to do so in this part of Surrey – Walworth and South-wark – where I have put down new roots in the course of my seven years as an apprentice. I have become part of the community here, and in particular of Mr Bincks's circle, most of whom of course, as you know, are members of the religious Society of Friends. My increasing sympathy with their way of life is something – and I know you will not misunder-stand me in this – which can better flourish now that my dear father has been taken from us. As an ardent member of the Church of England and faithful worshipper at All Saints, Wandsworth, his views on Dissent could not have been other than they were. I now look to you, dear Uncle Charles, in the absence of my late departed parent, to be my mentor and adviser, particularly as it is you who have been the first of the Drivers to devote your energy to the work of surveyor and valuer in which I also seek to succeed, allied with the practice of market garden-ing which contributes so greatly to estate management. I trust you will give me the benefit of your wide experience in Rotherhithe, and beyond, in all aspects of estate improvement, and in the part played by survey and valuation for the mode of improving roads through the new turn-pike trusts, and give very much needed confidence to

Your affectionate nephew,
Samuel Driver

Letter from Uncle Charles to Samuel Driver 2

Rotherhithe,
October 14, 1754

Dr Samuel,

You need have no fear that your father would have disapproved of your joining the Society of Friends and proposing to marry one of their number. I would say 34 was an admirable age at which to marry, and it seems you have found in Miss Purshouse a woman of exceptional qualities, with a captivating modesty combined with a refreshing wit and sense of fun which endear her to all who have met her. Your mother, I know, was enchanted by her. As it happens, I have carried out a number of surveys in the vicinity of Tipton where she was born and know well the part of Staffordshire where she spent her childhood. Mr John Purshouse, her father, and his wife Margaret, are held in the highest esteem in those parts. It is, I realise however, Mr Abraham Purshouse her bachelor uncle, to whom she is most beholden since living in Bermondsey – so uncles stand *in loco parentis* for both parties! I hope soon to make this gentleman's acquaintance either at his house in Mill Street, Southwark, or at Tom's Coffee House in Tooley Street of which I understand he is a member.

With Jane at your side your aspirations for a career in the line you have set your heart on cannot but be fulfilled. I will continue to help you, as I have done since you completed your time with Tom Bincks in 1741, in every way I can. I look forward to attending your wedding in Horsleydown Meeting House and to hearing from you the date and time as soon as these are fixed.

Sincerely, your affectionate uncle,

Charles Driver

Journal of Samuel Driver 2

November 29th, 1754

Ours was one of the first Quaker weddings to take place after the 'Rules for Proceeding in relation to Marriage' had been printed and circulated to all meetings to make a general practice uniform throughout Britain. A wedding is not made a separate occasion as in the Church of England; there was no 'service' and no ritual. At the end of the midweek 'meeting' at James's meeting house at Horsleydown in Bermondsey yesterday morning, we rose from the front wooden bench on which we had been sitting and stood hand in hand before them all. 'In the fear of the Lord and before this assembly, I take this my friend Jane to be my wife, promising through divine assistance to be unto her a loving and faithful husband until it shall please the Lord by death to separate us.' Thus I declared, and Jane followed in identical terms. We then sat down. It was all over save for the signing of the certificate and the congratulations of my dear mother, brothers and sisters.

Entry in Register of Quaker Births

30.8.1755

Driver, Abraham Purshouse   Kent Street Road, Parish of St George the Martyr, Southwark

Name of parents: Samuel and Jane

Occupation: Gardiner

1.7.1758

Driver, William   Kent Street Road, Parish of St George the Martyr, Southwark
Name of parents: Samuel and Jane
Occupation: Gardiner

Letter from William Driver to his brother Samuel Driver 2

Wandsworth,
July 17th, 1761

Dr Samuel,

  I am not a great letter writer as you know, but as head of the family I am moved to write to you on the occasion of the death of our dear mother in anticipation of all of us meeting at All Saints for her funeral. I know of your views as a Quaker of our forms of mourning and our service of burial, but I know this will not deter you and Jane from being with us all at the graveside of our beloved parent on Friday. I realise in the seven years since you completed your apprenticeship you are very much more than the market gardener and nurseryman which Mr Bincks taught you to be, and that your knowledge of local land tenures and values has led to a demand for your services as land-surveyor and valuer in a way our dear father became involved in a minor way through his Garden at Creek's Mouth. I hear you have on occasion conducted auction sales of the property of some of those to whom you have given advice on means of improving their land by the growing of timber. The scope here for your talents is obviously very great – very much greater I must admit than bakery, though of late I have branched out into confectionery and pastry and have met with some success with my brides cakes. I have little time for coming to the metropolis these days but we made a special excursion by river last month to see the coronation procession of King George III – it was the first time I had seen the new bridge at Westminster (I realise it was built in 1750 which shows my attachment to rural life in Wandsworth!), but it is good at last to have a second crossing of the Thames. The news sheets assert the Young Pretender was in the crowd that watched the procession – could this have been so?

  Our dear mother, now departed, was, I know, very proud of your advancement, Samuel, and looked to you to bring lustre to the Drivers, as I know you will, in a way that can never be accomplished by

Your affectionate brother
William

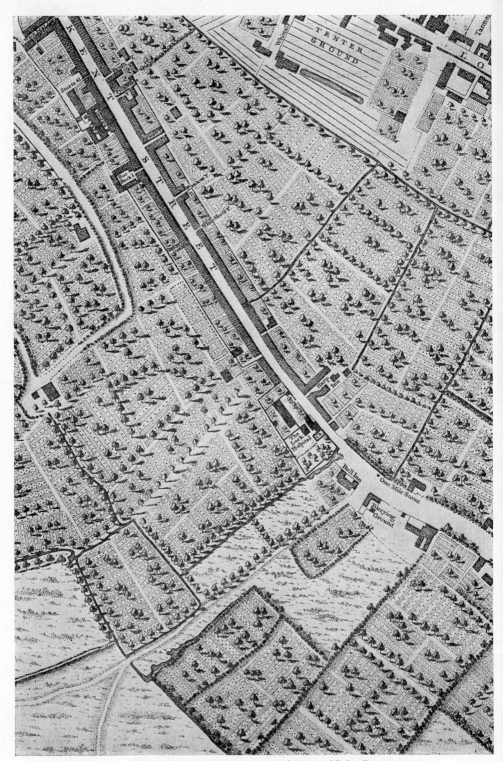

Part of Kent Street from 1746 Map of John Rocque

24

July 22nd, 1766

Probate has been given to the will of my dear Jane's uncle Abraham who died earlier this year. A bachelor, he had no son to whom to leave his property, and he has bequeathed a large parcel of freehold land off Kent Street Road to Jane. It seems to me that we should build houses here – one perhaps for ourselves – and develop it as the beginning of our own 'estate', using the arts we have accumulated in developing the property of others. I trust there will be occasion for me to employ my skills in land valuation in which I am more and more occupied, in the new form of inland navigation made possible not merely by improving *rivers* but actually cutting *artificial waterways* through land which has to be surveyed and acquired for the purpose. The first of these 'canals', as they are calling them, which the Duke of Bridgewater has devised to link his Worsley collieries with Manchester, and the even earlier Sankey Brook Canal, are now in operation. Before this was possible a very great amount of work must have been done by way of survey of the land as to its feasibility and its eventual purchase. I can see these canals becoming a great source of work for us land-surveyors; civil engineers will be employed in the construction, but we should be brought in for negotiating the land purchase and settling the many disputes which the cutting of artificial waterways running across the country are bound to give rise to.

In the meantime, increasing call is being made on my services as an auctioneer for which I seem to have an aptitude, and I confess I enjoy for its involvement with people as opposed to paper and figures, and for its drama. I went by coach on Monday to Reigate to make the final arrangements for the sale to take place later in the week at the Devil Tavern, Temple-Bar of the manor, and lately dissolved priory, belonging to the late Mrs Parsons. I joined the coach at the Golden Cross, Charing Cross and my companions in the inside compartment were a lady of uncertain age, a young attorney and rough looking farmer who as soon as we were on the road lit up a cigar whose tobacco fumes were soon filling the coach. In as polite a manner as I could muster I asked the smoker to desist in deference to the lady, but to my complaint he paid no heed. The attorney said that if he wished to smoke he should exchange his for one of the outside seats, but the lout insisted that he had paid for an inside seat and there he intended to remain. At Worplesdon where we stopped to change horses the young attorney immediately alighted and returned bearing two tallow candles in his hands. As soon as we were once more on our way he lit one of the candles, and as soon as it had burnt down he lit the other one with it and then blowed it out, whereupon the wick emitted a dark cloud of smoke of such a stench, as anyone who is familiar with the acrid fumes of tallow can testify, that we all held our breaths. The young man asked the dear lady if she had any objection, and she, cottoning on, protested that she had none. The atmosphere inside the coach was now unbearable but we suffered it in silence in the hope of the intrigue succeeding, which it did. For at the next stop our farmer friend took the hint and climbed into a vacant seat on the roof where he could puff away till only his lungs, and not the close confinement of the coach, were filled with the smoke of the burning weed.

The sale of Reigate Priory was a complicated matter which required detailed preparation if the auction, already planned to cover two days, was not to take a week. The priory itself was not a large estate, only some 76 acres in the occupation of one Richard Dalton, whose lease expired at Christmas, but Mrs Parsons' estate included several freehold and copyhold lands, tenements and hereditaments in Surrey, Sussex and Middlesex. There were nineteen lots to be sold and apart from the Priory included several farms with around 100 acres each – one, Hungerford Farm with 180 timber trees, willows and pollards, was at Nutfield where we Drivers were once said to have been yeoman farmers ourselves, and I was of a mind to purchase it myself.

The Conditions of Sale were the usual ones of the premises being put up in the condition they were now, no bidding being taken less than five pounds for each lot. The purchaser – the one who had made the highest or best bid – was to pay ten pounds per cent on the purchase money as a deposit, and the remainder on a legal conveyance before November 26th 1766. The vendor was to pay all taxes, rates & c of all the lots other than the Priory up to September 29th; on the priory up to December 25th.

At the invitation of Mrs Bedwyn, the daughter of the late Mrs Parsons whose estate was being disposed of, who had been supervising the final details with me at the Priory, I returned to town in her chaise. It was now the end of the day, and dark. As we passed through a lane overhung with trees a figure on horseback pushed by between the chaise and the hedge on my side. 'Stop!' he cried, and as he did so, realising his business, I had the presence of mind, before letting down the glass, to take out my watch and stuff it within my waistcoat under my arm.

'Your purse and watches' said the man.

'I have no watch' said I.

'Then your purse.'

It contained eleven guineas and I gave it to him. I could not see his hand in the darkness, but I felt him take it. He then asked for Mrs Bedwyn's purse.

'Don't be frightened' said he, 'I will not hurt you.'

'Indeed!' I huffed haughtily.

'I give you my word I will do you no hurt' said the gallant highwayman. Mrs Bedwyn gave him her purse and was about to add her watch but, before she could do so, he said, 'I am much obliged to you! I wish you good night!' pulled off his hat and rode away.

'You took that all very calmly' I said in admiration of her cool composure throughout the ordeal.

'On the contrary, I am in terror lest he may return, for I have given him a purse with only bad money in it that I carry on purpose for such an occasion as this.'

She smiled when I showed her the watch I withdrew from under my arm, but I could feel her trembling with apprehension as we continued our journey towards town.

August 17th, 1769

Abraham, the son and heir of whom I am justly proud, showing as he does all the Quaker virtues of application and industry, is now 14 and must soon be entering on a term of apprenticeship which will determine the course of his future activity; and in order to introduce him to the wider world of market gardening as practised beyond my own nursery I arranged with my Quaker neighbour – and competitor! – Mr James Maddock (who hails from Warrington in Lancashire and is the proprietor of the extensive Walworth Nursery which contains 320 sorts of gooseberry tree) for us to take him on a little tour of some of the leading gardens and nurseries in London. We visited first The Forty Acres at Kennington part of which is the oval plot of the nursery belonging to Mr William Malcolm begun by him in 1757. When Mr Malcolm told me that this year he had supplied plants to the Princess Dowager of Wales for the Kew Garden, I could not but be envious as, though I now have a considerable connection with the landed aristocracy, I would greatly value an entree to royalty and the prospect of being appointed, say, one of the surveyors of the Crown Estates. But as this was my first meeting with Mr Malcolm through the courtesy of James Maddock, I did not presume to press for details as to how he had obtained his order from the Princess.

We moved to George Neal's Pinery Nursery in Camberwell which specialises in pineapples, and then to the 18 acre Vineyard Nursery which Lewis Kennedy and James Lee run at Hammersmith. James Williamson showed us round his Kensington Nursery. These are all certainly larger than anything we know in Wandsworth or Battersea, though in Walworth and Southwark our gardens are assuming very large proportions. The increase in the population of London – I am told it has almost doubled from five to ten million since the Revolution of 1688 – is straining the resources of London's market gardens to the utmost; though the improvement of the roads which lead to Westminster and the City by the turnpike trusts is making it possible to bring produce from more distant gardens than hitherto, and I suppose the day will come when London no longer has room for its market gardens.

Young Abraham was, I think, duly impressed by what he saw and heard, and from what he told me is determined to become one of us, appreciative as he is of the promise that the business of nurseryman holds out for improvement in his own status through involvement to an ever increasing extent in the realm of estate management – he came with me on my survey of Dane-end Farm at Weston, Herts, last year.

February 10th, 1770

'There was an occasion, sir, when my father, warmed by claret, debated with the steward of Viscount St John at Battersea – the father of the infamous Bolingbroke you will remember – whether land converted to a burying ground could strictly be regarded, at the end of it all, as *improved*. I put it to you, sir, warmed by no more than the ale of the landlord of the George whose hospitality we are now enjoying, whether the removal of the entire hamlet of Milton to satisfy the aesthetic sensibility of the one-time James Damer Esquire now Baron Milton, and doubtless soon to become Earl of Somewhere or Other, who has become obsessed with the overriding importance of a fine vista from his morning room window, is not so far from being an improvement as to be capable of being condemned as an outright act of vandalism.'

'From the day I first set eyes on Milton Abbey and Milton' said my drinking companion, 'it was evident to a trained eye such as mine that the land had great capability of improvement.'

Mr Lancelot Brown, Royal Gardener, had still not lost the use of the phrase which had earned him the sobriquet by which he had been universally known these twenty years. In supplying him plants and trees for his many exercises in landscape gardening I had effected a casual acquaintance with Capability Brown, but had never before had an opportunity of a serious discussion with him over the morality of much of his work, from the standpoint of a Quaker, in particular the wholesale transformation of large areas of land of which his god-like treatment of Milton was a notorious example. The lords of Stowe, Castle Howard and Nuneham Courtenay had removed villages which blocked a clear view, but only a few houses had had to go. At Milton, in Lancelot Brown's opinion, the whole village stood in the way, containing more than a hundred houses.

'If it takes us twenty years, as well it may, his lordship intends to carry out my scheme' he said.

'*Pace* Mr William Harrison,' I could not resist interjecting. He was the Milton solicitor who was refusing to surrender his lease and was defying Capability and his master to demolish his homestead except over his dead body.

'We can wait for Mr Harrison.'

In any event it would probably take them the remainder of that modern Village Hampden's lifetime to level the other village houses, the School House, the market place, the King's Arms and the George Inn at which we were sitting, sow the empty space with lawns and plant the hillside with trees, and build a new village out of sight of his lordship's line of vision, to which the Jacobean almshouses, for fear of upsetting the Commissioners for Charitable Uses, were to be removed stone by stone. I wondered whether the Royal Gardener had read William Cowper's verse.

> Improvement too, the idol of the age,
> Is fed with many a victim. Lo, he comes!
> The omnipotent magician Brown appears!
> Down falls the venerable pile, the abode
> Of our forefathers . . .
> He speaks, the lake in front becomes a lawn;
> Woods vanish, hills subside and valleys rise,
> And streams, as if created for his use
> Persue the track of his directing wand.

And I was aiding and abetting this vandal! He had read Cowper's strictures and was unrepentant. Who was I to pit myself against Capability Brown! The boldness of my opening declaration deserted me and I never learnt what moral basis, if any, he claimed for the rightness of projects such as that at Milton. But back at home and reading once again of the plight of The Deserted Village as described by Dr Goldsmith published last month, my indignation returned. What of the village master who, it seemed, was aspiring to do the work of the surveyor?

> The village all declar'd how much he knew;
> 'Twas certain he could write, and cypher too;
> Lands he could measure, terms and tides presage,
> And even the story ran that he could gauge.

> . . . The man of wealth and pride
> Takes up the space that many poor supplied;
> Space for his lake, his park's extended bounds,
> Space for his horses, equipage and hounds;
> The robe that wraps his limbs in silken sloth
> Has robb'd the neighbouring fields of half their growth,
> His seat, where solitary sports are seen,
> Indignant spurns the cottage from the green.

Journal of Abraham Driver

June 18th, 1779

It is difficult to believe it can be the Will of God to remove so active a parent at the early age of 59 and to shift the responsibility for the variety of activities in which he was engaged as nurseryman and land-surveyor on to my inexperienced shoulders at the age of 24. But to maintain what he built in his short lifetime, and to build on it yet again, must be my sole concern, and that of my brother William who joins me in partnership on achieving his majority this year. Now that I am myself just married — Ann Neale honoured me with her hand last year – and I am the father of an Abraham Purshouse Driver 2 to perpetuate the line, the burden is heavier still, but with the help of God I will carry it – and relish the challenge of Providence.

Ann and I have built ourselves a handsome modern brick house with an elegant and spacious conservatory 240 ft in length and 24 ft width behind it, on the land she inherited from her uncle Abraham on the southern side of Kent Street Road opposite the One Mile Stone and beside Lock's Fields – Mr John Rocque in his map of London, Westminster and Southwark of 1746 indicated The Lock Hospital which abuts our land and the neighbouring Bull Inn. My brother William remains with my mother in the family home only a few yards distant on the other side of the lane which enters Kent Street Road at this point, concerning which there are rumours that there is an intention on the part of the Surrey authorities to make it into a public highway linking Kent Street with Walworth Road. [*See* map page 24.]

Indenture of December 30th, 1780

Sale of premises in order to make a public highway from Kent Street Road to Walworth by the Bishop of Winchester the landlord to John Pardon, Surrey Treasurer in trust.

The land represented in the drawing in the margin of the deed in green consisting of a certain lane called East Lane situate in the parish of St Mary Newington Butts containing in breadth thirty feet as the same is now marked and staked out and intended to form part of the road . . . and also that piece of land marked in the plan blue consisting of a certain close or parcel of land called Lock's Fields containing a breadth of thirty feet . . . also land marked red consisting of such part of certain closes of land situate near the dwelling house of Abraham Purshouse Driver in St George Southwark and part of the Nursery Garden of the said Abraham Purshouse Driver and in his occupation, and containing in breadth thirty feet and intended to form the residue of the said road . . . The road is to be a public highway.

Journal of Abraham Driver

December 30th, 1780
'So we too, Tom, in the midst of Walworth and Southwark are as much the victims of compulsory purchase as any countryman who has had to surrender to Enclosure!'
The other signatory to the deed of sale for the purpose of the new highway between Kent Street and Walworth was 'Thomas Clutton of Walworth, gentleman' kinsman of William Clutton son of the vicar of

Horsted Keynes who been articled as a land-surveyor to Robert Chat-field of Cuckfield, and we are having a drink together after the signing at Furnival's Inn Coffee House in Holborn.

We had just lit our pipes when we were joined at our table by a young man who on hearing the word 'enclosure', lit his pipe at the wax candle on our table and launched into a diatribe which left us little room for interruption.

'You gentlemen, like I, have doubtless read in this coffee house the pamphlet published last week entitled *An Enquiry into the Advantages and Disadvantages of Enclosures*. What an erroneous picture that pamphlet depicts of the plight of the cottagers! These I can assure you, as someone acquainted with the true state of affairs at first hand, are habitations of squalor, famine and disease, and command no sympathy. Seats of cleanliness? On the contrary they are fruitful seminaries of all kinds of vice. A common an Arcadian field, with shepherds living in Arcadian purity and innocence? A romantic dream. Are peace, plenty, good humour, philanthropy, religion to be met with there as the pamphleteer asserts? Are we really to believe that to give property to the poor will make them happy? To be led by the laws of charity will only lead to confusion, the encouragement of fraud, the destruction of justice. *Time* has condoned the encroachment of the labouring man who has erected his cottage on the common land; but the forbearance of the real owner has not established the encroachment as "property". This is no time for sentimentality. We have a National Debt of £70 million and the distress of the people must increase whatever the outcome of the war with the rebellious American colonies. What is needed is a general Act of Parliament for the enclosure of *all* the lands of England worth cultivating, in place of these time consuming individual bills.'

Tom Clutton and I sat and listened to this outburst with what we considered to be composure. Neither of us had in fact read the pamphlet in question, being less frequent visitors to the coffee house than our friend, so we found it difficult either to agree or disagree. In any event before we could hazard an opinion, we were joined by the man we had hoped to meet and who had introduced us to the Furnivals's Inn Coffee House in the first place, Thomas Stone, whose views on Enclosure we knew to be decisive, and hearing the last part of our friend's speech had no hesitation in making *his* point of view eminently clear.

'Enclosure of common fields' said Tom Stone, 'will be proved to be attended with good or bad consequences to the community in proportion to the good or bad management which is adopted on the occasion.'

'And it is for us, the land surveyors and valuers who have studied the best means of such improvement to provide the gentlemen of landed property with that technical advice they lack' I said.

December 4th, 1782

I was in Norwich to-day in connection with a valuation of an estate for tithes, and was introduced to Rev James Woodforde rector of the Norfolk living of Weston Longeville, who yesterday had had his Tithe Auditt. Learning of my business, he was pleased to tell me of the previous night's 'Frolick' as he described it, and I pressed him for details, as I had not hitherto heard of what occurred on these annual occasions when farmers actually paid over their tithes in person, my acquaintance with such matters being confined to the bare figures on paper. He received tithes, he said, from 25 farmers who had paid over to him yesterday £265 3. 0. They had all dined with him at Weston. He gave them salt fish, a leg of mutton boiled and capers, a knuckle of veal, a pig's face, a fine surloin of beef roasted, and plenty of plumb puddings. They drank six bottles of wine, five bottles of rum besides quantities of strong beer and ale. Parson Woodforde dined with the farmers in the great parlour; his clerk James Smith dined with his own folk in the kitchen, and his niece Nancy who lives with him and looks after him – the reverend is a bachelor – dined by herself in the study. I asked him how it had all gone.

'Much as could be expected' he said, 'but Farmer Forster behaved so insolent towards me I don't intend to have him ever again at my Frolick. And poor Jonathan Buck broke one of my decanters. But that was of no consequence. They had their fill – and I got my tithe. A good time was had by all.'

Letter from Ezekiel Townley to William Driver

Hounslow,
June 17th, 1784

Dr Mr Driver,

Crossing Hounslow Heath yesterday I came across a detachment of soldiers sweeping clear a wide path. Seeing, as I understand it, that a treaty is about to be signed with France at Versailles, and we are to recognise this new 'United States' of America as an independent state all of which is designed to produce peace after so many years of fighting,

I was apprehensive that the presence of soldiery on the heath might presage a new outbreak of hostilities – at home? – in anticipation maybe of a hostile reception to any opposition to Mr Pitt's measures for Parliamentary Reform. But on making a few discreet enquiries I learnt that they were preparing the ground for the measurement of a five mile line to be the base of a series of triangles from London to Dover to connect with those already executed in France. Our new friends the French, it seems, have submitted a memoire to our government urging the necessity of this in order to determine the relative positions of the two most famous observatories of the world. The Royal Society were consulted and they recommended that the government finance the preliminary field work and that this should be undertaken by Major General Roy, lately returned from fighting in America, and soldiers of the Royal Engineers. *This* is what is now taking place on Hounslow Heath! I suppose peaceful triangulation is a more desirable occupation for His Majesty's army than strangulation, but hardly what they have been trained – or paid – to do! The 'Ordnance Survey', as they are calling it, would seem to be merely a cheap way of mapping Britain by the use of the military, which takes away the bread and butter of us professionals who have now been 'pipped to the post' on a project we should ourselves have initiated years ago. Mr Jesse Ramsden I hear has made a 100-foot steel chain supplemented by deal rods which are to be changed to glass, to measure some 27,400 feet.

Yours etc.

Ezekiel Townley, surveyor

Journal of Abraham Driver

December 2nd, 1788

My brother William married Ann White earlier this year, and he and I have been taking account of the extent of our property in Southwark, and it seems that our nursery grounds adjoining William's house at the east corner of East Lane, now the new road, consists of about 40 acres. We are assessed on our two holdings at £36 and £33. We also have now the piece of land in Orford Row on the west side of Kent Road which we are about to develop. 'Drivers Seed Shop' has been incorporated into William's house, and is doing good business. On sale here as well as seeds is the revised edition we have edited this year of *The Pomona Britanica, or Fruit-Garden Displayed.*

Cartouche of Samuel Driver's map of Weston Estate, 1768

THE

POMONA BRITANICA;

O R,

FRUIT-GARDEN DISPLAYED:

CONTAINING

Scientific Defcriptions of all fuch FRUIT-TREES and FRUIT-
BEARING-PLANTS as are cultivated in *Great-Britain;*

W I T H

OBSERVATIONS and DIRECTIONS for their Management and Improvement,
agreeable to the beft and neweft Methods of the moft fkilful Practitioners.

WITH A

BOTANICAL LEXICON,

Explanatory of all the Technical Terms ufed in BOTANY, agreeable to
the Syftems of LINNÆUS and other celebrated Writers.

The Whole collected from Obfervations on real Practice and Experience.

By SEVERAL HANDS.
Revifed by A. and W. DRIVER, NURSERYMEN, *Kent-Road.*

———— " the downy Peach, the fhining Plum,
" The ruddy, fragrant Nectarine, and dark,
" Beneath his ample Leaf, the lufcious Fig.
" The Vine, too, here hangs out her Clufters; and
" The juicy Pear lies, in a foft Profufion."————
THOMSON.

L O N D O N:
Printed for the PROPRIETORS, and Publifhed by WILLIAM DARTON and Co.
White-Lion-Court, Birchin-Lane, 1788.

Title-page of *Pomona Britanica,* 1788

Our responsibilities are now considerable and seem to be growing; but I now have four sons, Abraham, Edward, Samuel and Charles, who one day one hopes will help share the burden, though it remains to be seen which of them will elect to enter the firm and learn from us the arts of surveying and valuing which occupy us so fully.

To-day William and I have signed an indenture between ourselves and Alderman Richard Clark of New Bridge Street giving us a licence to dig brick earth in a parcel of land at Walworth belonging to Mr Clark and leased by him in 1763 to several people of whom one is my friend Thomas Clutton of Newington Butts, described on the deed as 'brick-maker'. We are now engaged in building for speculation and this licence gives us liberty to 'fell, root up and destroy all and singular the trees, bushes, garden stuff and herbage growing on this piece of land for ten years; to dig up the soil, brick earth and gravel, and convert it into bricks and tiles; and erect kilns and sheds for the purpose, on the understanding that the bricks and tiles we make from the earth is not removed from the site but 'employed in the erection of good and substantial dwelling houses on part of the land; and that part of the land on which no buildings are erected shall be levelled and rendered fit for the cultivation of grass and other vegetable productions.'

The land consisting of nine acres in Walworth belonged to Richard Adams and Thomas Clutton and was occupied by William and myself.

Letter of Abraham Driver to his wife Ann

Royal Inn, Winchester
June 7th, 1794

My dearest Ann,

I was concerned that urgent business necessitated my leaving you so shortly after your safe delivery of our new son – I heartily concur incidentally that we should add 'Neale' to 'George' as his forenames out of respect of your dear father so recently taken from us. I like the sound of George Neale Driver!

With all the reports of the outbreak of waylaying post-chaises in the neighbourhood of London, you will be happy to hear that I reached Winchester last night without incident, and am to-day to have the meeting which I trust will settle once and for all the final details of the *General View of the Agriculture of Hampshire* which William and I have produced for the Board of Agriculture, and they are anxious to publish later this year.

Post-chaises attract highwaymen because it is the belief of these rogues that only the more wealthy travel in them, and probably two or three at a time only and one of them a female. But chaises are less liable to overturn and break down than coaches and are far faster. But then all types of carriage travel more expeditiously these days, because of the great improvements in our roads; and as an investor in more than one turnpike trust I am proud to be contributing towards this improvement, apart from having assisted, as you know, with several surveys and valuations. But of course there will always be detractors of anything the majority of us like to consider 'progress'. In the smoke room here this morning I was reading one of Arthur Young's *Farmer's Letters*. 'To find fault with good roads' he writes, 'would have the appearance of paradox and absurdity; but it is nevertheless a fact that giving the power of expeditious travelling depopulates the Kingdom. Young men and women in the country villages fix their eyes on London as the last stage of their hope. They enter into service in the country for little else but to raise money enough to go to London, which was no such easy matter when a stage coach was four or five days in creeping an hundred miles. The fare and expenses ran high. *But now!* a country fellow, one hundred miles from London, jumps on a coach box in the morning, and for eight or ten shillings gets to town by night which makes a material difference!'

You can rest assured there will be no delay in returning to Kent Street and the bosom of his family with its new addition, as soon as the business in Hampshire is concluded, on the part of

Your loving husband,
Abraham

Minutes of Partner's Meeting, March 21st, 1797
Tom's Coffee House, Tooley Street

Present: Abraham P. Driver
William Driver

Mr A. P. Driver said he and his brother had come to the conclusion that the firm having achieved the eminence of being appointed one of H.M. Surveyors of Crown Estates demanded more regularisation of their conduct of business, hitherto considered unnecessary, in particular the recording of discussions and decisions by partners on the occasions when they met to talk over their professional affairs; and that accordingly they had decided to institute the writing of formal minutes of these deliberations to supplement the record of financial transactions, in and out, in the books kept by the counting house staff. Mr William Driver agreed that the time had come to practise the precepts the firm preached to clients whose estates they were engaged to improve by way of better management and closer control.

Mr A. P. Driver said Messrs Driver had received a warrant from John Fordyce Esq, Surveyor General of His Majesty's Land Revenue, to execute a survey of the Parish of Romford in Essex, and that he had arranged a first visit to the site on April 3rd.

Mr William Driver submitted a list of the property auctions which Messrs Driver were so far committed to hold in the following six months.

The partners reviewed the situation concerning the terraces of houses, designed by Mr Michael Searle, the building of which on the Surrey Square site owned by the Driver family had been completed at the end of last year, and the effect of which had universally been acclaimed as outstandingly elegant. It was decided in principle to offer certain of the houses to members of the Driver family and to let the rest at the most advantageous rentals. The oblong piece of ground in the centre of the square would be laid out by Mr Edward Driver. Consideration was given to the acquisition and development of the adjacent ground – a church?

The matter of the coming retirement of Jack Kettle as supervisor of the Kent Road Nurseries was discussed and the suitability of his replacement by Oliver Balding, at present his principal assistant. The meeting decided that in view of the popularity of pineapples stimulated by Mr Abercrombie's recent book *The Hot-house Gardiner on the General Culture of the Pine-apple*, to increase the production of this fruit at the Kent Road Nurseries.

The meeting ended with both partners deploring the circumstances which had led Mr Pitt to introduce a tax on all legacies of personal property to collaterals, and the struggle with the post-Revolution France of General Bonaparte which looked like becoming protracted.

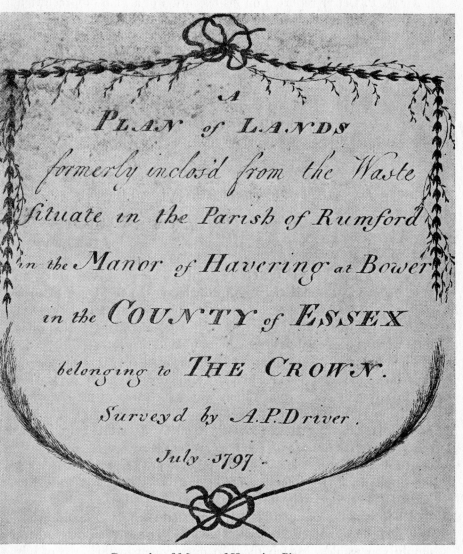

A

PLAN of LANDS

formerly inclos'd from the Waste

situate in the Parish of Rumford

in the Manor of Havering at Bower

in the COUNTY of ESSEX

belonging to THE CROWN.

Survey'd by A.P.Driver.

July 1797.

Cartouche of Manor of Havering Plan, 1797

Minutes of Partners' Meeting, December 14th, 1799
210 Kent Road, Southwark

Mr A. P. Driver reported on his execution of a Plan of Greenwich Powder Magazine commissioned by the Surveyor General, and submitted a copy.

Mr William Driver deplored the fact that the 18th century was ending with Mr Pitt levying a ten per cent *Income* Tax; but Mr A. P. Driver was sanguine that it would be raised as soon as the war with France was terminated. With a National Debt of £240 million (with a population of 20 million, some £12 a head) direct taxation of some kind, designed to reduce it, was likely to continue for many a year yet.

Letter from Abraham Driver to his son Edward

Worcester,
May 3rd, 1801

Dear Edward,

To-day I have been in the very extensive orchard at Rose Hill near here belonging to one Richard Burlingham who has come upon a Composition for dressing peach and nectarine trees to ensure the growth of good, kind wood early in the season, and prevent blight making what little wood is produced so diseased and unkind that little fruit is forthcoming. I was sufficiently impressed with the results of Mr Burlingham's experiment to promise to give him any testimonial he might require for me in advertising the composition which he plans to market commercially. I shall not be returning home for some time, and I have told Mr Burlingham that I am requesting you to make this matter your concern, and that if he sends you the proof of the advertisement you will draft suitable wording for a 'certificate' over my name recommending the composition. He intends sending out the advertisement sheet to potential purchasers to invite subscriptions of one guinea to entitle them to a bottle of the composition with instructions how to apply it, for delivery in due time for next season. I have said if he sent you an adequate supply you would dispatch them to nurserymen in this area of our acquaintance; and that you would undertake to receive subscriptions both at Kent Road and our new Physic Garden in Queen Street, Southwark.

I made Mr Burlingham aware that though you were only 18 years of

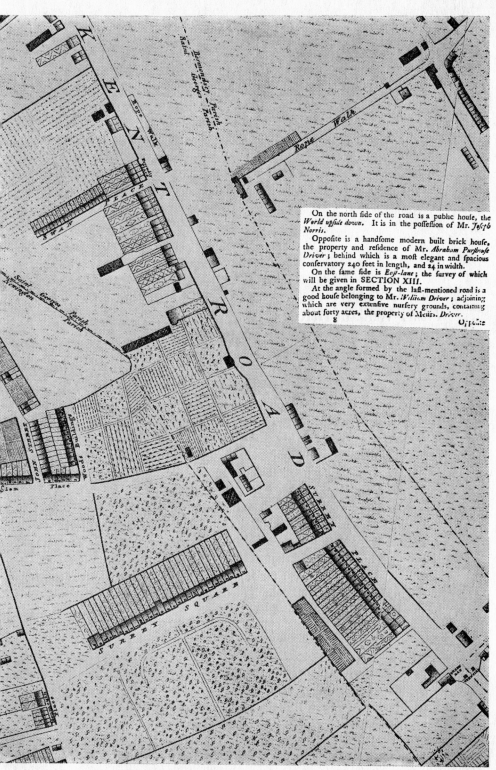

On the north side of the road is a public house, the *World upside down.* It is in the poffeffion of Mr. *Joseph Norris.*

Oppofite is a handfome modern built brick houfe, the property and refidence of Mr. *Abraham Purshouse Driver*; behind which is a moft elegant and fpacious conservatory 240 feet in length, and 24 in width.

On the fame fide is *East-lane*; the furvey of which will be given in SECTION XIII.

At the angle formed by the laft-mentioned road is a good houfe belonging to Mr. *William Driver*; adjoining which are very extenfive nurfery grounds, containing about forty acres, the property of Meffrs. *Driver.*

8   Oppofite

Part of Kent Road from Richard Horwood's map of 1799
(*Inset*) Entry in *Companion from London to Brighthelmston* of 1801

age, you were apprenticed to Messrs Driver in their role of Nurserymen and Seedsmen and fully competent to take in hand a project of this nature; and that when you had achieved your majority you would be joining us as a partner in our principal business of surveyors, auctioneers and valuers. Abraham and Samuel are showing little interest in our activities, so your uncle William and I look to you and George to carry on the family traditions in the new nineteenth century we have just entered, in which I can see more reward for our professional services than our horticultural products.

Ever, your affectionate Father

Memorandum

To: A. P. Driver   *Date:* August 10th, 1802
From: William Driver

VALUE OF BESTWALL TITHES

On July 5th 1790 expired the lease of the Corn and Hay Tithes of Bestwall in East Stoke near Wareham in Dorset which Mrs Margaret Sampson had held from the Crown for the previous 31 years, an estate formerly in the possession of the lately dissolved monastery of Sheen. Through her attorney Mr John Symes, Mrs Sampson sought the renewal of this lease, and to this end petitioned the Lords Commissioners of H.M. Treasury who referred the matter to John Fordyce Esq, Surveyor General of H.M. Land Revenue, whose clerk Mr William Harrison was ordered this year to instruct Messrs Driver to carry out a Survey and Valuation of the tithes at this date – the delay in time being due, it appeared, to the absence in Mr Fordyce's office of any information concerning the tithe (hence our commission).

On June 14th of this year (1802) Mr Harrison wrote an aide memoire in red ink in his own hand, which he has since shown me, headed 'Search in the Exchequer' which read as follows:

This search was made previous to the ordering of the Survey of these tythes, for the purpose of giving proper and "Authentic" Instructions to Messrs Driver respecting the Property Tythable of which the office contained no satisfactory account. One of the tenants doubted if Hay was included which this search clearly decided; and the result has been that the office has obtained what it never before possessed, a clear and distinct and well authenticated account of these Tythes which is detailed in the late Report to the Treasury, with a reference to these proceedings at Law, by which the Tythe, if it should ever be questioned in future, will at once be established beyond all doubt.

The document – the report on the search – on which this note is written, which I have also seen, confirmed that the last lease was granted on October 25th, 1759, expiring July 5th, 1790, but that Mrs Sampson continued to receive the profits up to to-day. It continued:

Mr Driver, it is presumed, will readily learn on enquiry at Bestwall which are the lands of which Mrs Sampson is Tythe Owner. In some papers concerning these tythes they are said to consist of those portions of tythes in Lower Bestwall, North Bestwall and South Bestwall. Mr Driver will examine into that fact and state the particulars accordingly in his Survey and Report to the Office.

At our partners' meeting on May 30th it was agreed that I should carry out this work, and I duly wrote to Mr Harrison on June 11th telling him I would be in Dorsetshire all the following week, and that if he would forward the instructions to my brother-in-law Samuel White in Poole, I would get them there.

Accordingly, Mr Harrison wrote to Mr Symes, Mrs Sampson's attorney, as follows:

Land Revenue Office, Whitehall
12th June, 1802

Sir, The Surveyor General has directed a Survey and Valuation to be made of the Bestwall Tythes, belonging to the Crown, preparatory to a sale thereof, and I shall be much obliged to you to favour me with the name and address of Mrs Sampson's Agent at or near Bestwall or of her principal Tenant or other intelligent person to whom the Surveyor may apply for the information he will want on the subject. He is now in Dorsetshire and it is meant that he should transact this business before he leaves the County.

P.S. If Mrs Sampson happens to have any Survey or Particular of these Tythes or of the Lands from which they arise it will be very obliging to favour me with the loan or a Copy of it. Any letter or Packet of whatever weight will come free directed to John Fordyce Esq, Surveyor General, at this office.

However, the dispatches of Mr Harrison, which one would like to think, from being on H.M.'s business, as having preferential treatment by H.M.'s Postal Services, were in fact subject to the delays we all are heir to.

I duly carried out the necessary enquiries and submitted my report to Mr Harrison to-day, in which I observed that the tithes were not being taken in kind but rented, and that no Quit Rents issued from the tithes. The present lessee of the Crown for the tithes was not the proprietor of the land, and of course there was no other advantage to her than the profit put upon the advance rent to her under-tenant. I should therefore think it far more advisable for the owners of the Land either to rent or purchase the tithes. The total area of the estate as you will see from the report, a copy of which I attach, is 419 acres with an annual value for a lease of £65.

Memorandum

To: A. P. Driver   *Date:* 11th October, 1802
From: William Driver

OWNERSHIP OF BESTWALL TITHES

There has been an epilogue to our report on the value of the Bestwall Tithes. Mr Harrison of the Surveyor General's office wrote to me on September 30th saying Mr Fordyce wanted to know who was the real proprietor of the estate at Bestwall. 'If you have this information send it to him by return post' he ended. So I wrote off to the Mr Thomas Brown I met when I was down at Wareham and seemed to be the most knowledgeable of those I spoke to; and I had a letter from him dated October 9th which said that Rev John Morton Colson is the owner of North Bestal (as he calls it), William Speke of South Bestal, and John Mace of East or Lower Bestal Farm. 'When you was at Wareham' says Farmer Brown, 'Elizabeth Chapman was owner of Lower Bestal who died a few weeks since and 'tis said gave it by will to Mr Mace.' I do not regard Farmer Brown as the most reliable of sources, but I have sent his letter to Mr Harrison for what it is worth. When I was down there I told the Reverend Colson of the purport of my mission and advised him it would be in his interests to offer to buy the tithes.

I would just like to put it on record that I was very glad to have the assistance – and companionship – of Edward on my last visits to Bestwall. He was of considerable help and showed great interest in the work, which augurs well for our hope that he will agree to join us as a partner in just over a year when he achieves his majority. He has also been with me on numerous occasions in the first stage of the Burnham Abbey survey. He is well liked by all he meets. He has a tidy mind and an ease of expression which should bring great benefits to Messrs Drivers, Surveyors, at a time it seems there will be rapid development in every sphere of life, to keep pace with which will need all his youthful enthusiasm and 'drive'.

Minutes of Partners' Meeting, October 18th, 1802

Present: Abraham P. Driver
William Driver

The partners discussed at length the advisability or otherwise of continuing to run the nursery side of the firm's business in view of the overwhelming demands on their time and that of their staff with their activities as surveyors, auctioneers and land agents, and in view of the fact that so large an area of what was market garden has been developed for building. The significance of terminating the market gardening which had been the foundation of the Drivers' fortunes was fully appreciated, but in the circumstances the partners considered they had no alternative. Their attentions were divided, and each side of the business suffered.

It was *Decided* therefore to run down the nursery operation as from this date, and gradually to dispose of staff, stock, catalogues, equipment and buildings; and to make an announcement of this decision to the public in the newspapers. Mr A. P. Driver said he would instruct Mr Tomkins to alter the firm's letterhead, and to notify the publishers of directories & c to adjust the firm's entries, though he was aware that for many years yet these notoriously unreliable publications would continue to designate Drivers 'nurserymen, seedsmen and surveyors'.

Mr William Driver said, though commercial exploitation would cease, he would keep certain of the greenhouses in commission, and parts of the kitchen garden and the vineyard, for his own domestic use, and take the head gardener Frimley on to his personal staff at Surrey Square.

45

Advertisement

Announcement by Messrs Driver that the estates side of their business has developed to the point where, in consequence of very great increase of engagements with several branches of their profession relative to groundwork, surveying and the disposal of landed property, they have decided to relinquish their nursery business in the Kent Road.

The Courier, October 30th, 1802

The Nineteenth Century Drivers

———◆———

SERVING THE CROWN

Edward, then Robert

1802–1812

Letter from Edward Driver to Emily Searle

Kent Road,
June 2nd, 1803

My dearest Emily,

I still bless the day your father introduced me to you when I was occupied with the flowers in the open garden in front of his beautiful terrace at Surrey Square. I say 'his' advisedly because to me the architect is the true creator of a building and no one will deny that the concept of these noble façades was his and his alone. They will stand as a monument to him, I feel sure, for all future generations, which is unlikely to be the case however of my poor efforts at landscaping – 'Capability' Driver!

Seeing you again on one of those hard, commonly grained settles they provide for buyers on that dingy first floor saleroom at Garraways Coffee House yesterday where my father was auctioneering those 'Sundry Very Improveable Freehold and Copyhold Estates' to be found in remote parts of Essex bearing improbable names like Little Parndon and Northweald Bassett, made bright a day of dull routine. But this, I suppose, must soon fill my time, as it does my father's, now we are committed exclusively to The Land. My elder brother Abraham has opted out of it all – perhaps wisely. But once there was romance at Garraways, you know – at the time of the Forty Five Rebellion which my grandfather lived through, subscriptions were opened there for the benefit of the soldiers, and they raised £19,000.

I am being indoctrinated slowly into Surveying and Valuing and Auctioneering and I confess I regret that we are abandoning Market Gardening altogether. But the latter had necessarily to give way to the former as the population of London mounted – the building of your father's Surrey Square houses on what was once a market garden was symbolic of the inevitable. But with you at my side I know I could face

49

the future, whatever it may bring, with equanimity and great assurance.

Your devoted

Edward

P.S. Let us meet at the Royal Surrey Gardens next Friday.

Memorandum

NEW RATING ASSESSMENTS, MICHAELMAS 1803

The Newington property of A. P. Driver and W. Driver has been jointly rated on four separate parcels as follows:

£30   plus £1 stock
£20   for 5 acres
£12   for 9 acres
£12   for 4 acres

W. Driver at Surrey Square has been separately rated on a rental of £50 plus stock at £2.

Memorandum

To: Edward Driver   *Date:* 3rd April 1804
From: A. P. Driver

BURNHAM ABBEY ESTATE

Now you are 21 and we have made you a partner – Messrs A., W., and E. Driver – your uncle and I would like you to complete the outstanding work on the survey of the above by yourself. This is the one-time monastery site which the Earl of Jersey leases from the Crown in Buckinghamshire, some three miles from Windsor. It was granted to Lord Villiers, the Earl's ancestor, in the reign of William III for 99 years, and it expires at Michaelmas this year. It consists of closes of arable, meadow, pasture and woodland, 399 acres in all, and is occupied by a tenant called Edmund Winder. The Earl has sent a memorial to the Land Revenue Office requesting a renewal of the lease, and for the estate to be reduced to 365 acres, hence the Surveyor General's need for an up-to-date survey.

You have seen the document 'A Description of the Premises from the

50

Cartouche of Kingston Bargeway Map, 1804

Lease and from the Particular of 1649' sent to us by Mr Harrison of the Land Revenue Office, and I attach the Instruction and Warrant dated March 20th we have received from Mr Fordyce, the Surveyor General, to view His Majesty's estate at Burnham 'and make forth a Plan, Particular and Valuation of the premises' verified by our oath or affirmation.

Would you please write to Mr Harrison to-day telling him of your readiness to go down to Burnham whenever convenient. The most important people there as far as you are concerned are Mr Baine, Lord Jersey's surveyor, and Mr Alexander Murray, his agent. When you return from visiting the site, we will discuss your observations and suggestions, and consider what recommendations, based on your findings, we should submit – I will be asking you to draft a letter to Mr Fordyce for my signature.

Journal of Abraham Driver

June 17th, 1806
'How is it, in spite of that General Enclosure Act, they are still going about it piecemeal, and landlords still have to go to all the trouble of posting individual notices on church doors and inserting advertisements in local newspapers?'

Young Edward's enquiring mind was quizzing me over punch and sandwiches in the Drinking Room of Garraway's after a particularly gruelling series of auctions; and I was glad to witness this symptom of his growing interest in the varied aspects of our profession, and of the opportunity of giving him the information so far as I was able.

'That General Enclosure Act of 1801' I told him, 'did not dispense with individual bills of enclosure. Much of our business would have gone by default if it had. It directed that in each case commissioners should be appointed to make "a true survey, plan and valuation" either by themselves or someone they appointed –'

'Like us.'

'Exactly. On the occasions when I have been appointed Commissioner I have often myself carried out the survey, as I was doing in Bedfordshire last month, where it was proposed enclosing something called Ampthill Warren, a 340 acre piece of waste land belonging to –'

' "His King's Most Excellent Majesty in Right of His Crown" – I know that part of it by now!'

I, Abraham Pinshouse Driver do solemnly affirm that the Survey or account hereto annexed was faithfully and impartially made by me; that the Value of the Property of the Crown therein contained is justly estimated therein according to the best of my Skill and Judgment and that all the Particulars stated in the said Survey or account are true to the best of my Knowledge and belief

A C Driver

Westminster
to wit.
Affirmed at the Land Revenue
Office the 24th day of August
1809 before me.

Affidavit regarding Windsor Waste Survey, August 24th, 1809

'And leased to the Earl of Upper Ossory, who as tenant is entitled to the "Right of the Soil" on the commons which in the course of time have become subject to "divers Encroachments and Trespasses" and in their present state are quite incapable of improvement.'

'The word still subsists – even in this wonderful 19th century of ours! It has had a long and useful life. And they propose making it *capable* of improvement, I suppose, by enclosing it, is that it?'

'It is thought it would be beneficial to the various owners if the commons and waste lands were allotted "in proportion to their respective Estates, Rights and Interests", and then "conveniently laid together and enclosed".'

'And that cannot be done without a parliamentary bill?'

'Precisely. Such a bill would require two gentlemen to be appointed Commissioners "for valuing, dividing, allotting and enclosing" the land and exonerating from tithes any that were tithable.'

'What if the two of them disagree?'

'A third would be appointed to give his view – only on the points in dispute.'

'How do the commissioners go about it?'

'We take the market room at the local inn, let it be known that we are in session, and under the authority of our Act of Parliament summon before us anyone who is able to tell us what encroachments have been made on the waste land in the last forty years.'

'And there is never any difficulty in finding such "informers"?'

'The informers are the people who have an interest in seeing the encroachers de-croach, if there is such a word.'

'But surely some of it is left for public use?'

'At Ampthill we allotted about two acres for public stone, sand and gravel pits, and land for roads to serve them; another two acres for public marle, clay and mortar pits.'

'And you said something about tithes?'

'We allotted tithes to the rector – Great and Small – and gave him ten acres for a parsonage house.'

'*Ten* acres?'

'For a minister of the Church of England the cure of souls is an exhausting activity, which demands the greatest room for recreation.'

'And room to put his hunters.'

'The commission generally includes making an estimate of the annual value of all the homesteads, gardens and orchards belonging to each proprietor. When that is so, I get Mr Kennedy in the counting house to ascertain from the *London Gazette* the price of a Winchester Bushel of good marketable wheat in that county over the last 21 years, and have him work out what quantity of this wheat, according to the average price he has calculated, is equal to a fifth part of the annual value of all the arable land – got that?'

'Yes' said Edward, taking a deep draught of punch to concentrate his thoughts.

'And what is equal to one-ninth of all the rest of the land. Mr Kennedy then takes these two amounts and applies them to each holding; and added together they represent what the proprietor of each holding has to pay the rector.'

'You mean as a once-and-for-all payment?'

'Exactly. Thereafter these lands are exonerated from tithes.'

'I hope the rector appreciates the work he is creating.'

'I cannot see the system persisting long. The day must come, not too delayed, when tithes will be abolished altogether. At the moment, to facilitate the future regulating of yearly rents by the division of any estates by sale, commissioners have to make a Schedule of each estate with the name of the owners, the exact measure in acres, roods and perches, the yearly rents issuing out of each estate, and the quantity of wheat to govern each rent.'

'General tidying-up?'

'Parts of the warren at Ampthill – not more than 16 acres of it – we allotted as small gardens and areas which would produce a supply of fuel for the poorer inhabitants of the parish. One twentieth part of the commons and one third of the warren went to the King and his lessee the Earl of Upper Ossory; and all the rest was divided among the interested proprietors in the proportions we adjudged to be just compensation and satisfaction for their Lands, without abrogating Rights of Common.'

'Presumably the rector's ten acres were fenced off from the rest?'

'And so were the parts designated for the poor – and the sheep. No one could cut turf or furze on the common lands without a licence from us; and we also determined how much cattle was allowed. We ordered drains to be dug, ditches to be widened, bridges to be built.'

'And how much do Messrs Driver profit from this very onerous and responsible work?'

'As a commissioner I pay my own expenses, but received £2 12s 6d a day for every meeting.'

'The main reward must be knowing you are trusted and known to

Engraved Map of the Manor of Lambeth.

THIS DAY is PUBLISHED, PRICE THREE GUINEAS,

By Mr. EDWARD DRIVER.

A COMPLETE MAP

OF THE

Manor of Lambeth,

From actual Admeasurement, made by Order of the Commissioners, under an Act of Inclosure passed in the Year 1806: neatly engraved and printed on Six large Sheets of the best Wove Paper; with a complete Reference of above Two Thousand Lines; distinguishing (by a Number referring to the body of the Plan) every House, Yard, Building, and Inclosure, of each person's Property, and the exact Quantity thereof. Together with all the Allotments, and also the several Parcels of Land which have been Sold under the Act.

The whole MAP comprises a District which extends from WESTMINSTER BRIDGE to the Southern Part of NORWOOD COMMON, adjoining the Parish of CROYDON, being a distance of Seven Miles in length, including a great Part of KENNINGTON, STOCKWELL, BRIXTON, CAMBERWELL, HEARNE and DENMARK HILLS, and NORWOOD.

The above MAP will contain a complete Delineation of every person's Estate within the said Manor, distinguishing the FREEHOLD from the COPYHOLD, and may be had by application at the Office of Messrs. DRIVER, Surveyors and Land Agents, KENT ROAD, or No. 5, AUCTION MART.

KENT ROAD
MARCH 1st, 1810.

Front Page of Leaflet for Edward Driver's Lambeth Map, 1810

be impartial – and thus invited to undertake so important a public duty.'

I downed my punch in embarrassment at this unsolicited testimonial from my son, but in doing so was put in mind of how I could return the compliment.

'Thank you Edward. Seeing you are now fully informed on this most intricate of subjects, I am prompted to entrust *you* with a part of a commission which we have just received regarding the Manor of Lambeth, due for enclosure under an Act passed this year. You will remember when we were talking just now I said these exercises were threefold – the survey, the plan and the valuation. What better way could we deploy your undoubted talents than by instructing you to execute entirely on your own, with the help of such draughtsmen and others on our staff as you may need, and maybe enlisting your young brother George who needs to be gradually introduced to our affairs and this would be a good opportunity – to execute A Complete Map of the Manor of Lambeth, covering the seven miles from Westminster Bridge to Norwood Common, indicating every estate and its owner, and which is freehold and which copyhold. Apart from the original which you submit to the Enclosure Commissioners you can have it engraved, and solicit the purchase of copies from every property holder shown on it –'

'At –?'

'What about three guineas a copy?'

'I await your instructions.'

Minutes of Partners' Meeting, June 26th, 1808

Present: Mr Abraham P. Driver
Mr William Driver
Mr Edward Driver

Mr A. P. Driver stated that at the end of the auction of the Hookwood estate at Limpsfield, Surrey, he conducted at Garraways on Friday, he had been introduced to Mr John Greenwood, the secretary designate of a syndicate formed to promote what he called an 'Auction Mart', the support of which he solicited from Messrs Driver. The plan was to erect a building in Bartholomew Lane for which the land had already been purchased, and to institute a system, in Mr Greenwood's words, 'pregnant with benefit to the Landed, the Commercial and the Monied Interests of the Kingdom'. It would be found, Mr Greenwood had told

57

Mr Driver, that from the retrospect of less than half a century sales by public auction were originally very circumscribed, seldom extending beyond a gallery of pictures, a library or such miscellaneous collections of the Arts, manufactures and merchandise as were adopted to gratify the curiosity or the propensities of the Age.

Mr Driver circulated to the meeting a draft of the Prospectus of the proposed Auction Mart. He himself felt the firm should give the project their support, but he invited the views of his fellow partners.

A variety of concurring circumstances, however, have rendered the business of an Auctioneer, eminent, conspicuous, and important—a generous Public has honored the individuals engaged in it, with unlimitted confidence; and placed them in situations the most responsible. Public Auctions have likewise been adopted, as an impartial, and just medium,—for the exercise of competition—for accelerating the Transfer of Property—opening the Channels of Commerce—and promoting the spirit of Enterprize and Speculation.

From Prospectus of *The Auction Mart*, 1810

Letter from Abraham Driver to William Clutton

210 Kent Street,
October 13th, 1812

Dear William,

That we should have sat together as Enclosure Commissioners for Betchworth and Brockham parishes last week, alongside the redoubtable George Smallpiece, squire of Guildford, gave me no little pleasure, as you will appreciate, not the least for the opportunity the occasion afforded of renewing a bond between our two families which stretches back at least half a century. We Drivers have come up in the world since then! I well remember my father telling me how *his* father had felt so demonstrably inferior to a character at Wandsworth aptly called Hawty or Hawtin, or some such name, who flaunted his "Esquire" round, when in the list of parishioners grandfather Driver only appeared as 'Mr'!

It was kind of you to congratulate me on my recent election as Master of the Clothworkers Company. I suppose this, as much as anything else, could be said (though not by me!) to be symbolic of a new-won status.

I am grieved, as I know you are, that the King's illness should have reached a permanence which has forced Parliament to pass an Act of Regency, particularly when there is no alternative candidate for Regent than the debauched profligate who calls himself Prince of Wales. I understand from the Land Revenue Office that the Prince has conceived a grandiose plan for a new street which would make a triumphal way for His Highness from Carlton House to Marybone Park. His architectural extravagances at Brighton seem to have gone to his head! The final Crown Lease in Marybone Park, that of the Duke of Portland, expired in January of last year. In anticipation of this the late Mr Fordyce – his death in 1810 was a sad loss – as long ago as September 1793 offered a reward of £1,000 to whatever person submitted a plan of development for the park, which covers 540 acres, which was adopted; but not a single plan was submitted. Since the official 'competition' lapsed however three plans have been drawn up: by Mr John Nash, by Mr Thomas Leverton and Mr Thomas Chawner, and by Mr John White, the Duke of Portland's agent. These came as a result of a letter these people received from Mr Milne, Mr Fordyce's successor as Surveyor General, in October 1810, inviting a plan and a report 'to unite the objects of present and growing improvement in point of revenue with the advantages of forming a handsome, elegant and commodious addition to the metropolis of the empire as the ground seems to suggest'.

Mr White had already written unsolicited in April 1809 giving Mr Fordyce his ideas for improvement in heroic terms.

When I have considered the advantages which the inhabitants of the metropolis derive from their free access to the Parks and Kensington Gardens, I could not but admire the wisdom and liberality of the age when they were so appropriated, and the reflection has induced me to hope that two years hence when the lease of Marybone Park expires, the officers of the Crown will be inclined to a similar appropriation of that beautiful and convenient portion of public property.

etc etc.

Paragraph III of Mr Milne's questionnaire to the architects is the one in which I have been particularly interested:

You will, in forming your opinion, consider the Subject, first as connected with the measure of a new, convenient communication by means of a broad street in direct line from about Charing Cross to the southern boundary of the estate . . . and you will, when viewing the subject in this light, suggest such plan or plans as may seem to you most eligible and most practicable for opening such a Communication.

This, I think, adumbrates a certain amount of work for this office by way of land purchase; but be that as it may, the only way in which we have so far become involved in the Marybone Park project is with the building of the proposed canal – the promotion of a company formed for the purpose – which will connect the Thames at Limehouse with the Grand Junction Canal at Paddington. Work began this month. By Act of Parliament and with the consent of the Crown it is to enter the Regent's Park, as Marybone is to be called, between Lord's Cricket Ground and the Burial Ground of the Parish of St Marybone.

Mr Thomas Lord was very upset by the decision, and he told me at a stormy meeting at which he tried to persuade me to use what influence I had to have the line of the canal altered, that he would now almost certainly have to take up the turf at the ground he had moved to when the Duke of Portman had raised his rent on his first cricket ground in Dorset Square, and move to yet another site, the third 'Lord's'. He had his eye, he said, on a field at the corner of St John's Wood Road and Grove End Road, to the north of the line the canal would take. He hoped this would be his last move, and that this would become the permanent headquarters of the Marylebone Club so long as cricket endured, which he was sanguine would be for many generations yet. I told him then the decision was final and that he should accept it with as good grace as he could.

Have you ever played cricket, William? It is becoming increasingly popular these days and land is being sought for it in the most unlikely places. Why even that oval market garden I remember visiting as a boy with my father at Kennington has become a cricket ground. 'Improvement'? Certainly using that desolate Black Heath with its gravel pits and quarries as a golfing ground could be so construed. Golf certainly takes up more room than cricket; golf 'links', as they call them in Scotland, would seem to constitute a potential source of land development which, should the game ever cotton on down here as it has in the north, we should watch.

Very sincerely yours,
Abraham Driver

1811

EXTRACT OF MR NASH'S REPORT ON THE
PROGRESS OF THE WORKS IN MARYBONE PARK

Extract	*Minute*
Page 12: Mr Nash states he presumes that the Regents Canal Company have paid for their Canal and Towing Path and Banks	They have paid for a certain quantity of land to be occupied by the Canal & Towing path, but if more land is used in that way the Company are to pay for the excess at the same rate.
	q/ – has any money been paid for banks and slopes? Messrs Driver have been ordered to ascertain the respective quantities.
	q/ – Should not Drivers be called on for their report?

1812–1833

Journal of Abraham Driver

February 12th, 1814

'You state, Mr Driver, that you are interested in land and the part that can be played in its development by builders on speculation.'

Mr John Nash, the architect, had come into Mr Milne's room at the Office of Woods and Forests where I was receiving instructions regarding the work we were doing in connection with the development of Marybone Park.

'Building on speculation has had its day, Mr Driver.'

'But Mr Nash –'

'Hear me out, sir. There was a time when it was of general benefit to seller and buyer. But to-day the builder on speculation has no qualms about the disservice he does a public to whom the superior allurements of the interior – a few flimsy marble chimney pieces and the like – are sufficient to procure a sale, which after all is all the builder is concerned with. So, to such finery everything out of sight is sacrificed.'

'Out of sight, Mr Nash? What are you hinting at?'

'I am *asserting*, sir, that such builders ensure that no defects as there might be in the constructive and substantial parts shall make their appearance while the houses are on sale.'

'It is a damaging imputation.'

'It is nonetheless a true one. And for want of these essentials, which constitute the strength and permanency of houses, a very few years will exhibit cracked walls, swagged floors, bulged fronts, crooked roofs, leaky gutters, inadequate drains and other ills of an originally bad construction. And it is quite certain that without renovation equal to rebuilding, all those houses long, very long, before the expiration of the leases, will cease to exist, and the reversionary estate the proprietors look for will never be realised. For it is not till the end of the builder's term that the proprietor of the fee will be entitled to the additional ground rents laid on by the builder.'

'You exaggerate, sir'

'And you apply such strictures' said Mr Milne, 'to the type of development which should take place in Marylebone Park?'

'I do indeed' said Mr Nash. 'In my opinion, it is not in the interest of the Crown that Marylebone Park should be covered with buildings of the type that I have just described; nor that it should let out the ground by the acre for builders to seek their profit by sub-dividing it into such streets as will best answer their speculations, however large the amount of ground rents which builders lay on may appear on paper, and in the course of time perhaps be realised by them upon the supposition that those ground rents would revert to the Crown.'

'Some builders on speculation may be of this type, but not in my opinion all of them' I said, feeling Mr Nash should not be allowed to have the field entirely to himself.

'It is not so much their ill intent' said the great man, 'as that the current price of labour and materials prevent them from erecting houses capable of enduring a building term of 99 years, or even 61 years; and therefore those ground rents will not be realised by the Crown.'

'The day will come, will it not' said Mr Milne, 'when the inflated prices will deflate?'

'That may well be, but they alone are not the whole cause of the trouble. There is a much more delicate circumstance behind the trend – fashion. So precarious is the value of houses from the change of fashion only, that those which were not quite out of fashion last year are abandoned for those which are something more characterized by the newer fashion.'

His argument was proving more sympathetic. 'There is much in what you say, sir' I said, and he launched to develop his thesis.

'Nothing is more common' he said, 'than to see old houses covering large spaces of ground with ample yards and offices, and most substantially built, deserted for houses slightly built on contracted spots and with small and inconvenient offices, on no other account than that the latter have the polish of newness and fashion, and that the former are clothed in the respectable garb worn 40 years ago. If this is true with regard to houses of infinitely more intrinsic value, the state of request 40 years hence of the slight and flimsy buildings of which the modern enlargement of the town is composed, may be very easily imagined.'

Mr Milne, whose brief in regard to Marylebone Park, as indeed to all

63

Crown Estates, included ensuring a substantial revenue as well as providing a public amenity, had reservations about the ability of any plan which Mr Nash might proffer to satisfy him on this point, and he said so. He was not recommending the total exclusion of houses, said Mr Nash, only that arrangement of them which did not divide up the whole area into streets and destroy its character as a park.

'My recommendation' he said, 'is that the Crown should not trust to those forced and unnatural means of procuring buildings to be erected in Marylebone Park, but to advert to the advantages and circumstances belonging to the place itself, and to advance and improve those, and to endeavour to create such others as are obviously the motives operating on the wealthy part of the public in the choice of situations for their houses, or which shall hold forth advantages to the industrious and inferior classes.'

'What do you consider to be the motives of the wealthy in their choice of situation?' I asked.

'The parts of the town which the great and opulent prefer are the west side of Arlington Street, the upper end of Piccadilly, Park Lane and Grosvenor Place; and they do so not because they are nearer the court or the houses of Parliament *but because they look into Hyde Park, the Green Park and the Queen's Garden.* We should build houses that *look into* Marylebone Park not stand in it.'

Diary of George Neale Driver

Christmas Evening, 1816

I have been one whole year a partner in what is now 'A., W., E. & G. N. Driver'! And what a momentous year – with the Bourbons, who thought they were safe back on their throne, having to flee all over again, and then Bonaparte losing the final gamble at Waterloo! What times to be living in! I saw the defeated Emperor on the British frigate which had brought him from France and was anchored in Torbay Harbour while the Prime Minister and Lord Castlereagh were thinking what to do with him.

The services of 'Messrs Driver' as surveyors and valuers have been in such demand that it is no longer practicable to manage the volume of business, nor house the staff required to handle it, in our house at Kent Road, and our festivities to-night were as much a Christmas dinner as a 'farewell' party to mark the removal of the counting house, drawing

64

offices and the rest to new premises on the other side of the river just north of Blackfriars Bridge – which father says he remembers seeing built! It was opened, he says, in 1769 when he was a boy of 14. I do not think three bridges across the Thames is enough – what about a 'Waterloo Bridge' so everyone can remember the Iron Duke's great victory?

The street we have moved to is called New Bridge Street which was built over the old Fleet Ditch. Our house is no. 13 – but no one dares make a joke of it for fear of upsetting the senior partners! Hearty brother Charles, who is not with us in the surveying business and thus unaware of father's sensitivity on such matters, nearly remarked on it in the speech he made at dinner to-night about the Driver market gardening activity which had been gradually allowed to die since 1802 now being physically severed from surveying, but was luckily headed off by Edward's Emily.

It was a great family gathering – the dining room was full of the choicest floral products of the Driver nursery and we ate the rarest out-of-season fruit forced in Uncle William's East Lane greenhouse. When Fanny brought in the Christmas cake father was heard to murmur something about it being the usual Driver mix, which my sister Louisa, who was sitting beside me and looking very elegant in her 'Empire style' gown, said was a reference to a family tradition that grandfather Samuel Driver was a baker in Wandsworth.

The speeches went on all night. Father may be a Quaker – both he and my brother Abraham still carry the Purshouse name, so we cannot forget it though none of us are any longer 'Friends' except in name – and success and prosperity have made him neither flamboyant nor over-indulgent, but he knows how to enjoy himself on formal occasions such as this and revels in playing the paterfamilias. We toasted the King, but could not with any sincerity wish him a long life in his troubled state; and no one felt disposed to drink the health of 'Florizel', as Abraham's wife Grace disrespectfully calls the Regent; though considering the work the firm has done in connection with what is now to be called 'Regent's Park', to say nothing of the work we hope to derive from the building of the Regent's new street from Carlton House, we are greatly in that Prince's debt. We toasted the Duke of Wellington and drank a bumper three times three to the British Army. Father toasted the Driver Family; and Abraham, as son and heir, responded. Uncle William toasted the Driver Firm coupled with 13 New Bridge Street, the new centre of our activities, and Edward responded.

65

Charles finally married Ann Manning four years ago, and last month they produced a baby boy; so I proposed a special toast for this latest addition to the dynasty – the fifth generation? – 'Robert Collier Driver', over whose future as a surveyor I waxed lyrical as befitted the general conviviality. We looked to him, I said, not only to *carry on* the family tradition but to develop the scope of Drivers' activities in the changing world of the 19th century, from which the Disturber of Europe had been finally removed ('We *hope!*' interjected mother), and in which we could now settle down to reap the benefits of a lasting peace. The population would go on growing – six-week-old Robert Collier Driver was a symbol of that growth – and land development and building would have to increase to keep pace with it and the march of civilisation. I saw father take his watch out of his pocket at this point, and saw fit to resume my seat, but not before I had turned to 'Charles Burrell Driver', the father of this great prodigy, and recited the verses which I had composed specially for the occasion:

> A loving father he, no seer,
> Survey'd his new-born babe,
> And swore he saw inside his mouth
> A silver astrolabe.
>
> He'd be as fam'd and capable
> As any Brown could be;
> No longer fruit and vegetables
> But pleasure domes decree.
>
> We cannot tell what heights he'll reach,
> And yet he can but crawl;
> But this we know, our Robert here
> Will sure outlive us all.

The two cousins, both called Samuel, (my brother, and Uncle Will's son Samuel White Driver) together with the brothers James Horne, husband of Uncle Will's daughter Mary, and Thomas Horne, husband of my sister Ann, then sang a quartet, and this great evening came to a close.

Memorandum
to all staff

DEATH OF MR WILLIAM DRIVER

The New Bridge Street office will be closed all next Wednesday to enable staff to attend the funeral of Mr William Driver at All Saints, Surrey Square. It is hoped that as many of those who knew Mr Driver during his 40 years as a partner of the firm will see fit to pay their last respects to a man who has been taken from us at the early age of 61 and has been held in affection by all with whom he came into contact in and out of the office.

April 10th, 1819

Journal of Abraham Driver

March 25th, 1820

The building of the new 'Regent Street' is, I am glad to say, completed.

I am 65. My younger brother has died before me at 61; H. M. King George III mercifully passed on at the end of January. Mindful therefore of man's mortality, I have to-day made my will – which I should have done before, but my mind has always been so fully occupied with things present. I have made Samuel, Edward and son-in-law Tom Horne my executors, stipulating that they must allow my dear wife Ann to reside in this Kent Road home here for the rest of her life if she so wishes, and have the full use of the garden and paddock. Eventually the estate can be sold and the proceeds divided equally between my five sons and two daughters. I am glad at last to have applied myself to this uncongenial task and settled my affairs in the way my attorney has been urging for many years now. My health seems robust, but I must admit I am finding the auctioneering, of which I still insist on taking my share, an increasing strain.

Manuscript

'NOTES ON AUCTIONEERING'
(FOUND AMONG A. P. DRIVER'S PAPERS)

Licence

1. Anyone wishing to 'sell by outcry, knocking down of the hammer, by candle, by lot, by parcel or any other mode of sale by auction where the highest bidder is held to be the purchaser' *must obtain a licence* (12s) A licence for an 'Appraiser' costs 10s.

Duty

2. Three days before sale, give Collector of Excise *notice in writing*; and within six weeks an account of the amount sold and 'make oath of truth thereof'.

3. Duty is imposed on the *bidding* – the highest bid – and is liable whether there is a sale or no. It is Seven Pence for every 20s of purchase money bid – a shilling in the £ for furniture & c. Auctioneer may make it condition *purchaser* pays duty, but is entitled to claim allowance if the owner 'buys in' his estate (without hint of collusion though). If sale is void (if 'owner' is not in fact owner) auctioneer must get remission of duty from J.P. No duty if sale is after sheriff has seized estate for creditors, or if sale of a bankrupt.

Responsibilities

4. Must use utmost diligence; if penalty incurred, auctioneer must pay it himself.

5. He must obtain the best price which the property being sold is fairly worth. If the vendor specifies a price, auctioneer not justified in selling for less. The printed conditions of sale will say the highest bidder is the purchaser, so if the auctioneer has secret instructions not to sell under a certain sum, this secret limitation is a fraud on the purchaser and contrary to the express condition of sale. If the auctioneer disobeys secret instructions, he is in the right.

Case of vendor of an estate writing down the lowest price he was prepared to sell on a piece of paper and putting it under a candle stick at the time of sale 'with the privity of the Auctioneer, but not signed by the owner nor any notice given in writing to the auctioneer of the price so set down, and the Auctioneer had not given previous notice of sale to the Collector of the duty as required by the Act'. In this case, where no bids reached the price written on the paper under the candle stick of which auctioneer was ignorant, and the owner withdrew the property from sale, it could not be said there was 'no sale' in the legal sense and the auctioneer was still liable for duty.

'Puffing'

6. Puffing is illegal. If an owner employs puffers to bid for him without declaring he has done so, it is a fraud on the real bidders and the highest bidder cannot be compelled to complete the contract.

Lord Mansfield said in the case of Bexwell v. Christie 'the basis of all dealing ought to be good faith.' Public confidence was impossible 'if the owner might secretly and privately enhance the price by a person employed for that purpose; yet tricks and practices of this kind daily increase and grow so frequent that good men give in to the ways of the bad and dishonest in their own defence'.

You make what conditions you like, but they must be printed in the handbills for all the public and potential bidders to see. Lord Ashburnham had it inserted in the conditions of sale of his estate recently that he himself might bid once in the course of the sale, and as soon as the proceedings opened he straightway bid £15,000. This was fair, as the public had been apprised and knew on what terms they bid.

A. & E. Driver, 13 New Bridge Street

July 1820

Diary of George Neale Driver

November 28th, 1821

Father passed away to-day. With Uncle William gone, the whole responsibility for 'Messrs Driver' devolves on Edward and myself. I pray God to give us strength and right judgement to maintain their standards and high sense of public accountability. The Land Revenue Office will have reason to mourn the removal of one who, as a Surveyor of the Crown Estates for more than a quarter of a century, has given them honourable and painstaking service. The reputation he has won for the firm as trusted servants, accurate and shrewd in their assessments and appraisals, as a result of the surveys and valuations carried out for them in this period, has brought 'Messrs Driver' to the front rank of their profession – and we who are the heirs of their competency must never let them down.

The earliest I have note of is the survey at Romford of 1797 and of the Greenwich Powder Magazine of 1799, and there followed Burnham

Monastery (1800), Reading Hundred and Town (1801), Portland Manor (1803), Castle & Lands, All Hallows, St Peters and St Leonards (1804), Biggleswade Manor (1807), the Waste Land at Windsor (1808), Ampthill Manor, East Hendred Manor and Moreton & Ock Hundreds (1812), Bray and Cookham Manors (1814) – to mention a few of those I happen to know of.

A. P. Driver is dead – and *requiescat in pace* – but, as witness the poster which lies before me for tomorrow's sales at the Auction Mart of the 'Genteel Residence' at Ringwood with its coach house and pleasure gardens of 15 acres, and the estates at Wateringbury and Mereworth, the living must needs be served and 'A. & E. Driver' are there, as is their pledge and will be for many a generation to come, to see they are not disappointed.

LOT VII.

Another valuable FREEHOLD GROUND RENT,

Issuing out of a large FREEHOLD HOUSE; held under a Lease granted to Mr. WILLIAM DRIVER, for a Term of *Sixty-Three* Years, of which *Fifty-two* Years will be unexpired at *Midsummer* next, at the Net Annual Rent of £30, and an addition of 15s. for Land-Tax; but which Lease is now in the possession of Mr. SAMUEL WHITE DRIVER,.. 30 15 0

Particulars of Sale of Driver Kent Road Estate, June 12th, 1823

Letter from Edward Driver to his cousin Samuel White Driver, son of William Driver

Surrey Square,
12th June, 1823

Dear Sam,

We held the auction of the freehold ground rents of the family estate in Kent Road this morning as advertised, and in accordance with father's wishes – 'by the direction of the devisees in Trust under the will of Mr A. P. Driver', as the lawyers had it. All went smoothly. The estate was divided into 13 lots involving a hundred dwelling houses off Kent Road in Friendly Place, Swan Place, Cornbury Place, Orford Row, Brunswick Place, Nursery Place and Alfred Place; and Stanford Place off East Street. The whole produces some £300 a year. We made

70

Map of Driver Kent Road Estate, 1823

your house 'Lot VII' and described it as a 'large freehold house under lease to Mr William Driver for 63 years of which 52 will be unexpired at midsummer at net annual rent of £30 and 15s for Land Tax, but lease now in possession of Mr Samuel White Driver'. This means your father had the 63 year lease in 1812, expiring in 1875.

How quickly this part of Surrey has become built over! Annie and I were looking at a map of the area as it was in 1746 made by John Rocque [see page 24]; the estate was all orchards and market gardens save for 'The Lock Hospital' comprising three large-sized buildings. 'The Bull Inn' was at the north corner of Kent Road and East Street and a 'Burying Ground' on the south corner just about where your home is now – I hope you have not seen any ghosts! On Horwood's map of 1799 [see page 41] there is no sign of the Lock Hospital, Bull Inn nor Burying Ground. But Friendly Place is marked – so named perhaps by the Quaker Abraham Purshouse, our grandmother's uncle, whose land it originally was – and Swan Place, and of course our Surrey Square which the map shows as a single row or terrace. The whole of the area between Kent Road and Woods Buildings is shown as a cultivated market garden and nursery, the one worked by grandfather Samuel Driver 2, who was born, if I remember rightly, in 1720. So here we are spanning more than a century. 'Nursery Place' alone reminds contemporaries that once it was all nursery.

My regards to Margaret,

Ever yours,
Edward

Diary of Edward Driver

January 10th, 1825
'Mr Currey, I presume?'

The man in the rough knee britches paused as he stretched to pull a beam from out of the rubble and turned towards me. I put out my hand and walked towards him. 'Driver' I said, 'Edward Driver. I'm the surveyor sent by Mr Milne's office on behalf of the Crown Estates to come and make the valuation.'

He was expecting me, and shook me by the hand. Edmund Currey was the man who had purchased the materials of the house on the Swinley Park estate in Berkshire which the Crown was proposing to let to HRH Prince William Frederick, Duke of Gloucester, and here he was personally supervising the demolition and the carting away of the stone and wood that was once a fine mansion.

He clapped his hands together to knock off the dust, and a big red Irish setter came bounding from the bushes and leapt up at him.

'Down boy, down! If you like to follow me I will show you round.'

Though the mansion house had been pulled down, what Mr Currey called 'the homestead' was to remain, and I recognised it from the Particular as the 'compact and well-sheltered substantial brick-built Dwelling House' which the Crown had decided to retain as a residence for the Keeper. We made a tour of the other 'outhouses' which were to be similarly retained – the Housekeeper's House, the Coach House, the Coal House, the Stabling with its eleven stalls, the Knife House, the Larder, the Wood House, the Poultry House, the Chaff House, the Cow House, the Granary. I made notes as I went, appraising the value of each for its exterior as we made a circumambulation, and then the interior. We afterwards made a circuit of the entire estate, first taking his pony and trap to the furthest point of the adjoining wood which I noted contained large standing timber but little underwood. There was a good plant of ash, alder and other poles, but my attention was caught by small vacant places needing filling up in the coppice. Beside it were a series of fish ponds.

'Five acres, it says here' I shouted at Mr Currey through the wind, 'looks more.'

'Five acres too much, if you ask me' he said. 'In my opinion they would be materially improved if you drained the lot.'

Draining, I thought, could hardly improve them, merely remove them; but I considered this no occasion for so frivolous an observation. Perhaps keep one or two as a 'hazard', against the day when the land became one of those golfing grounds father was talking about – this seemed as likely a spot as any.

'Maybe' I said, jotting down the fact of his objection to the fish ponds on my pad.

We were now in the centre of the estate, and we looked around it from our vantage point of a slight prominence.

'Total acreage, 297 acres, 2 rods, 4 perches' I said reading from my paper.

'That is not including the deer paddocks – I think His Majesty wants to keep those for himself.'

It was true – though I was hard put to it to see H. M. King George IV stalking deer in this rough environment, or indeed anywhere else.

'Total rates and taxes £32 per annum, correct?'

Mr Currey nodded.

'Free of tithes? Land Tax £2 17s 6d? Poor Rate 4s in the Pound?'

He assented to these figures, and with a sweep of the hand I admired the condition of the fence surrounding the whole property.

'I would have thought however' I said seeking his approbation of what my experience told me was needed, 'that a good Quick Fence could be planted with advantage – new quicking of some 150 rods – and about half of the 40 acres of tillage could well be fenced with Pale Fence.'

Mr Currey was evidently not ready to give his opinion on this and held his peace. 'My grandfather' I said, 'was knowledgeable on fencing matters; he knew the best woods for the job. This was the basis of our transition from gardeners to surveyors you know, a process which began, incidentally, exactly a hundred years ago this year.'

He was not impressed. I do not believe in fact he was listening, searching as he was with his stick to dislodge something in the undergrowth at which his dog was barking loudly.

'To-day' I continued in spite of his inattention, 'a new Quick Fence can be done at 3s to 3s 6d a rod, and I think it would be prudent to do this here.'

His eyes lit up however when I mentioned I intended recommending cutting down some of the oak trees. He said he would be willing to take them at a valuation, so long as he could fell them at his leisure and use his own people.

'When strangers are admitted' he said, shaking his head, 'the preserves always suffer.'

He was glad to hear the homestead was going to stay and be occupied by the Keeper as it would be the means of securing the consumption of the produce of the estate; otherwise all the dung would be carried away and the land become exhausted.

'What of the Heath Allotment of 76 acres?' I asked him.

'It is of no value to the farm' he said, 'other than for planting with Scotch fir and larches. Time and time again it has been robbed of its top surface. It will no longer answer even as a sheep walk.'

We were now back to my chaise. He had one parting observation. It were better, he said, if the planting of new trees were done by the Duke of Gloucester and not by His Majesty, as in the event of any damage being done to young plants by game, it would be HRH's own loss.

I gave a final look round to fix the picture of the estate in my mind before leaving. If the lease was to be for 21 or 31 years, as opposed to a yearly tenancy, then the Crown would have to charge a higher rent, as the longer period would enable the Duke to carry out the very great improvements of which the estate was capable. My first thoughts were that £128 per annum would be a fair annual rent.

'I suppose the next time you come down' said Mr Currey with a twinkle in his eye as he helped me into my chaise, 'will be by one of these "railway" affairs we have been hearing someone has laid down between Stockton and Darlington. Is steam going to take over from your fine steed here? "Puffing Billy", is that it?'

I said I thought he was probably right, and bid him adieu.

NOTICE TO ALL STAFF

From May 15th the address of this firm will be:

8 Richmond Terrace,
Parliament Street,
Whitehall, SW

and from that date these offices will be closed.
E. & G. N. Driver
13 New Bridge Street, Blackfriars

May 1st, 1826

Letter from Edward Driver to his wife Emily

St Mary's, The Scilly Islands,
June 12th, 1829

My dear Emily,

One does not need the playwriting skill of a Mr Sheridan to set down the comedy in which I have been playing the leading role these past few days, but rather the reporting ability of a Mr Boswell to capture the dialogue as it was spoken in all its comic absurdity. I have come here, as you know, on instructions from the Special Commissioners of His Majesty's Duchy of Cornwall to carry out a survey of these islands off the extremity of Cornwall, the lease of which to the Duke of Leeds expires in November 1831.

I made the voyage from Penzance in a packet boat of diminutive

75

proportions, and the most incommodious it has ever been my misfortune to sail in, whose departure, subject on all occasions to the tide, was further delayed by inclement weather. I was pleased we should have decided against your accompanying me, as there was no accommodation suitable for a lady, the so-called 'cabin' being no larger than a closet. One could have borne this with equanimity for five or six hours, but in the event the voyage took 15 and it was, as you can imagine, almost beyond endurance. I cannot believe that anyone having once made the voyage, however delighted with their destination, would ever hazard it again – to the loss of the Duchy and the lessee. So with this tragic prologue, let the play begin.

Scene 1: Interior of Hotel at St Mary's

Mrs Gahan, the landlady. Good morning sir. I understand you wish to
    speak with me.

ED. Yes, madam. I have come from the mainland to make a survey –

Mrs G. For the Lord Proprietor no doubt?

ED. And who may he be?

Mrs G. The Lord Proprietor, sir. I know not his name. Everyone knows
    what is meant by the Lord Proprietor.

ED. Everyone except me. Would it by any chance be the Duke of Leeds?

Mrs G. Ah! (*clapping her hands together*) That is he.

ED. No ma'am. My duties concern His Grace, to whom I refer in my
    official reports as the Noble Lessee and you call the Lord Proprietor,
    but my instructions you might say, via his special commissioners, are
    from His Majesty (*thinks:* 'That will put the fear of God in her!')

Mrs G. (*curtsying*) And what can I do for you, sir?

ED. The King is the real proprietor or landowner of the Scilly Islands
    as part of his Duchy of Cornwall, and your so-called Lord Proprietor
    is his tenant.

Mrs G. (*forcing a smile and nodding*) Quite so.

ED. I have to make a start somewhere, and I have elected to do so by
    reading, and trying to understand, this Rent Roll here (*which lay
    before me on my desk*). My object is to trace the several houses in
    St Mary's from the order in which they are placed, and desirous of
    digesting the best mode of proceeding with my survey, I have
    attempted to find in it the name of this house, your hotel, madam, and
    I admit I am unable to do so. I was hoping that you could assist me.
    I have been down the columns and do not see a Mrs Gahan listed.

(I gave her the Roll and putting spectacles on her nose she runs her eye down each sheet, nodding her head and drawing in her breath at the end of each.)

Mrs G. You are correct sir. My name is nowhere.

ED. How can you account for that, madam?

Mrs G. *(taking off spectacles and putting on an act of thinking)* Maybe, sir, the house is listed in the name of Thomas Phillips.

ED. And who may he be?

Mrs G. He built the hotel.

ED. When?

Mrs G. Some 70 years ago.

ED. Been dead – ?

Mrs G. Some 40 years.

ED. You have been occupying the hotel all that time?

Mrs G. Yes, sir.

ED. Did he sell the house to you?

Mrs G. No, sir.

ED. To whom then does it belong?

Mrs G. To his two daughters.

ED. And where do they reside? Hard by?

Mrs G. One in Plymouth, the other in Falmouth. Both left Scilly many years ago.

ED. I note from this Roll that 15 years arrears of rent are due on this hotel at 2s 6d a year. Would you know how this happened?

Mrs G. Well sir, Mr John, the Lord Proprietor's Agent that is, has never applied to me for payment.

ED. You pay no rent then?

Mrs G. *(sniffing)* On the contrary, sir! I remit my rent regularly to the Misses Phillips in equal moities at Plymouth and Falmouth.

ED. I understand. This is how the original Ground Rent has been allowed to increase, through no fault of course *(beaming at her)* of yours, madam. If Mr John had properly made application to you as the occupier there is no doubt whatsoever that it would immediately have been paid. Would you be so good, madam, to inform me of the amount you are paying the ladies in Plymouth and Falmouth?

Mrs G. Formerly it was £35 a year, but after my husband's death it was reduced, since he had expended much money on the premises, and I now pay only £20 a year.

ED. In truth, madam, I can tell you that these ladies are no more entitled to this rent than any stranger, but that is no fault of yours but

77

the negligence of the personage you see fit to call the Lord Proprietor. And I feel sure there are many other cases of a similar nature to yours. I am greatly indebted to you, madam, for answering my questions so directly and may I say, with such charm (*you may have no fear of my being beguiled by her; she looked an ogress*). It would appear to me, madam, and I am only thinking aloud as you might say, that a ground rent of 2s 6d a year or indeed of five shillings for any house of any age, whether occupying a small or large space, has been what I would call 'injudicious', and I would give you a friendly warning that it is unlikely to continue at that rate for another 30 years.

(*Commotion outside the room; a knock on the door to which I call* 'Come in!' ; *enter an overdressed man of middle age who says something to Mrs Gahan which I cannot hear.*)

Mrs G. There is a deputation outside, sir, who, apprised of your presence on the island, beg an audience to present a memorial to you.

ED. (*addressing the man who had entered*) Who, sir, do you represent?

Man (*whose name turned out to be Zachariah Legge*) We are eight of the principal occupiers of land and houses in St Mary's, and we wish to be afforded an opportunity, if your honour would so grant it, of having our situation as tenants under the Lord Proprietor considered, and of delivering a memorial signed, not only by us, but also by most of the respectable inhabitants of this island.

ED. I should very much welcome meeting such a deputation. Mrs Gahan, please be so good as to admit his companions. (*They file into the room, in their best clothes and decidedly awkward in them.*)

Zachariah Legge. Our wish is that we should have our leases for three 'lives' or 99 years.

ED. I can say at once that there is little expectation of that being granted for buildings already erected; but in the event of the Scillies becoming a place of resort for strangers, which I consider not at all improbable, those who might be desirous of treating for land to erect lodging houses, baths or other public buildings, might expect leases of three lives or for fixed terms of 60 or 70 years. I would advise, however, for your own long term advantage, that you find some way of abandoning the system which seems to be the tradition on Scilly of subdividing the land on the death of the occupier. It is making the land more and more unworkable; and such underlettings and subdivisions make it impossible for a surveyor such as myself to undertake the survey of the land and name the tenants, which will enable you to look to improvement. I would also take the opportunity of suggesting that those who live in the smaller islands where there is distress help to alleviate it by agreeing to take work other than fishing, which I understand most are reluctant to do.

William Hoskyns. I would like to take the opportunity, sir, if I may, of raising the question of 'Branch Pilots'.

ED. I am not sure they are within my jurisdiction, though it seems my survey will cover as much as Domesday before I am done. What, pray, are Branch Pilots?

WH. A nondescript name given by the Trinity Board to the persons, with little or no experience of the sea, whom they have taken upon themselves to appoint, if you please, to rescue valuable cargoes from wrecks round these shores.

ZL. A job for centuries undertaken by *any* seaman who inhabits the Scilly Isles. (*General 'Ayes' from all the deputation who obviously were very disturbed by this innovation.*)

WH. We do the risky work of taking the wrecked ships into the roads and then the b—dy Branch Pilots take charge of the vessel and dismiss us without so much as a by your leave –

ZL. And without allowing us any recompense for our exertions.

ED. For how long have the Trinity Board been exercising this right of appointing Branch Pilots to handle salvage?

WH. Some 20 years. There are 32 of them and their nomination rests with the Officers of the Custom at St Mary, namely the Collector, the Comptroller and the Surveyor.

ED. I cannot see this strictly as falling within my brief, but personally I sympathise with the complaint and I will note it in my report.

Scene 2: The Garrison on the Hugh

ED. I apologise, General, for my tardiness. The road hardly encourages rapid travel, as you will know. It is not only narrow and irregular, but, for no particular reason that I can see, climbs over the higher parts of the island, making it ill-suited for horses though not maybe for infantry on the march. It scarcely admits a carriage however. Besides, my watch was damaged on the perilous voyage from Penzance, and I have not seen a public time-piece by which I could tell the hour.

General Smyth, Officer Commanding the Garrison. There is no clock in any public place in these islands. The bell which you saw hanging over the entrance to the garrison as you came in tells the people of this island what o'clock it is. It *rings* at six, nine and twelve noon, and at three, six and nine after noon – that is, the bell is swung so that peals ring out for a minute or so. The number of each intermediate hour is *struck* – a clapper knocks the outside of the bell.

ED. I have just heard it strike ten then. But I thought I heard it ringing as I was coming along that dreadful road.

General. That would have been to give notice of a church service.

ED. But is not the church the one I passed on the way, some mile distant?

General. It is. It has no bell of its own.

ED. Even if it had, I do not imagine the rector would wish to abet the ravages of the sea in bringing about the final disintegration of its fabric with the reverberations of a bell in its bell-tower. I would have said it were better to anticipate the incursion of the sea and pull it down before it is washed away; and build another, with maybe a bell of its own, on an altogether safer site.

General. That is for the Bishop of Exeter to say. His Reverence has signalled his intention of making us a visit.

ED. I trust not in an attempt to influence appointments to the Mother Church of St Mary's, or to lay his hands on any of the Scilly tithes. Though I think the tradition that the islands are 'extra parochial', that is free of Episcopal Jurisdiction, is ill-founded, it would, in my opinion, be very inadvisable for the Bishop to interfere.

General. All the islands are tithable, but only St Mary's is specifically charged. Would you let that sleeping dog lie too?

ED. I would have to be better informed in order to express an opinion. I am more concerned with rates than tithes, and that all the islands should be considered as one parish instead of each sustaining its own poor. There should be a single workhouse for The Scillies and a General Rate made so that St Mary's could contribute to the support of the poor in the other, less prosperous islands.

General. So you are concerned with politics as well as facts?

ED. It is a question of good management. Scilly is an estate – a Crown Estate – just as any other I am called upon to survey in order to recommend means of improvement. If my advice to His Majesty's Commissioners for the Duchy of Cornwall is to have any value, it must take into account the whole circumstance of life here as it is to-day; and if much of this has been shaped by past custom and tradition which has been allowed to continue, but in the interests of His

Majesty in this year of grace 1829 should be terminated in my opinion, I should so report.

General. Fish is tithed, but by custom it goes not to the Church but to the Lord Proprietor's Resident Agent.

ED. Mr John?

General. None other. Tithe of Kelp is due, but never insisted upon.

ED. Kelp?

General. It is the ash of burnt seaweed which is sent to the mainland for processing and used in the manufacture of glass and soap – and a medical preparation known as iodine.

ED. What tithes do St Mary's pay, and on what?

General. Ten shillings an acre for potatoes and wheat; six shillings for barley; but none for hay. The farms are mostly small. A large crop will be 20 bushels an acre; but an average is 16.

ED. That seems very meagre.

General. Scilly Bushels of course – double your Winchester Bushels. An average crop is 32 Winchester Bushels. But tithes are not my province.

ED. 'Our' Winchester Bushels. You regard yourselves as a world apart over here, eh, General? An El Dorado with no Land Tax, no Window Tax, no Game Licences, no Liquor Licences.

General. It is all very satisfactory, I must confess.

ED. You are, are you not, a Lieutenant General in His Majesty's Army and Commanding Officer of this Garrison, and appointed as such by His Majesty's Government? But I see you also have the title of Lieutenant Governor, which seems to indicate a wider, a civil responsibility over and above the military one of commanding the soldiers of the garrison and defending the island against attack.

General. Magisterial authority is exercised by Mr John the Agent.

ED. That, as I see it, is as it should be. There is a Council, is there not, to conduct the business of local government?

General. It appoints church wardens, but does little else. The precise nature of the civil authority is undefined, and Mr John is very doubtful as to what powers the Council has, with the result that he makes no impact at all.

ED. You consider you should be running the Scillies?

General. That I should be unable to act outside the walls of this garrison, except in a military emergency of course, seems to me ridiculous.

ED. In my opinion you should be one of the magistrates, but not the chief one. The power of 'Presidency', if I may so call it, should reside with the Agent of the Noble Lessee, the Duke of Leeds whom you call the Lord Proprietor. St Mary's is not a garrison and is not subject to martial law, only this part of it – a hundred acres or so? – for which incidentally I understand the Government pays no rent to the lessee. I see you have converted most of it, general, to agricultural use and enjoy it rent free. Very 'satisfactory', I agree. But not for the Duchy of Cornwall who should be paid some £130 to £150 a year for this land I reckon. Your house – the best on the island I would say – with its large garden – has the commander of the garrison always lived here?

General. The Military Commandant, as he was then called, originally lived in that house down there (*pointing below*). It is now occupied by the serjeant and his wife who act as our servants. Mr John built this house some 15 years ago. The ground rent is five shillings a year.

ED. It would be let for agricultural purposes at 40s a year. I would assess £3 a year as a fair ground rent. At least five shillings is paid here, but I understand that no rent at all is paid for the land that the lighthouse stands on at St Agnes, nor the lighthouse keepers' cottages; no rent is paid either for the land of that Telegraph Tower on Newford Downs. All should be made to pay their due. We do not live rent-free, you know, in England.

General. So you intend to milk The Scillies to enable His Grace the Duke of Leeds to live in even greater luxury, is that it?

ED. On the contrary. My advice will be to extract what is due in order to finance schemes whereby the Scilly Islands may be brought into the modern world of the eighteen twenties, and out of the backwater into which they have been allowed to slide by inertia, indifference, weakness, ignorance and downright folly.

General. And you have some schemes in mind?

ED. Prime object is to attract strangers to the Scillies with money to spend, who will come not only as holiday makers but residents; and to do that you will need a very much larger and more commodious steam packet boat with accommodation suitable for persons of respectability and ladies, whose sailings are regular and swift – five hours say instead of fifteen – and not dependent on tides and weather. You need a new pier from The Newman to Bacon Lodge for which the harbour dues will be increased –

General. (*rubbing hands*) I am glad to hear that!

ED. And the right of the *Duchy* to these asserted. I could not do other, General, than recommend that the present practice of the Lieutenant General taking them in his stead should at once be discontinued – the

1. Samuel Driver, 1720–79 – seedsman, nurseryman and surveyor, whose marriage to Quaker Jane Purshouse brought the Drivers property in the Kent Road.

2. Abraham Purshouse Driver, 1755–1821 – surveyor and valuer, who re-linquished the Kent Road nursery in 1802 and was in great demand by the office of His Majesty's Woods and Forests and in tithe commutation and enclosure cases.

3. Robert Collier Driver, 1816–96 – the portrait presented to his wife in 1893 by the Land Surveyors Club in recognition of his service as treasurer and honorary secretary for forty years (*see* page 189).

4. Henry Jonas, son of a Cambridgeshire farmer, who was made a partner of Messrs. Driver in 1878 and died in 1928.

5. Maria Robson 'Cissie' Jonas (*née* Driver), 1854–88 – a daguerrotype taken at Ramsgate in 1860 when she was six. Her marriage to Henry Jonas in 1878 linked the Drivers and the Jonases (*see* page 190).

6. Harold Driver Jonas, 1879–1953 – Henry's son and father of Philip.

same advice as I will give in relation to the fish tithes which quite irregularly go, as you have informed me, to Mr John.

General (*conceding a smile*) You would make a good serjeant-major, Mr Driver.

ED. The known sources of gold in your El Dorado must be diverted to their rightful owner; then new sources found to add to them, to enable him to bring about the improvement from which *all* will benefit.

General. Such as?

ED. Simple things – a Rope Walk, a Basket Factory using the wood of the oziers and willows you will plant, a Brewery. Open up the granite quarries. Build a hotel and lodging houses at Porth Mellyn Bay and make it into a fashionable Watering Place and bathing resort. Many invalids, in my opinion, would find very great benefit in the climate here. Those who, for many complaints, are ordered by their doctors to Madeira or Lisbon, the South of France or Italy, might well find equal advantages in resorting to this island.

General. It will take time – to realise your dream.

ED. It is no dream; it *will* take time – and effort and enthusiasm and appreciation of what is required and what will result from it, particularly on the part of the Lord Proprietor, if His Majesty is to grant a renewal of his lease. So much supineness has been manifested in these islands, it will need a concerted effort to pull them up – and into line with the wind of change that seems to have passed the Scillies by these forty years or more.

> (*Garrison bell ringing the midday hour, Lieutenant Governor and the Duchy of Cornwall's Surveyor resolve to put aside their differences, and toast the health of King George IV in rich brown Madeira, and the brighter future of the Isles of Scilly which they both had at heart.*)

So there you are, Emily my dear. I will tell you the rest when I see you and have done that terrible crossing again.

Your loving, Edward

Diary of Edward Driver

June 28th, 1830

Our drinking the good health of his Majesty on the balcony of the Governor's House on St Mary's, Scilly, that hot morning last summer was not enough to extend that voluptuous monarch's life more than a twelvemonth; for I read in my newspaper to-day that the First Gentleman in Europe died on Saturday at Windsor and that the Duke of Wellington went at once to Bushy Park to bring the Duke of Clarence the intelligence of his Illustrious Brother's decease and of his now being King William IV. Whereupon the latter drove to St James's Palace in a plain carriage and four looking very pale and much fatigued.

There has been no false respect or sorrow shown by the papers, who have not hesitated to express openly what all the nation has thought of George IV throughout his brief reign and his regency: 'set religion, morality and even decency at defiance' – 'he thought of nothing but personal ease. . . . He consented to the Popish Bill on the same principle that he had shaken off poor Mrs Robinson. Protestantism and Perdita were voted bores; they disturbed his peace.' As a lapsed Quaker I am glad to see contempt dispensed where contempt is due, and no unworthy *Nihil de mortuis nisi bonum* cant wasted on so ignoble a character.

Robert Collier Driver – articles of apprenticeship for five years as a land surveyor with James Marmont

February 1st, 1832

Articles of apprenticeship and agreement entered into between Charles Burrell Driver of Cornhill in the City of London, stationer, and Robert Collier Driver (son of the said Charles Burrell Driver, a minor of the age of sixteen years or thereabouts) of the one part, and James Marmont of the City of Bristol, land surveyor, of the other part.

Witness, that the said Robt Collier Driver of his own free will and by and with the consent and approbation of his Father, Doth put and bind himself apprentice to the said James Marmont to serve him in the business, practice and profession of a Land Surveyor and in all things incident thereto from this date for full term of Five Years. . . . and that the said Robt Collier Driver will keep the secrets of the said James Marmont and readily and cheerfully obey and execute his lawful and reasonable commands and shall not depart or absent himself from the employ of the said Jas. Marmont without his consent first obtained, and shall be just true and faithful to him in all matters whatever, and in no way wrongfully use, detain, lend, lose, waste or destroy any moneys, goods or things whatever belonging to him or knowingly suffer the same to be done by others, but shall conduct and demean himself with all due diligence, honesty, sobriety and temperance, and as a faithful apprentice ought to do.

Diary of Edward Driver

July 3rd, 1833

The House of Commons Select Committee on the Present State of Agriculture has been sitting since May 10th. 'Edward Driver Esquire' (!) was the first of two witnesses to be heard today, followed by 'Mr Smith Woolley'. They will have questioned 51 witnesses before they have done – there are only two more days to go – of whom 11 were Esquires and 40 Misters. My old friend George Smallpiece of Cobham, Guildford, is to be the last witness of all – he has been occupier of land for at least 40 years and he and his brother farm some 1,000 acres. Only a few landowners have been heard, mostly rent payers like George and land surveyors like me.

It was a hot day and the room in the Palace of Westminster where the hearings took place was excessively stuffy, and hardly conducive to the lucidity of mind required to answer with any degree of accuracy and objectivity the questions which rained upon one in quick succession. It was something of an ordeal I must confess – they must have asked me well over a hundred questions, and I trust the strain did not show. Though the committee consists of 37, five constitute a quorum, and this morning Sir James Graham Bart presided over some nine or ten of them, none of whom I recognised or knew except, I think, Lord Howick and Mr Gilbert Heathcote. There was a moment when the questioning came to the Corn Laws that I was gratified to see Sir Robert Peel enter the room and occupy a chair for a period, though it was not for long.

I told them 31 years was the usual term of a Crown Estate lease and that I was employed as Receiver in 18 counties. Many leases which had expired in the last three years had not been re-let but sold. Most tenants were paying 'war rents' for which they had contracted at the top of the war price. Most Crown estates were let in large parcels to individuals who afterwards re-let them. The Crown Estates were not extensive; the whole amount of my receipt did not exceed £15,000 a year. One of the largest was at Eltham in Kent which had been let in 1808 for 31 years. The lessee had been refused a reduction in rent as he was underletting the farm in a way that was very unsatisfactory to the tenants. But when a Crown Estate in Sussex reverted to the Crown for want of a male heir, and a relative had made the discovery to the Crown, this gentleman became the tenant at a reduced rent as a reward, and thereupon sub-let the several farms.

Crown property, I said, always sold at a higher price and more readily than estates belonging to private individuals, because the title was so simple and so good, and the charge for the conveyance so extremely moderate.

I told them I thought the condition of labourers was better than two years ago but worse than 10 years ago. The poor rate was highest in Sussex and increasing most in the 18 counties I knew. The advantages of letting small tracts of land to cottagers were not so great as I had expected. The evil which had resulted from this was the dissatisfaction of farmers who found labourers employed on their own grounds more fatigued and less able to perform the labour which they were paid to do by their employer.

Question: 'The dissatisfaction is with the farmers not the labourers?'

Answer: 'Not with the labourers.'

Question: 'Nor with the owners of the cottages or gardens?'

Answer: 'No. I offered 20 acres to divide into small lots, and I did not get one person to take them.'

There was a great deal of land on the market at the present time, I said. I had great difficulty in selling land, especially any with inferior soil. For the last three years the capitalist had been unwilling to advance money. There was never a more favourable opportunity for the investment of money in land than the present. Funds had been so high a price and rents so much reduced, there should be no objection in the minds of capitalists to make investments, but such was not the case. The reason was the uncertainty that seemed to prevail in the minds of all as to the stability of rents in land; and the reason for this was the question of the Corn Laws being so much in agitation. Capitalists' opinion was that any alteration of the corn laws would produce a very serious reduction of rent.

Question: 'They do not fancy a property tax?'

Answer: 'I do not know. If the corn laws remain as they are, present rents should be maintained. In some cases present rents may be too high for the present price of corn, but not much too high. Some landlords make abatements, others not. But over the last ten years there has been a general reduction. Over the last ten years most have not realised the rent on expectation of which they purchased. If corn falls below the

Jovis, 4° die Julii, 1833.

THE RIGHT HON. SIR JAMES GRAHAM, BART.

IN THE CHAIR.

Edward Driver, Esq., called in ; and Examined.

11661. YOU are a land-surveyor?—Yes, I am.

11662. Residing in London?—Yes.

11663. And in extensive practice?—Yes.

11664. Throughout what district does that practice extend?—I think I may say generally all through the country ; I receive, for instance, rents for the Crown in 18 counties.

11665. How long have you been so extensively employed in those counties?—For the Crown ever since the Act of Parliament passed, in 1817, for the appointment of receivers, which is now 16 years ; and I was long before so employed for many private individuals.

11666. In the transaction of your business do you visit in the course of the year all, or the greater part, of those counties?—Yes, I do.

11667. Have you been in the habit of so doing since you have been a receiver of rents?—Yes, I have.

11668. Making such distinctions as you think it right to make in your answer, with respect to different counties, should you say that the general agriculture of those counties which you visit annually, and in which you receive rents, has been going back lately, and if so, from what period has it began to go back?—I think I may say generally that it has been going back, and certainly I think more in the last 10 years than at any former period.

11669. Bringing to comparison rather a later period, since the passing of the last Corn Bill, which was in 1828, has the agriculture of these 18 counties been going back since that?—I think the distress that they feel has increased since the period of 1828.

11670. With respect to the gross produce raised in the 18 counties, should you say that that had diminished since 1822, in average seasons?—I think in many of them it has certainly diminished, from, I should say, the land having become in a poorer state, having been more neglected of late years, and consequently less productive.

11671. Does that observation apply to all qualities of soil, that it has been more neglected, or to any particular soil?—No ; I think I should say to the inferior soils, such as the cold clay soils and thin soils, more than to the better soils.

11672. To the cold clay soils more than to the least inferior soils?—I do not think the light inferior soils have suffered so much in proportion to others.

11673. The stiff clay land requires more labour?—Yes ; and the seasons have been particularly unpropitious for those lands for several years back.

11674. Do you know any considerable tract of cold clay land that has gone out of cultivation in those 18 counties?—Not in one district, but I think in a great many districts there have been small portions that have gone out of cultivation.

11675. But no considerable tract within your knowledge?—No, certainly not.

11676. Within the last 16 years what should you say had been the abatement of rent, speaking generally?—I think from 20 to 25 per cent.

11677. Is that upon the highest war-rents, because 16 years would not carry you back to the war?—No, it would not; and I think in some upon the war-rents there has been more reduction than 25 per cent.

4 A 2

11678. Ha

average of the last three years there will be a still further reduction of rent. The price of land has been falling for some time; so capitalists are inclined to obtain a high rate of years' purchase. The interest obtained for a large investment in land is $3\frac{1}{2}$ per cent. I would have no difficulty in getting this; but I would not get 4 per cent.'

It was more easy, I said, to find vendors than purchasers now. It was from fear of the law regulating the price of corn. There was as much money in the market as there were estates to sell, but there was an unwillingness to purchase. Respectable tenants could be found for good land, but not inferior lands. For the last ten years tenants generally had been regarding leases for a fixed term of years as binding one side and not the other. A tenant of good substance had rented a very large farm of 1,500 acres in Cambridgeshire, perhaps the finest in the kingdom, but he soon considered the rent too high when the landlord refused to make an abatement, the tenant complained he was losing money and threatened to leave the country and go to Van Diemen's Land. I was obliged in these circumstances to negociate with him, rather than have the farm vacated, which would be a serious injury to the estate. We had to let him off his bargain. We divided it into three farms and let them to three good tenants at a sacrifice of 10 per cent reduction in rent. A change had come about recently in the opinions and habits of tenants, I told them. They seemed to regard their own characters less than heretofore, largely owing to their distress in their farming.

The scale of rent was not linked to any given price of wheat. I said I knew of a farm in Sussex near Battle with cold clay soil where the rent to-day was the same as it had been in 1787 – six shillings an acre. But the poor rates had increased and the highway rates, though the tithes were the same as in 1787. But only one-twentieth of all Crown estates had the same rents as in 1787. Those that had been raised since 1787 were much too cheap for to-day's conditions, but such tenants were even now grumbling. Though rent on poor clay land like at Battle might be 6s an acre, on fine lands it was 18s to 20s.

Question: 'They do not complain at 6s an acre?'

Answer: 'They all complain. Some are tithable; others tithe-free. The 6s an acre land bears 16 bushels of corn an acre on average. A good crop is 20 bushels. Complaining tenants say "If times are not better, we shall not go on long". The habits of farmers are more expensive than they were in 1787, but that is not the case with the very small farmers, the working farmer, what we call "round-frockmen". They would suffer if wheat fell to 50s a quarter. They suffer with their present rent and are never backward in making observations on it, but most complain of the increased poor rate – in Sussex the poor rates are 15s to 20s in the pound.'

Question: 'Is the ten per cent increase in rent due to improvement in husbandry and easier mode of extracting crops?'

Answer: 'Mainly due to better land. I cannot agree that by an improved system of husbandry less good soils can be brought under cultivation. Improvements have not taken place more upon the poorer soils than the richer.'

Note
on Report of the Select Committee on Agriculture

August 2nd, 1833

'The Agriculture of the kingdom is the first of all its Concerns, the foundation of all its Prosperity' – a generally held principle.

Produce of Great Britain is unequal to Consumption, and is partially dependent on Wheat from foreign countries. Average price of wheat in 1821 was 54s 6d; highest price in last five years 76s 7d; lowest 51s 3d; average 61s 8d. Average price in 1833, 53s 1d.

In their report the committee observe critically on the practice of giving the Father of the Family an increased allowance on the birth of each child; a Premium is thus indirectly offered to improvident marriages and to an increase in the population. The Law of Settlement tends to prevent the free circulation of labour and to chain it to the spot where it is not wanted, and to check its natural flow to the place where it is required. The labour of the poor man is his only commodity, and the reasons should be cogent which justify any legal impediment to his carrying it to the best market he can discover.

'Your committee are of the opinion that the present reluctance to purchase land, or to take it on lease, is to be ascribed to losses recently sustained in agriculture and to the uncertainty supposed to exist with regard to present Corn Laws . . . and uncertainty on a subject of such vital importance where stability and confidence are essential produces others hardly less disastrous than Change itself.'

Letter of Edward Driver to his nephew, Robert Driver

8 Richmond Terrace,
September 20th, 1833

Dear Robert,

Your apprenticeship with Mr Marmont at Bristol – our second largest town, is it not? – cannot but be rewarded with qualification of the highest sort, and Uncle George and I are delighted that you should have chosen to follow the profession which, in that youthful speech of mine on your first Christmas day, of which I regret to say we are continually reminding you, I fervently hoped you would adopt, and that there will be another Driver to whom we can hand on the torch before we finally withdraw.

I thought it would be helpful if from time to time I sent you an account of some of our activities at Richmond Terrace which would not only help you in your studies, but keep you informed of how we are serving clients whose affairs we have been taking care of for very many years and are likely still to be serving when you come to join us here.

The first assignment I had entirely on my own after attaining my majority in 1804 was going down to Burnham Abbey, the Crown's estate in Buckinghamshire, to make a survey before Lord Jersey's lease expired. Exactly another 21 years later, as it happened, in 1825, I was down there again to make another appraisal after repairs had been made to the farm – the attached letter of December 17th, 1823 refers. Lord Grenville of course was the Whig Prime Minister who in 1806 led the so-called 'Ministry of All The Talents' and will go down in history as the man of whom our present king, as Duke of Clarence and Lord High Admiral, said 'Lord Grenville at one blow destroyed, by the abolition of the Slave Trade, the maritime strength of the country' – one of many such pronouncements which earned him the name Silly Billy.

I have just returned from the Auction Mart where to-day I have sold the 430 acre farm at Burnham in seven lots – the climax to some eight years' activity which constitutes an interesting 'Case History', involving Tithes, Dilapidations, Turnpike Trusts and other matters, from which I think there is much to be learnt. I thought therefore that this would make a suitable opening for the series of such studies which I hope to send you in the course of the next five years. The 'A. Milne Esq' to whom most of my letters are written is, of course, the Surveyor General.

From your vantage point in Bristol I hope you will be able to reciprocate by keeping me informed of the progress made by the committee formed last autumn to forward the scheme for a Bristol and London Railroad, the name of which I see was changed last month to the 'Great Western Railway'. At the same time I am endeavouring to establish a relationship with the Mr Charles Saunders who has been appointed secretary of the project's London Committee. With a Driver at each end of the line we ought to accomplish something between us!

I am glad at least that you were not in Bristol for the terrible riots of the year before last demonstrating against opposition to the Reform Bill – I am told it was the nearest thing to civil war in this country since the House of Commons debated the Grand Remonstrance in 1641. But with the Bill receiving the royal assent last June I hope things will be quieter, though for many, I realise, it does not go far enough and of course it does not do much to relieve agricultural distress. We do not want a return to the Mobbing Winter of 1830. I know Sir Robert Peel has ideas about setting up a new kind of 'Police Force' and though this may help the Lord Lieutenant to keep law and order in his county, again it will not alleviate the sufferings of the farm labourers or bring them the 14s a week I consider they rightly deserve. I had no sympathy with the idle fishermen of Scilly who refused all work but fishing, but the distress of those for whom work should be found on the land over here cries out for relief and *action* by those in authority.

Your affectionate
Uncle Edward

1833–1835

Enclosure to letter of September 20th, 1833

CASE HISTORY: BURNHAM ABBEY ESTATE,
1825–1833

1. Dilapidations

At the beginning of 1825 the extensive programme of repairs to Burnham Abbey Farm were completed. They included new weather boarding and quartering in the north end of the Old Abbey, blocking up window openings, stripping and tiling the new lean-to and patching up the floor of the loft. The plastering of the Little Barn was repaired; also the tiling on the Barley Barn, the brick nogging of the Oat Barn, the underpinning of the Wheat Barn, the brick work to the Farmhouse and Brewhouses. I reported to the Office of Woods and Forests that this had been carried out to my satisfaction on January 31st, 1825; but three years later I was down at Burnham and noticed that a barn, which is the only building on the 220 acres leased by a Mr Horatio Waller, was in a very bad state. I had reason to admonish him in regard to other matters too – lopping some large branches off several of the trees in a very improper manner.

2. Recommendation to Sell

On May 17th 1831 I wrote to Mr Milne recommending that the Crown would do better to sell Mr Waller's 224 acres than continuing them upon lease. It would be desirable, I said, to offer the land by auction in June. They accepted my advice and a date for the sale, later than I had hoped, was fixed – August 13th.

3. Liability for Tithes

We had to determine, before the land could be offered, whether it was tithable. It was said it had been tithe-free for 150 years, but we received a letter from the Crown Estate solicitors saying that this supposition was based on a survey made by the Commissioners of Enquiry during the Usurpation (that is, Oliver Cromwell's Commonwealth), but in spite of that document tithes were in fact due, and to the Crown. They assured us that the estate could be sold in that understanding. However we took the precaution of commissioning a gentleman named Mr Caley whom I made the mistake of calling an antiquarian when I should have said antiquary, to search the records in the Augmentation Office to ascertain how the exemption from tithes arose.

Mr Caley reported that Burnham Abbey had been founded in 1265 by Richard King of the Romans, and that it had been either a Benedictine or Augustine order. The Crown took the estate during the reign of Henry VIII on the surrender of Alice Baldwyn the last abbess on – he had the exact date! – September 19th, 1539. On November 31st the following year the estate and tithes demised to the Crown, who let it to one William Tyldesley for 21 years at an annual rent of £32 15s 9d.

This information took some time to uncover and the auction fixed for August 13th had to be postponed. I took the opportunity afforded by this further extension of time to ask Mr Charsley, Mr Waller's agent, to make some enquiries among the other tenants regarding the payment of tithes, in order to establish the *practice* quite part from the legal rights and wrongs of the matter. One tenant only, reported Mr Charsley, had told him he had not paid tithes although demanded of him; but my impression is that in fact no one has ever paid tithes, but will not admit it.

4. Expiration of Lease – Necessary Precautions

The Crown Solicitor advised postponing the auction indefinitely until the Crown's title to the tithes was ascertained for certain, and the services of Mr Caley were enlisted once again to make further searches for evidence. This meant Mr Waller's lease would expire before we were able to offer the land for sale, and on September 16th we suggested that one of us attended at the estate on the day the lease expired to receive possession on behalf of the Crown and arrange valuation of the Ploughings and other labour performed by the tenants. Proceeding in this way the Crown would not be prejudiced in their right to enforce any claim from either of the lessees which might be due for dilapidations or mismanagement contrary to the covenants in the lease. This would not preclude the Crown from entering into fresh negociations with the present tenants.

5. Attendance on Expiry Day

Arthur Spigott of our office attended on October 10th to receive possession of the lands at Burnham on lease to Horatio Waller which expired that day. On the 15th I wrote to Mr Milne to report that the estate was now in the possession of the Crown, and that we had left a person in charge. I wrote further: 'We feel it an imperative duty to call the especial attention of the Commissioners of Woods & C to the great inattention which has been manifested in the non-observance of the covenants in the lease for the cultivation of the land; and submit this is an instance which ought not to be passed over because we gave notice two or three years since. . . . The land has been cropped with two white strawed crops in succession in several instances. The whole of the straw and other produce of this year's crop has been carried away from the farm and not any dung brought back in lieu thereof, consequently the farm is very much prejudiced and compensation ought to be required, especially as the lessee is a Gentleman of very large property and his agent is fully sensible of his liability and I believe willing to make any reasonable compensation. We should be allowed to negociate with him for payment.'

6. Further Recommendation to Sell a Misjudgement

In November we again recommended that the property should be advertised and sold without delay. By now Mr Waller was no longer the lessee. We fully expected, we wrote, that there would be very good competition for it. We fixed the date of sale as March 9th, 1832.

I regret to say however we misjudged the situation, and no bids were made – so no sale. See my letter to Mr Milne of March 9th.

7. Surrender of Lord Grenville's Lease

The lease of the land which Lord Grenville rented at Burnham was due to expire on October 10th, 1835, and in January this year (1833) we advised Mr Milne's office to treat with Lord Grenville for the surrender of the remainder of his lease at once and put the estate up for sale this spring. The property was adjoining the High Turnpike Road to Bath and was near to Windsor and Maidenhead, so the full value should be obtained by offering it in competition in lots. The purchaser would be able to take possession at Michaelmas.

On February 19th we heard from Mr William Chisholme, Lord Grenville's solicitor, that he was willing to enter into a treaty for surrender of his lease from October 10th. The Crown agreed to pay the difference between receipts from tenants (£577) and the rent paid by Lord G. to the Crown (£437) – an annual profit of £139 7s 6d.

Richmond Terrace
9th March 1832

Lands at Burnham

Sir

I regret to be obliged to report to you there was not any competition at the Auction held this day for the above Estates & scarcely any Bidder for either of the Lots – that consequently no Bidding being offered, at all approaching to the Minimum Prices which had been fixed for the respective Lots – no Sale of either has been effected –

We shall probably have some application, to treat for the whole by Private Contract –

I remain Sir

Your Most, Obedient Humble Sert.

Edwd Driver

A. Milne Esqre

Letter of Edward Driver re sale of Lands at Burnham, 1832

95

8. Further Postponement of Sale

The auction was advertised for July 13th (1833), but was again postponed owing to the uncertainty over the tithes. A new Act was coming into operation on August 16th which would give the Crown the right to prescribe for a general exemption from tithes on the ground of non-payment. Counsel's opinion was sought this time but the learned gentleman did little other than resurrect the Cromwellian Survey of 1650 which stated it was tithe-free, and recommend that the sale should be postponed until after August 16th when we could say 'tithe-free' without the prospective purchaser fearing that he might have to litigate the question. He also recommended that Messrs Driver should be consulted before the Particular was settled.

9. Preliminaries to the Sale of September 20th, 1833

So we come – at last! – to to-day's sale. On September 9th we sought guidance from Mr Milne's office on the minimum price we should ask and it was of course for us to make suggestions. We were unashamedly optimistic; in view of the 'excellent neighbourhood' we said we should expect higher prices by competition than by private contract. We estimated a total of £21,080 for all seven lots and suggested allowing a latitude of five per cent under this sum.

Prospective purchasers visited the site, and one of them a Mr J. B. Monck, wrote to say he was well satisfied with the land but that the farmhouse was in a most deplorable and almost inconceivable state of dilapidation.

'Lord Grenville' wrote Mr Monk, 'is no doubt bound by covenants to deliver up the premises in good and substantial repair or to pay the Crown a sum for doing the repairs. If the sum due from Lord Grenville were transferred to the purchaser by the conditions of sale I should be glad to be a bidder, otherwise I must decline. The money that I have to lay out on land is trust money. I may invest this money on the purchase of an estate in good condition and in good repair, and pay for it accordingly; but if I buy land out of condition and where intensive repairs are wanting, I cannot improve the land and make the repairs out of the trust money subsequently to the conclusion of the purchase.'

Our reply to this was: 'We cannot advise the Crown to enter into any engagement that the purchaser shall be put into the situation of taking the benefit of any claim the Crown may have against the lessee in respect of any dilapidations, but it will be better that they assert such claim for their own benefit; as it is our opinion that the property is likely to produce quite as much at the auction in the manner it is proposed to offer it, as it would do were the right of claim to be given to the purchaser.'

10. Accusation of 'Mistaken Description'

Mr Milne's office referred to us a letter they had received from a Mr Hamlet Henry Hawthorn, Master of Burnham Gore National School, who called their attention to article 10 of our conditions of sale: 'if any mistake be made in the description of the property or any such error whatsoever, such error or mistake shall not annul sale, but a compensation given'. For nine years Mr Hawthorn had served the Honourable Hudson Bay Company as Accountant at their Settlements in America, and at the termination of his agreement with them was solicited to take charge of the school at Burnham Gore. In 18 years he had educated 600 children from surrounding parishes, showing altogether '27 years of arduous servitude to my King and Country'. He became acquainted with Mr Hollier of Burnham Abbey Farm in 1818 and agreed to rent from him Lent Cottage which was part of the Burnham Farm estate and 'separated from the dwelling house about one gun shot'. He agreed to undertake repairs costing £90 and pay £20 a year rent. Confiding in declarations and oath of Mr Hollier, he entered the premises and started to do the repairs 'not suffering to arise in my mind any doubt of the honesty of him who was to deliver me a fair and honest lease at Michaelmas 1819'. He received a 14 year lease, but without the privilege Mr Hollier was to have put in it, namely the two acres of land occupied by John Williams and Henry Newell which constituted Lot 5 of our sale. Nonetheless he signed the lease in September 1819; but when after seven years he had to leave Lent Cottage to go and live at the Gore School, Mr Hollier refused to make him any allowance for the unexpired seven years. Thereupon Mr Hawthorn let the tenement to 'an unprincipled man', Henry Newell, who refused to pay rent until Mr Hollier ordered him to. When Mr Hawthorn demanded rent from his 'tenant', Mr Hollier told Newell, in front of a constable as witness, not to pay him, and further asserted that the lease he had given Hawthorn was 'false', declaring 'Now do your best!'

At this turn of events, admitted Mr Hawthorn, his power to act ceased; but on reading article 10 of our conditions of sale he 'accepted the invitation' as he put it, of making known his grievance 'which has borne down the mind and body of your very respectful Declarationist' now an invalid of three months. There was of course nothing which we could do as auctioneers of the property to meet Mr Hawthorn's grievance or to justify our paying him the compensation referred to in the conditions of sale.

11. Sale of Burnham Abbey Farm at Auction Mart,
    September 20th, 1833

The prospectus declared the property to be tithe-free as you see, and exonerated from Land Tax, and thus peculiarly well adapted either for investment or occupation. The occupier Mrs Mary Ann Hollier had received notice to quit on October 10th next.

This time there was spirited competition for Lot 1, the farmhouse, which we sold to Mr John Pocock for £16,700. Mr Harry Grover bought the land he was occupying (Lot 2) for £1,620. Lots 4 and 5 (which included the unprincipled Henry Newell's Lent Cottage) were sold to Lord Grenville for £1,980. The whole estate was sold for the gross amount of £22,720 which we had reason to believe was very satisfactory, and not all that distant from our estimate. All that was left for us to do was to charge the various purchasers for the timber on their land – Mr Pocock naturally had most to pay (£542) and the total did not exceed £750. Mr Pocock also had to pay £267 for Tillage.

Diary of George Neale Driver

June 21st, 1834

'All right, we are all concerned chiefly with agriculture and we are all based on London.'

'What about auctioneering? Are not auctioneers to be admitted?'

'So long as he is primarily a land surveyor, and a competent one at that, no one should be *dis*qualified, to put it negatively, by also pursuing the business of auctioneer.'

'*Business*, eh? Auctioneering is a very large part of *our* business. There is nothing "inferior" to it, compared, say, to valuing.'

'Many would so regard it.'

'Chain surveying and plotting is certainly inferior.'

'It is not a question of what is inferior but what is not "professional". Auctioneering is "commercial" – you know, buying and selling. The land surveyor has *clients*, not customers. He sells advice. He provides services.'

'What about land *dealing*? Does that put a land surveyor beyond the pale?'

Edward, William Blount and I were drinking our brandy after lunch at the club, and arguing about the type of people who could be admitted to the 'Land Surveyors Club' which Will Blount had once propounded after a particularly good dinner in this very room, and was now on the point of being institutionalised. Will had thought there was room for a society of professional men in the world of land surveying which shunned the cosy, eating and drinking character of the Architects Club (while not entirely eschewing that aspect of any band of brothers), but would primarily advance the dignity and position in society which he considered our due. We were *consultants*, and should be so treated; we were in the market to give advice to anyone who saw fit to consult us, as opposed to the 'land agent' retained as a servant or official by a single employer. It was a worthy object, but when it came to defining precisely what we meant by 'Land Surveyor' in the context of the proposed 'Land Surveyors Club' it was not at all easy – hence the argument.

The point had not been resolved of course by the time we moved to 12 Cumberland Street for the meeting at which a formal resolution was passed – and minuted – to establish a club with six founder members, of which Edward was one. It would have been undesirable to have had two partners from the same firm, but it was decided this afternoon that the Club should hold its first meeting at the Freemasons Tavern next Friday (the 27th) when I should attend and be proposed as Treasurer. Following our argument, Will Blount said he thought he, Edward and I should undertake the task of framing the rules of membership and attempt a Definition of a Land Surveyor. Will said he saw the Club as the body which eventually might draw up a Scale of Charges for valuation, estate management, measuring and the rest.

I think we all realised, though none of us were prepared to say so, that we were too anxious to emphasise our agricultural connection. To many of us it was a matter of pride almost, as if association with the landed aristocracy – being consulted by them on tithe matters and the like – imposed a status which somehow made us 'superior'. I am eleven years younger than Edward, and I think I can discern, as perhaps he cannot, that times are changing, that the importance of agriculture is beginning to recede and we must look to the towns and to industry for the future centre of our activity. Apart from that, these railways cannot but transform our lives. The combined opposition of Eton College and the Middlesex, Bucks and Berks landowners is unlikely seriously to impede the passing of the Great Western Railway Bill which had its second reading in the Commons in March, though after the Committee stage the Lords will do their best to reject it, I am sure of that.

Diary of Edward Driver

October 17th, 1834

So that room I gave evidence in to the Select Committee on Agriculture is no more! – burnt to the ground along with the rest of the Palace of Westminster – except Westminster Hall, thank goodness! – in the conflagration that swept the building and reduced it to ashes last night. Someone has said the cause was over-zealous stoking of the heating apparatus with Exchequer tallies. A likely tale! More certainly a latterday Faux, who learnt his business rick burning in Sussex and was paid by someone with a mind to accelerating the process of Parliamentary Reform and call attention to the inadequacy of the legislation of 1832.

I wonder where I shall attend if ever I am called on to give evidence to another Select Committee?

Minutes of Evidence

before the Lords Committee on the Act to making a Railway from Bristol to join the London and Birmingham Railway to be called

THE GREAT WESTERN RAILWAY

Lord Wharncliffe in the chair
Mr Sergeant Merewether for the Provost and Fellows of Eton College

Evidence of Edward Driver Esquire 2nd July 1835

EDWARD DRIVER Esquire is called in, and examined as follows:

(*Mr Talbot.*)   You are a Land Surveyor and Valuer?
Yes, I am.

And of considerable Experience?
Yes.

Have you been engaged for the Crown upon these Matters?
Yes.

Have those Examinations of the Value of Land been made for the Purpose of Purchase and Sale?
All Purposes.

Buying and selling included?
Yes.

You have been employed by the Directors to value a Part of the Land upon this Line?
I have been employed to value the Land from the River at Maidenhead to the Junction with the Birmingham and London Railway.

What Quantity of Land is comprised in that Distance?
189 to 190 Acres.

From whom did you take the Quantities that would be required?
From Mr. Brunel the Engineer.

What is your Valuation, – the Sum Total of that 190 Acres?
£39,446.

What does that include besides the actual Value of the Land?
All the Compensation for any Buildings that are interfered with; all Subtenants and Lessees Claims for Compensation, and for all Severance and consequential Damage of every Kind and Nature.

Is the Country a level Country generally in that District?
Exceedingly level.

Did you meet with many Obstacles in the Way of Houses and Buildings.
I think there is only One House upon the whole Line.

Where is that?
At Ealing Common.

You mean there is only One House actually upon the Line?
Yes; I am not aware that the Line will interfere with that; they may shift it; and there are One or Two Labourers Cottages in other Parts.

You say you have had considerable Experience in Land Valuations; have you had Land Valuations to make in this District?
Very generally.

Compared with the Estimates made on former Occasions, how is this Estimate, high or low?

I should consider it the highest I have made at all.

Have you been engaged upon similar Projects?
Yes.

Such as what?

Upon the London and Birmingham I was employed to value against them for the Owners of the Property.

(*By a Lord.*)   I think you say your Calculation was, from Maidenhead to London, 39,446*l.*
Yes.

Does that include simply the Width of the Cutting, or the Land which is occupied by the Width of the Cutting, Twenty-two Feet?
No, the whole of the Land.

Is that a Calculation of the Width throughout?

No; it is much wider where the deep Cutting is, and where the Embankment is; the Base is much wider; and the whole of that is included.

Have you calculated upon any Chances of Damage by Slips from the Banks?

I have; but I think the Ground is so very level upon that Line there is not much to be apprehended from Slips.

Let the Ground be ever so level, do you not think in all these Matters there must be, generally speaking, a Damage greater than that which you usually pay upon such Occasions?

I think the Estimate I have formed will cover every possible Claim that may be made for any Damage whatever.

What Proportion of the 39,000*l.* is for the Land alone, exclusive of the Compensation?
22,341*l.* for the Land alone.

Cross-examined by Mr Sergeant Merewether.

That leaves about 17,105*l.* for Compensation, does not it?
Yes.

Is that the whole of the Sum you have allowed for Compensation?

That is the whole of the Sum I have allowed for Compensation beyond the Value of the Land.

So that when you say you have taken into consideration every possible Claim that can be made for Compensation, and that with reference to the Land you have spoken of, is all covered by the Sum of 17,105*l.*?

Yes.

What is the Length of the Line you have valued?

I think it is about Twenty Miles.

When you made your Valuation of the Land, what Number of Years Purchase did you put on it?

Thirty-three Years Purchase.

(*Mr Talbot.*)   What is the Average per Cent. for Compensation per Acre? I make it between Seventy and Eighty per Cent.; is it so?

It would be very nearly that; as near as possible.

The Witness is directed to withdraw.

1835–1857

Memorandum

To: Mr J. Fawcett, Counting House   *From:* E. Driver

GREAT WESTERN RAILWAY – SURVEYING,
VALUING, AND SETTLING CLAIMS, 1835

I attach my notes of the name and owner and amount of claim of
each of the properties we have visited on instruction from the Great
Western Railway in connection with the above, and I would be glad if
you would make the necessary calculations as regards our fees, on the
usual scale of the first £100 at 5 per cent and pro rata, and have these
set out in columns, and the addition made, for formal presentation to
the G.W.R. directors.

I estimate we investigated 174 claims totalling £84,240, of which the
highest was by Mr Robert Palmer for £8,645 and the second highest by
John Leveson Gower for £4,521; and the lowest John Winch for £3 and
Mr Hawkins for £1. I have the impression that Mr Pascoe Grenfell
whose 12 acres in Berkshire I value at £2,020 will have trouble in
satisfying his tenant Messrs Louch. He is anxious to avoid the expense
of having to appeal to a jury, but I advised him and his solicitor, Mr
Naylor, that Messrs Louch would probably press for a verdict on compensation for their loss by this means in the absence of a satisfactory
offer from him.

I reckon our fee from percentages should be in the region of £1,200.
To these you will add our charges for miscellaneous services such as
assisting Mr Smallpiece and Mr Cooke in preparing their valuations to
give evidence before a jury, and making plans of their property;
attendance to be sworn in the House of Lords and special attendances
to give evidence on the amended bill before the Committee; attending
the Sherriff's Office when the juries were appointed; attending at

Hanwell as Shewer to the Jury; attending juries all day on two other occasions – as detailed on the attached sheet.

To the total you will add a sum for Travelling Expenses which the directors have agreed shall be computed at the rate of 10 per cent upon the bill.

14th August, 1835

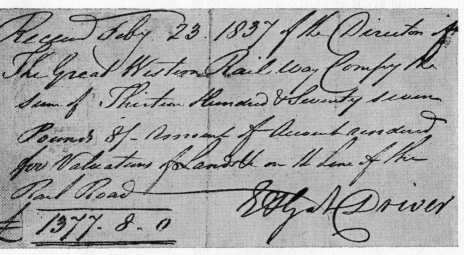

Receipt to Great Western Railway, 1837

Letter of Edward Driver to Robert Driver

8 Richmond Terrace
June 21st, 1837

My dear Robert,

So you are 21 at last! – your Bristol apprenticeship successfully completed (Mr Marmont speaks very highly of you), and ready, I hope to take up your partnership, after perhaps a well deserved vacation. Your Uncle George and I will welcome you here at Richmond Terrace next week or the week after – and I know your father is greatly looking forward to having you at home again.

The death of the King yesterday morning and the succession of the young Princess Victoria, marks, I think, the passing of an era – if you manage to arrive in London by Thursday you will be in time to see the funeral. The change cannot but be for the good. After all, William IV came to the throne at the mature age of 65 and he was so excited by the exaltation he nearly went mad. From all accounts our 19 year old sovereign – and, as owner of the Crown Estates, royal client – who might well be either dazzled or confounded with the grandeur and novelty of her situation, seems neither the one nor the other, as Mr Greville was heard to remark, and behaves with a decorum and propriety beyond her years, and with all the sedateness and dignity the want of which was so conspicuous in her uncle.

Come and help to make what I suppose we must get used to calling the 'Victorian' age a prosperous one for Messrs Driver and

Your Affectionate

Uncle Edward

Memorandum

To: Mr Andrew Spigott   *Date:* 2nd October, 1837
From: E. Driver

GREAT WESTERN RAILWAY

Mr Saunders tells me he has had a letter from Mr Lewis Reid of White Waltham, agent of Mr John Leveson Gower, a copy of which I attach. Mr Saunders wants particulars of the 'bargain' which Mr Reid alleges I made with Mr Leveson Gower in respect of a payment of £800 for a bridge across Mr Gower's freehold land in Mille Field, Ruscombe, plus £27 for timber, less £40 for two cottages standing within the line which Mr Gower seems to have bought from the railway company (?), making £787 due to him in all. It seems the church also has some claim on the sale of the bridge.

It is some time since these events, and I would be obliged if you would recover such papers as relate to them, and discuss with me at your earliest convenience what advice I should convey to Mr Saunders of the GWR who is seeing Mr Reid at Cornhill tomorrow afternoon.

Memorandum

To: E. Driver   *Date:* 14 August, 1838
From: G. N. Driver

Here is a copy of the 'Statement' which I have been working on for so long setting out the price of wheat per quarter in Britain since the year 1043 (when I reckon it was 6d) to the present day, and since 1790 the nature of each year's crop and the price of five other crops as well as wheat, and wool, meat, cheese, hops and linseed. My information shows that in this first year of Queen Victoria out of the 77 million acres in Great Britain (including the whole of Ireland), 47 million are cultivated, 14½ million are capable of improvement and 15½ million barren and unprofitable, with a population of nigh on 27 million. To think that wheat reached 122s a quarter in 1812 (the highest on my list)! It was down to 63s in 1815, and 39s in 1835 (the lowest since 1790). It is back to 64s this year.

This has been a Herculean task as you can imagine, and I am glad it is over. But I am sure it was worth doing. I hope another member of the family will think it worth bringing up to date – say in another 25 years time.

Diary of George Neale Driver

April 17th, 1839

Scene: The Land Surveyor's Club Morning Room.

Discovered: E. Driver, G. N. Driver, and Will Blount, arguing as usual.

'If we are not a pressure group, we are a self-admiration society.'

'We all agreed that sponsoring a Scale of Charges would be one of our functions, and here we have the opportunity of making the club an authority to whom our governors will listen, and we stand divided.'

'We shall be a laughing stock. Downing claret and swapping stories of Lord This's cows and Earl That's fish ponds, that is all the Land Surveyors Club are capable, they'll say.'

'They *are* saying.'

'They consulted us on what we considered a reasonable rate for consultancy on tithe commutation; we told them three guineas a day, and they chuck it back in our faces. Into the Bill goes *two* guineas.'

'What can you expect from a Parliament of landowners? *They* are our clients; *they* are going to have to foot our bill, so naturally they opt to pay two rather than three guineas. They can make it the law of the land, and they damn well have!'

'So what do we do? Sit back and take it? Become a Study Group?'

'They pass a Tithe Commutation Act whenever it was – 1836? But remember, it is *commutation* not abolition. Cutting out tithes and forgetting them once and for all would mean nothing for us. But with commuting, and not abolishing them they need us very badly. They want us on their side – and the best of us. Working out that "rent-charge", which is to take the place of the tithe, in terms of bushels of grain converted into money by a seven year price average – you will not get your stewards and land agents taking a hand at anything as complicated as that. I tell you, they need *us*. Or they will be losing more than they gain.'

'They will need maps too – "award maps" .'

'The wholesale making of maps might lead to a cadastral survey of all Britain.'

'It might indeed, but not by us, my dear sir. This soldier fellow – Dawson, Lieutenant Dawson, is that his name? –'

'He is a captain now.'

'*Captain* Dawson then, has already recommended such a survey be made under *his* supervision, if you please, to ensure uniformity and accuracy. And what is he proposing paying us? Our rightful 1s 6d an acre? Ninepence. *Ninepence* an acre. And he is saying he will not have anyone in the scheme who has ever made a voluntary agreement.'

'I have been responsible for many voluntary agreements; but they are all over with now, they had to be completed by last October. Never mind about the so-called 'Ordnance Survey' scheme – let the army get on with that if they have the mind to. For tithe commutation they want us for valuation not cartography. The principal work of dealing with disputed commutation still lies ahead, with its compulsory awards, commissioners and the rest.'

'It is Enclosures all over again.'

'And the Canals.'

'And the Railways.'

'That tithes should have survived into the Railway Age amazes me. A levy of ten per cent on gross output a year, that's what it amounts to – for the good of our souls, eh? To keep the parson in port.'

'But at least two-thirds of all agricultural land in Britain is now tithe-free.'

'Even so, the process of commutation, which means a deal of work for us, is only just beginning, and I can see it lasting for at least a decade. And remember, there was that other Act passed in 1836 too, the Parochial Assessments Act – *that* is going to bring us public valuation work – rating assessments can only be done by *experts*. You Edward, and you Will, and me.'

Memorandum

To: Mr Andrew Spigott   *Date:* April 27th, 1839
From: Edward Driver

I was in Kent yesterday and had luncheon with Mr Tom Camell the
Sevenoaks solicitor whom I have known a number of years. He was
recently instructed to place an advertisement in the Maidstone and
other Kent papers, which appeared on March 4th, inviting tenders for
the work of measuring and mapping the parish of West Peckham in
accordance with the requirements of the Act for the Commutation of
Tithes. The surveyor whose tender is accepted enters into an agreement
with the several owners of land in the parish with not less than three
fourths of the total subject to tithes, to make the survey before July 1st,
'drawn accurately, carefully and skilfully on the scale and in the
manner mentioned in the instructions issued by the Tithe Commissioners
for England and Wales'. He also has to make a 'Book of Reference' to
the plan, in which he specifies the name and description of each parcel
of property, with its true quantity or contents in statute measure, the
names of the owners and occupiers, the state of cultivation, whether
arable, meadow or pasture, wood, coppice or common land, gardens,
orchards, hop grounds. The plan and the Book of Reference have to be
delivered for approval to the Tithe Commissioners before July 1st. The
latter also require the surveyor's 'plain working plan with the lines of
construction, names and reference figures shewn thereon, together with
his genuine and original field book, so that the accuracy of the plan
may be tested without expense to the landowners'. Which shows how
much they trust us! I suppose some of our fraternity have been sketching
what they see on the ground, and then when they get home, fabricating,
in collaboration with the landowner, a plan which shows the property to
better advantage in regard to the 'rent-charge' they will receive in lieu
of tithes.

Once the Tithe Commissioners approve the plan and put their seal
on it, the landowner pays the surveyor for it at the sum per acre agreed
in the contract, plus an amount at a lower rate for copies. In the event
of the plan contracted for not being completed in time, the landowner
is entitled to engage another surveyor and receive compensation from
the defaulting one for the extra expense to which he is put.

Mr Camell told me his advertisement had attracted the attention of a
number of surveyors both in Kent and in London. All offered to under-

take the work at differing rates of remuneration, and for the most part, I regret to say, much below the 1s 6d an acre scale which, as you know, we are trying to establish as the norm. A Mr John Darbyshire of Chatham for instance, who had been employed by the Royal Engineers in the Ordnance Survey of Ireland and claimed fully to understand Trigonometrical Calculations, was prepared to make a plan with book of reference for sevenpence an acre, and the copies for three halfpence. A Mr D. A. Nicholson of Bough Beech with an office in Edenbridge said he would engage to furnish a plan and book at ninepence an acre and copies at 1½d. He had just finished similar work at Chiddingstone and was well acquainted with Captain Dawson of the Royal Engineers who was now Assistant Commissioner at the Tithe Commission Office. In his letter Mr Nicholson said he considered himself perfectly competent to do the work 'although a great many surveyors have utterly failed, greatly to the annoyance of parishes and the protraction of the time for settlement'.

A London surveyor, Richard Dixon of Bedford Row, said he would do the work, copies and all, for a shilling an acre, and finish the measuring of the land so as not to interfere with the crops by May 10th, and deliver books and maps by June 10th. He had already done the Ightham Survey (2,400 acres) and he had just had his Hasketon (Suffolk) map declared sealable. A shilling an acre was also the charge proposed by Frederick Drayson of Sittingbourne, but he would ask twopence an acre for each copy in addition. He was currently surveying the parish of Yalding and had work in hand for the Tithe Commissioners on a scale of 12,000 acres a month (£610 ?). He was also well acquainted with Capt. Dawson. Mr Carrington Robinson of Sevenoaks asked 1s 4d an acre – a more respectable sum!

This information was given to me by my friend Mr Camell in confidence of course, and I pass it to you under the same seal for your instruction and for the edification of the apprentices under your care. There is undoubtedly a certain amount of profit for our office from Tithe Commutation work, though not at a very high rate if the lowest of these tenders is representative of that to which someone in Mr Camell's position would award the contract. I understood from him that he will probably see fit to engage Mr Darbyshire at sevenpence an acre. Be that as it may, I suggest you scan the principal Sussex, Kent and, maybe, Essex newspapers for advertisements inviting tenders for Tithe Commutation surveys, and make submissions according to the availability of our staff. In the event of one of our tenders being accepted, the drawing of a plan and the preparation of the Book of Reference will prove good discipline in field work for the younger members of the office. I am sending a copy of this memorandum to Mr R. C. Driver who will take the matter under his administration.

Letter from Edward Driver to Miss Annie Mear

3rd May, 1843

My dear Annie,

Hard work, as I am always telling you, is still the best balm for this hurt mind, not yet fully recovered from the shock of Emily's death, in spite of so much time having already elapsed since that mournful event. I do not know if it is my sombre mood which has made the locations I have been visiting of late appear so depressing, but so they have been. The week before last I was down at what I had always regarded as an unpretentious but pleasant seaside resort, Hastings in Sussex, but my duties on behalf of the Chief Commissioner for Her Majesty's Woods and Forests were concerned with a derelict part of it known as the Priory Ground or America Ground – why 'America' I know not – which has recently been awarded to the Crown. It is marsh more than ground – the sea receded from it and no one claimed it – and until 1836 was occupied by 'squatters' living in shacks and shanties who put up numerous ropewalks on the beach. There were still signs of some of the 'half-boats' which had been used by many of these beach-dwellers as their habitation – boats sawn asunder at midships during searches for smuggled goods. It had been a derelict wasteland of this kind since the 15th century – think of that! In 1823 the position of these squatters, whose encroachment had only been condoned by time, was regularised by their being given short tenancies, on the termination of which they had to leave. The population of the parish of Holy Trinity in which it lay fell from 1,076 in 1831, to nine in the last census of 1841! The ground was cleared, drained and enclosed. Some now call it The Desert or The Government Ground. A footpath has been made through it, use of which is only by permission, so others call it The Permission Ground. Lord Carlisle the Chief Commissioner now wants to build on it, and my mission was in preparation for this. It will be a match for Benjamin Kaye's fine Pelham Crescent erected only some 20 years ago, and James Burton's elegant St Leonards Hotel which he quickly renamed the Royal Victoria when our present Queen announced her intention of paying the town a visit when still a princess in 1834. They will be having a railway line from Brighton before very soon – as you know, I have been buying all the land for the London and Brighton Railway and am familiar with these matters. So it is time Hastings drew a veil over the more squalid aspects of its past and faced the realities – and graces – of the modern age.

I met Mr Patrick Robertson, the Member of Parliament for Hastings, by arrangement in the Royal Victoria, and he told me that he would be very glad to take a lease of the Priory Land from the Crown once it had been cleared, and develop it on the lines we both had in mind. I think he is set on having a 'Robertson Terrace' and a 'Robertson Street' in Hastings by which his constituents and posterity can remember him! And no doubt we shall have a Carlisle Parade before we are finished. After all, if the Queen has given her name to a railway station I do not see why Mr Robertson and Lord Carlisle should not have their streets!

Then on Wednesday I was at Windsor where the Queen has been advised to *buy* various freehold and copyhold estates – she is more usually selling her property. The Commissioners of Her Woods and Forests have recommended that she acquire the manors of Clewer, Brocas and Dedworth Mansel in Berkshire (New Windsor) belonging to a Mr Frederick Keppel, and they sent me down to look the premises over and make the usual report and valuation. All was in near ruin! I have never seen such dilapidation in all my life. I do not imagine any repairs can have been done for a quarter of a century or more – since George IV succeeded at any rate. And as for the land, a quagmire. I shall have to put 'underdrained' in my report, but it is the conventional understatement they will understand at the Land Revenue Office. It has been totally neglected – I cannot hazard for how long, but no attention can have been given it for many, many years. I found great difficulty in riding over it to make my inspection. No wonder Mr Keppel wants to get rid of it!

My brother George has high hopes of our being commissioned to make a large scale survey of London to help them plan the proposed new sewerage system. That would subscribe to my state of depression indeed! But in the light of Mr Chadwick's offensive *Report on the Sanitary Condition of the Labouring Population* of last year which castigated surveyors as inefficient, incompetent and expensive, and praised the Corps of Engineers and Sappers for their skill and economy, I suspect the work will be entrusted to the latter. Indeed we 'civilian' surveyors have already resolved to send a deputation to Sir Robert Peel in the hope of finding the rumour of the engineers' employment untrue, and are holding a protest meeting next month in Grays Inn Coffee House.

The Land Surveyors Club which George and I helped to found with such high ideals in 1834 has never thrived – mostly from laziness and a refusal to co-operate with other sections of our profession. Now another attempt to close our ranks – against the soldiers – is being made by others, but I cannot see it meeting with any greater success than Willy Blount's effort. But forgive me, my dear; such pessimism is no doubt only a product of my melancholy, which soon must pass.

Sight of so much decay in these last two weeks has soured my outlook, but writing of it to you, my dear, has already brought welcome relief. I hope for more in this regard by *seeing* you at Dr Lanchester's soiree on Monday, a prescription designed not only to dispel all gloom but make glad the heart of

Your loving
Edward

Minutes of Partners' Meeting
7th February, 1845

Present: E. Driver
G. N. Driver
R. C. Driver

Mr E. Driver said he had called the meeting to impress upon all partners the significance to the firm of the Lands Clauses Consolidation Act which had received the royal assent at the end of last year. By it all future railway land purchase, so large a part of which was being undertaken by Messrs Driver, would be regulated. Its object was to introduce uniform procedures, to replace the ad hoc methods which had grown up with the development of the railways, but out of fairness to railway company and landowner alike needed a degree of standardisation imposed by law which they had hitherto lacked. Under the Act the companies would still be able to make private bargains with property owners if they could; but if they failed, they either had to go to arbitration, appoint an umpire or 'oversman', or refer the case to a jury of 25 summoned by the sherriff or a special jury of 13.

Legally required procedure such as this would be likely to be entrusted only to those who had had experience in the 'old' methods, and gained reputations regionally and nationally as trusted valuers, negotiators and arbitrators. There were not many such in Britain in 1845 said Mr Driver, but Messrs Driver was one of them. Work would come from either of the two 'sides', the railway promoters or the owners whose land was being compulsorily purchased.

Mr R. C. Driver observed that Mr John Clutton seemed to manage to hunt with hare and hounds, representing as he had done both the South Eastern Railway and landowners.

Mr G. N. Driver said landowners could expect more from the railway companies than the canal makers because railways were pure speculation for profit. There was no 'social service' aspect in them as there had been in canals.

Mr E. Driver said he was due to give evidence before a Select Committee of the House of Lords on Saturday, May 31st on Compensation for Lands compulsorily taken or injured by railways.

DIE SABBATI, 31° MAII 1845.

The EARL FITZWILLIAM in the Chair.

Mr EDWARD DRIVER is called in, and examined as follows:

265. YOU are a Surveyor?
I am.

266. Can you give the Committee any general Information respecting the Rates at which Land has been purchased by Railways, distinguishing the Price of the Land from the Severance and Damages?
I think I am in a Situation to give your Lordships Information upon the Great Western Line, in which I was concerned, having purchased about the first Sixty Miles from London, and the Portion of it from London to Maidenhead. I gave Evidence upon that before Parliament, and subsequently treated, and purchased the same, and kept an Account of the Result; and I can give that Information. The Quantity of Land was 190 Acres from London to Maidenhead. My Estimate and Evidence before Parliament upon the Average was 208*l.* an Acre, including every Description of Expense. I found afterwards, by taking out the Figures, that it came to the following Result:— that 117*l.* an Acre was the Cost

7. The terrace off Old Kent Road in South London, all that remains of
Surrey Square built by the Drivers on land which came into the family from
Abraham Purshouse, uncle of Samuel Driver's wife Jane – a 1975 photo-
graph (*see* page 38).

8. 8 Richmond Terrace, Whitehall, in 1975 – the office of E. & G. N. Driver
from 1826 to 1850.

9. The Surveyors Institution building which stood on the 12 Great George Street site near Parliament Square, London, before it was demolished at the turn of the century, showing the portico for which R. C. Driver donated the cost, £140 (*see* page 190).

Five Guineas
REWARD.

WHEREAS,
Mr. Driver's Garden,
In the Kent-Road,
Was Robbed,
On *Sunday Morning*, by Two Men, who were discovered and fired at by the
Private Watchman,
And as it is suspected One of them was Wounded, as he let fall Part of the Fruit, this is to give Notice, that whoever will give Information, so that the Offender may be convicted, shall receive the above Reward.

AUGUST 31, 1819.

Sorrell, Printer, 87, Bartholomew-Close, London.

10.

11. & 12. The presidential badge presented to the Surveyors Institution by R. C. Driver after retiring from the presidency in 1892 – to be seen today in the library at Great George Street (*see* page 190). The inscription reads: 'Presented by Robert Collier Driver Esq: President 1890–1891 to be worn by his Successors in the Chair on all Official and Public Occasions as a Mark of Distinction.'

13. Edward Driver valued and negotiated the purchase of much of the land required for the London and Brighton Railway, seen here being built across the South Downs in the 1840s.

for the Land only; but, including the Severance, it was 194*l.* an Acre.

267. That would make the Severance 77*l.*?

Yes; and the Tenant's Interest was 15*l.* That produced an Average of 209*l.* an Acre for the Land and Severance and Tenant's Interest, my Evidence having stated before Parliament an Average of about 208*l.*, so that I was within 1*l.* an Acre of my first Estimate, showing that I had formed a tolerably correct Estimate. Upon general Principle, my Mode is this, to charge the Land first at the full Rent; if it is worth 35*s.* an Acre I should call it 40*s.* an Acre. I then put it at Thirty-three Years Purchase. I add a Fourth to that for compulsory Sale, making Forty-one Years and a Half. Then I find a Moiety more must be added, making Sixteen Years and a Half Purchase more, to cover Severance, which makes Fifty-eight Years Purchase; and I have generally said that it comes to Sixty Years Purchase to cover every thing.

268. Have you ever been employed as an Arbitrator?

Yes, in several Cases.

269. Have you found that your Colleagues have thought that this was a right Principle?

I have found that they may have asked more; but they have always been satisfied when the Verdict has been to this Amount.

270. Have the Gentleman that you have met with in that Way admitted the Principles you have just stated?

Quite so.

271. This was at the Commencement of the Great Western Railway?

Yes.

272. There was more Opposition then to the Sale of Land for Railway Purposes than there is now?

We wanted to pay the full fair Price for every thing. We had only Two Juries in the whole of the Distance between London and Maidenhead, and those were both very different Cases; they were Market Gardens where the Profits were very enormous. The Grower or Occupier showed the Produce of Pears and Apples, and what they could get for them in Covent Garden Market.

273. Would you not say that that is rather valuable Land upon the greatest Part of the Line to Maidenhead?

It is more valuable than upon the Brighton Line; but I valued upon the Brighton Line also. I am quite satisfied that this Mode of Calculation would ensure full Justice to the Landowners, without introducing any fancy Value or extravagant Demands.

274. Have you any Notion in your own Mind that the Price paid for Land ought in any degree to be influenced by what are likely to be the Profits of the Railway?

I have always reprobated any such Notion. I never would allow any Argument of that Kind to be used, and we never can use it in the Reduction of the Demand of a Landowner, because it has always been held that the Advantages from a Canal or any such speculative Undertaking were never to be taken into consideration in the Reduction of the Compensation for the Land they have taken; therefore I never would admit that.

275. Or an Enhancement of the Value of the Land?

I think not; I think that ought to be left entirely out of the Question.

276. You do not take into consideration that the Property of the Individual is most likely benefited by the Railway?

I think not.

277. It is no doubt your Opinion that Landed Property is generally very much improved in Value by having a Railway run through it?

I think it is; I think it has equalized the Value of Land very much.

278. In letting Land for Building Purposes upon large Estates, the Ground Rents fixed have some reference to what are expected to be the Profits of the Builders?

In that Case the Locality is the Inducement to the Person to take the Land, and therefore it does affect the Value; but that is a Sort of private Agreement between Parties.

279. Does not the Railway stand very much in reference to the Land upon which it is placed in the same relation that Houses do to the Land upon which they are built?

As far as Residences go, I think it does.

280. Supposing that a Railway was to go through a Gentleman's Residence that he had just finished at the Expence of 10,000*l.*, how should you value what he ought to have; should you do it by reference to that Cost of 10,000*l.*, or upon what Principle?

If I felt that the Railway had prejudiced him, either as to letting or as to Sale, I should exercise my Judgment in considering what would be the Amount of the Depreciation on this Account.

281. Suppose it goes through the House and destroys it?
I should pay him the full Cost of the Building.

282. And the Value of the Land it stood upon?
Yes; and Compensation for any Inconvenience he sustained besides, or Disappointment.

283. In the Case of taking a Gentleman's Residence in that Way, would you be guided by the Amount of Money he had just expended, or would you be guided by the Rent which you might think that Gentleman might get for the House if he let it?
I think I should be guided by the Money he had spent, thinking that the Railway Company ought to pay for the whole Amount of the Loss he had suffered. I believe that has always been the Case.

284. You do not consider the letting Value of the Place to be the real Criterion of its Value to the Owner?
Certainly not; and particularly with reference to a Residence.

285. You do not consider that any large Country House lets for any thing like the Money which it has cost to erect it?
Certainly not. Gentlemen are always desirous of letting their Houses, if they can get a good Tenant, at a very moderate Rent, in order to ensure the House being kept warm. I have Houses which I should be glad to let upon those Terms. A House, if untenanted during the Winter, suffers most materially.

286. It may frequently happen that a Landed Proprietor of considerable Fortune may, from temporary Circumstances, wish to let a Residence for Two, Three, or Five, or a short Term of Years, in which Case the Rent he gets is no Criterion of the Value of the Property?
Certainly not. I should think the Rent would hardly be the Interest of the Value of the Materials to be sold, it is of so little Consequence.

287. In your Statement of the Amount of the Valuation of the Land down to Maidenhead, did you take in any Ground upon which Houses were existing, or was it all Land where there were no Houses?
I think we did not destroy any Residence at all, nor affect any Residence much.

288. Have you been employed upon other Railways besides the Great Western?

Yes. I bought the whole of the Land for the Brighton Railway. I am now negociating from Brighton to Chichester, and to Portsmouth.

289. Between Shoreham and Chichester you have been employed to purchase the Land?

I have been employed for the purchasing all of that. I think the Line from Brighton to London can hardly be considered a fair Criterion, because there were such extravagant Sums given by Companies. There were Nine Individuals who were paid above 136,000*l.* for the Purchase of their Property; it was Ten Times the Value, certainly.

290. That was before the Alteration in the Constitution of the Committees?

It was; and it was pending the Discussion in the Houses, and the Competition of Four or Five Railways. These extravagant Prices were agreed to be given by the Company as an Expediency to get rid of Opposition.

291. Was it not the Fact that the rival Companies at the Moment had got so very eager in the Chase that they would give any thing to beat the other Parties?

It was very much the Case.

292. What was the average Money that the Land between Shoreham and Chichester cost?

I have not the Means of telling the Average very accurately; but I should think it will amount to an Average of between 220*l.* and 230*l.* an Acre.

293. It goes through Parts of the best Land in the County of Sussex?
It goes through very fine agricultural Land.

294. Did you estimate the Land beyond Maidenhead upon the Great Western Railway?
Yes; about Thirty Miles beyond.

295. For that Thirty Miles beyond Maidenhead did you come to the same Result as you have stated with respect to the first Thirty Miles?

I have not ascertained that. I took particular Pains in making that Calculation as to the first District up to Maidenhead, and it was so much Trouble that I did not pursue the Investigation further.

296. Do you think that the Circumstances which guided you in

coming to Fifty-eight Years Purchase would equally guide you now if you had to do it again?

Precisely. I have gone upon the same Principle in valuing from Brighton to Chichester.

297. In that Distance to Maidenhead, can you state what was the lowest Value of any particular Lands, and what was the highest Value of any particular Lands?

In that District there was some very good Land; perhaps the Average would be about 50s. an Acre as the Rental for agricultural Purposes, and I do not think any was under 30s.

298. From your Experience, do you think that small Landowners, not being Men of Influence, get as much for their Land as Men of great Parliamentary Influence do?

I think that in all Cases where it is referred to Valuation they do. Where the large Proprietor and influential Men make Bargains of course they get more.

299. Would you see any Objection to a Clause in a general Act prohibiting private Bargains being made before the passing of the Act?

I should think the prohibiting it would be a very unnecessary and unwise Measure. I always recommend that private Bargains should be endeavoured to be made before the passing of the Act.

300. Do you think it would be advisable that the Value of the Land should be ascertained, prior to the passing of the Act, by some compulsory Mode?

It would be very desirable, if it could be done upon fair and equitable Terms; but I do not know how that could be managed.

. . . . . .

351. You would prefer that Parliament should enable the Company to purchase the Property at some fixed Rate?

Yes; by some fixed Tribunal, such as Official Referees, as alluded to, so that no Party should have Power of refusing.

352. In fact you want the Railways to have more compulsory Power over the Landowners?

Yes.

353. And that they should not have so many Opportunities of appealing to Parliament and delaying the passing of Bills?

Yes. There is an Instance of a Railway projected, upon which One Party has Eight Acres and Three Quarters of Land; the Value of it was easily to be ascertained. The Parties objected. Mr. Brunel is concerned, and he said to me last Night, these Parties say they are willing to come to an amicable Arrangement. He asked, "What do you want for it?" He replied, "I want 15,000*l*. for it." That is for Eight Acres of mere Agricultural Land.

354. Is not that for Injury to the Residence?
No. I have been upon the Line, and I do not think it is worth 2,500*l*. for the fullest Compensation of all Kind. I could not see the House along the Line.

355. Is there to be no Embankment?
No; it is almost dead Level. That is a Sort of exorbitant Claim that Railway Proprietors are often obliged, under certain Circumstances, to comply with.

The Witness is directed to withdraw.

NOTES ON REPORT OF THE SELECT COMMITTEE
OF THE HOUSE OF LORDS

appointed to take into consideration The Practicability and the
Expediency of establishing some Principle of Compensation to
be made to the owners of Real Property whose Lands etc may
be compulsorily taken for the Construction of Public Railways.

Witnesses state that to the marketable value of the property taken they add a percentage on the ground of the sale being compulsory. The committee consider a very high percentage – not less than 50 per cent on original value for compulsion only, to which seller is bound to submit.

'The public utility will prevail'. Nothing for loss of Beauty when line goes near ruined abbey – 'for the mere destruction of an object of Beauty or Interest pay nothing.' 'If it was beautiful land, he should get a station made near it and turn it into building land.'

Committee consider it necessary to consider land not merely as a source of income, but as the subject of expensive Embellishment and subservient to the Enjoyment and Reaction of the Proprietor. 'Public Advantage' may require such considerations to be sacrificed.

'In the case of the railways, though the Public may be considered ultimately the Gainers, the immediate motive to their construction is the interest of the Speculators who have no Right to complain of being obliged to purchase at a somewhat higher rate the means of carrying on their speculation.'

Price of land purchased a small proportion of sum for construction.

Committee said: return should be made of owners within 300 yards of the proposed works who had deposited written objections.

E. D.

July 1845

Circular Letter

Messrs Driver

8 Richmond Terrace, Parliament Street, Whitehall, London

2nd June, 1850

Dear Sir,

This is to notify you that from July 1st our address will be:

5, Whitehall, London

E., G. N., and R. C. Driver

Letter of Edward Driver to Mrs George Neale Driver

18th January, 1852

Dear Mary,

It is difficult to express the distress I experienced on learning of the seizure which has left poor George virtually paralysed. I know you are seeking the best medical attention available and that he will have all your loving care and attention. Do not concern yourself – and do not let him be concerned – at his incapacity to take any further part in the affairs of the firm. We are making the necessary arrangements to have his work taken over by senior and responsible members of the staff which of course is now of a considerable size. Robert, I need hardly say, is our chief mainstay and he will treat personally with George's principal clients. I have myself been of indifferent health these last few months – I am in my 70th year, you know! – and only go to the office once or twice a week. Samuel is a partner in little other than name, so Robert has been taking a large part of the burden for some time now. He is very able and much liked. They are making him Hon. Secretary of the Land Surveyors Club, and I know he, as no one else, will inject that semi-moribund society with a new sense of its responsibilities and bring it back to life, perhaps in a new guise, who knows? Have you met Maria Robson, his betrothed? They are to be married in Darlington – her home town – later in the year. She is a charming girl and should make him very happy. I only hope that Robert's father will recover from his illness which I understand is fairly grave, and that I have no recurrence of mine, so as to allow both of us to attend his wedding. We are all ailing, you see – for Edward, Charles and George Driver it would appear that 1852 is a year of destiny!

Annie sends her kindest regards and love, and all sympathy. Do let us know in what specific way we can help.

Ever, yours sincerely,

Edward

Letter from Samuel Driver 3 to Robert Driver

14th December, 1852

My dear Robert,

I have never been a very prominent member of the partnership but there was a time when I was more conspicuously active than I have been in recent years – that summer of 1814, for instance, when I and your uncle Edward helped our father and our Uncle William over the Leigh Swatch estate in Essex and between us we produced a plan based on one of 1762, which was finally designated as being 'surveyed and set out by Abraham, William, Edward and Samuel Driver'! It was not often that four Drivers were all engaged on a single project, though a few months later Uncle William, Edward and I did the survey of Sayes Farm, Chertsey.

And now there is only one – though of course for what remains of my life the style of the firm will be S. & R. C. Driver. But with Edward now gone and your Uncle George so tragically struck down with paralysis, on you, to all intents and purposes, my dear Robert falls the mantle of all of us. So much, as always in these matters, will depend on your good health and your good fortune. This letter is to wish you both in good measure.

I always regretted that your father felt unable to join us, and neither Charles, Thomas, Burrell nor Edward, your brothers, but we respected C.B.'s determination to be independent, and now that he too has passed on, the considerable success he made as a stationer can be seen in its proper perspective. There always seems to have been a Samuel in the family, and I am the fifth since the Wandsworth baker–market gardener whom we all regard as the first. With neither your father nor Uncle Abraham, the eldest son of the first Abraham Purshouse Driver, in the partnership, I am the only active partner of that generation left, though at 64 my activity, as you know, is very limited. But please do not hesitate to consult me on any matter with which you think I might be able to help, though I am well aware you are fully equipped to stand on your own feet. I have had a very good report of the survey you did in August down at Great Staughton in Huntingdonshire.

I was in the same part of the country myself only last week, and having occasion to visit the village of Ickleton was introduced to a leading farmer of those parts, Samuel Jonas by name, who is building up one of the largest farming areas in Britain. Within ten years he reckons he will be cultivating around 3,000 acres of arable. His centre is at Chrishall Grange at Saffron Walden some four miles east of Royston, but his land will soon spread over five farms belonging to four different landlords. They are all contiguous, and he aims to amalgamate them into a single unit. He likes big fields – several are more than 400 acres, few are under 60. The part I saw had a few whitethorn hedges, but what there were were new, trim and straight, occupying as little space as possible. They say no estate of equal size is more highly cultivated or yields a greater amount of production per acre. Samuel Jonas is no mere farmer, he is a scientific agriculturist! He has worked it out, he told me, that an average force of two and a quarter horses is sufficient for a hundred acres. He aims to have 75 or so horses to work the 3,000 acres of the eventual estate – and some hundred men and boys.

Building up this big farm holding has made him much more even than an agriculturist. He has become fully acquainted with the ways of land dealing and valuing. He is evolving into a surveyor in much the same way as Samuel Driver 1, the market gardener, became one by force of similar circumstances in the 18th century. He spoke very knowledgeably of the variety of forms of agreement required for different types of sale. He instanced what an outgoing tenant may and may not do by way of cultivation in the last year of his occupancy – the terms of quitting and valuation. I had much to learn from him. On such occasion the landlord would reserve all the trees and underwood, and the liberty with or without horses to cut and remove wood, to hunt and kill game and rabbits. The tenant would have to protect trees from cattle damage, not break up the greensward nor injure the training ground, but feed with sheep only; he must not mow the meadow twice in a year but cultivate the arable land in the four course system, &c., &c.

What particularly interested me was a schedule he showed me setting out the different customs in the counties thereabouts.

A stranger certainly has to have his wits about him – but Mr Jonas is no stranger, and no fool! The time of entry in Bedfordshire, it appears, is Michaelmas or Lady-day; in Cambridgeshire, Old Lady-day, the tenant retaining the use of barns and yards until Midsummer-day twelvemonth following; in Essex, Michaelmas; in Herts, Old Lady-day; in Norfolk, Michaelmas; in Suffolk, Old Michaelmas Day. Rent Day is half yearly in Cambridgeshire, yearly in Essex. In Cambridgeshire the incomer takes all dung free of expence; in Essex the incomer takes straw and chaff of the outgoer's last crop on paying for thrashing and conveying corn to the market, and pays for manure at valuation.

Samuel Jonas said he was frequently called in to act as umpire to assess what the executors of a rector had to pay the new incumbent as compensation for dilapidations at the rectory house. He had been recently involved in valuing land for the Diocese of Ely where the patrons were Cambridge University colleges, and it was intended to allow a rector to grant a lease under the recent Act for the Better Enabling Incumbents of Ecclesiastical Beneficies to demise the Lands belonging to their Beneficies on farming leases. In each case he had carried out a survey, often using as a base a map made for an Enclosure, hiving off part of the land he considered situated the most conveniently for actual occupation by the rector and valuing the land proposed to be leased. He made a full report to the Bishop of Ely who appointed him, naming the annual sum he considered should be the yearly rent demanded, and the terms. On the last occasion Mr Jonas said he had reserved for the lessor the right of sporting, of planting trees, digging turf, taking an acre of ground to build a school on, and not more than ten acres of the 24 acre Fen ground for poor allotments.

Mr Jonas knew of us of course, and indeed in his book of forms of Awards and Agreements which he had copied for guidance, he had as an example an 'Award of a Mr J. A. Nockolds an Umpire between Messrs Driver of Whitehall London and Mr Robt Franklin of Thaxted in the manner of a Valuation of Timber on an estate at Hempstead and Sampford in Essex.' I well remember this; it was a dispute which this Mr Franklin had over a valuation made by your uncle George Neale Driver for the timber in a sale we conducted at the Auction Mart on August 12, 1845. Franklin's case lent heavily on this very matter of 'the custom of the County'.

Asked to arbitrate over the allowance for bark to be made in the girth of an elm, Nockolds declared 'I find it is generally the custom of this County i.e. Essex, and the adjoining neighborhood, to use two straps in measuring Timber, one giving an allowance of $\frac{1}{8}$th for bark and the other $\frac{1}{12}$th. But I do not find it universally the custom to confine the former entirely to the elm and the latter to the oak. It was the practice of my late father and other valuers of his time (and I have followed it) to measure young smooth elm with the oak strap and occasionally very rough old oak with the elm strap, in fact to use either so as to get the actual quantity of the timber clear of the bark as occasion might require ... The actual quantity of the timber clear of the bark is the point at issue and I cannot as umpire admit that any custom – *not universal* – should operate to its prejudice.'

This is the sort of problem which would have delighted Samuel Driver I who became involved in such issues, we hear, as part of his parochial duties at All Saints, Wandsworth and the buying of timber for the repair of the church roof.

Samuel Jonas is obviously a man of parts, and someone whose acquaintance I consider to be well worth our cultivating. He was telling me of a Mr Fox Talbot's experiments with a *camera obscura* and the 'fixing' of the images it threw on to ordinary writing paper by making the latter 'light-sensitive', as he said, with common salt and something else. If such a process can ever be perfected think what a help it would be to us surveyors! So much truer representations than those 'artistic' engravings and lithographs. And what if you took a 'camera' into a balloon and pointed it at the landscape beneath – an instantaneous map! But I am getting carried away. Mr Jonas is coming to London next month to visit the Great Exhibition in Hyde Park – the Agricultural and 'Photographic' sections in particular – and I gave him my card and insisted that he paid us a call. It would be nice if you could be here when he does, so that you can make his acquaintance. I feel sure such a meeting would stand us in good stead. He has a young son, Henry.

These will be sad days for your dear mother, but I know your sisters will be attending her at Cambridge Place and bringing what comfort they may, and I know you will be over as often as your duties will allow. The character of Camberwell New Road has changed since your father and mother first went to live there, and I know you feel happier in Highbury, but of course, as you will be aware, your father was by no means well off – he left less than £1,000 – and the house in Cambridge Place is at least good security. And then his business took him to the City, yours to Westminster.

I am glad we were able to move to 5 Whitehall the year before last, so that you will not be troubled with further upheavals of a similar nature for some years. You will have had problems enough without administrative distractions of that kind – though you are very lucky in having a Head Clerk as reliable as Elisha Singleton. But I suppose we should draw comfort from not having to face in our survey work the worries of the kind I imagine will shortly be encountered by Dr David Livingstone when he arrives to chart the unexplored course of the Zambesi!

It would not appear to be a very auspicious moment for shouldering new responsibilities – the European scene is particularly disturbing with that fellow Louis Napoleon declaring himself emperor as Napoleon III and starting a 'Second Empire' (shades of 1814!), and with the likelihood of our becoming involved in the Crimea if Russia fails to patch up her quarrel with Turkey, whom we would certainly support. But come rain or shine, we look to you Robert to keep 'Messrs Driver' in business and, now you are married, to provide us with a sixth generation of surveyors!

My kindest regards to Maria,

Your affectionate,

Uncle Samuel

P.S. I enclose a list, by no means exhaustive, and made for what reason I do not know, of some of the principal surveys carried out by the firm for the Crown between 1787 and 1835 which I found among my brother Edward's papers, which I thought you might like to have, though of course, the full records will be in the Counting House.

(ENCLOSURE)

1.   1787   Geometrical Plan of the Forest of Dean, Gloucestershire, reduced from actual survey of one furlong to an inch taken by Abraham and William Driver.

2.   1787   Survey of New Forest, Hampshire, by Abraham and William Driver.

3. 1797 Crown Estate formerly waste in Manor of Havering-atte-Bower, Romford, Essex, surveyed by Abraham Driver.

4. 1798 Estate at Sellinge, Smeeth and Lympne, Kent, formerly property of Mary Gardiner, surveyed by Abraham and William Driver by order of Surveyor General.

5. 1798 Loddington and Thorpe Malsor, Northamptonshire, surveyed by Abraham and William Driver.

6. 1799 Part of Greenwich surveyed by Abraham Driver.

7. 1799 Ham, Frith Farm and Brampton Field, parcel of Manor of West Ham, surveyed by Abraham Driver.

8. 1799 Ham Farm, Baughurst, Hampshire, in possession of Sir Charles Pole, Bart., Crown lessee, made by order of John Fordyce Esq., by Abraham Driver – farm sold September 1800.

9. 1800 Hallowford Manor, Shepperton, Middlesex; map of 1785 by Thos. Richardson with particular and valuation by Abraham Driver, and 1830 by Edward Driver.

10. 1800 East Combe Farm, Greenwich, surveyed by Abraham and William Driver.

11. 1800 Burnham Abbey; map 3 chains to one inch, surveyed by Abraham Driver.

12. 1803 Little St John's Wood, Islington; particular and valuation by Abraham Driver.

13. 1803 Crown Manor of Egham surveyed by Abraham and William Driver.

14. 1803 Stapleford Abbots, Essex, surveyed by Abraham and William Driver.

15. 1804 Eweline and Nuffield, Oxfordshire, surveyed by Abraham and William Driver.

16. 1804 Upberry Farm, Gillingham, property of Mrs Fullagar, to be bought by the Government, surveyed by Abraham and William Driver.

17. 1804 Wallingford, Berkshire, surveyed by Abraham and William Driver.

18. 1804 Part of Bargeway between Kingston Bridge and Hampton Court, with particular and valuation made in 1804 and 1837 by Abraham, William and Edward Driver.

19. 1804 Tiddington Farm, Alveston, Warwickshire, surveyed by Abraham Driver.

20. 1805 Highbury Wood, Islington, surveyed by Abraham and William Driver.

21. 1805 Blackheath and part of Greenwich Park, surveyed by Abraham and William Driver.

22. 1805 Estate at Dagenham, surveyed by Abraham and William Driver.

23. 1805 Crown Estate at Great Staughton, Huntingdonshire, surveyed by Abraham Driver.

24. 1806 Crown lands at Eltham, Lee, Mottingham, Bexley and Royal Arsenal, 6 chains to the inch; surveyed by Abraham, William and Edward Driver.

25. 1806 Northaw, Hertfordshire, surveyed for Enclosure Award of 29th August by Edward Driver.

26. 1807 Walton Leigh Manor, Walton-on-Thames, lands leased from Crown; Plans E & F by Abraham, William and Edward Driver.

27. 1807 Watercourse on Hampton Common surveyed by William Driver.

28. 1808 Estate at Northfleet purchased by Commissioners of the Navy from Francis Wadman Esq., surveyed 18th March by Abraham, William and Edward Driver.

29. 1812 Crown Estate at Hitchin – two mills called Shotting and Port Mills, surveyed 3 chains to the inch by Abraham, William and Edward Driver.

30. 1812 Shefford and Campton Manors, Bedfordshire, surveyed 12th June by Abraham, William and Edward Driver.

31. 1812 Crown Estate at Steppingley, Bedfordshire, surveyed by Abraham, William and Edward Driver.

32. 1813 Gillingham, Kent, surveyed by Abraham, William and Edward and Samuel Driver.

33. 1813 Sellinge, surveyed for Enclosure Award of 16th June by Edward Driver.

34. 1814 Beomund Manor, Chertsey, surveyed for Enclosure Award by Edward Driver.

35. 1814 Leigh Swatch, Essex, surveyed and set out by Abraham, William, Edward and Samuel Driver according to plan of 1762.

36. 1814 Sayes Farm, Chertsey, surveyed by William, Edward and Samuel Driver.

37. 1815 Commons and Waste at Horsepath, Oxfordshire, surveyed by Abraham, William and Edward Driver.

38. 1817 Woodland belonging to Crown at Cuxton and Halling in Kent, surveyed by Abraham and Edward Driver.

39. 1818 Demesne lands at West Molesey, manor on lease to Lord Hotham and Sir G. H. F. Berkley, surveyed by Abraham and Edward Driver, as sold to lessees October 1820.

40. 1819 Crown Estate Swanscombe, surveyed by Abraham and Edward Driver, with a note on King's Bench case of 1835.

41. 1819 Frogmore and Shaw Farms in New and Old Windsor, surveyed by Abraham and Edward Driver.

42. 1820 Highham House, Walthamstow, surveyed by Abraham and William Driver.

43. 1820 Hive Estate, Northfleet, surveyed by Abraham and Edward Driver.

44. 1824 Bishops Marshes, Gillingham, surveyed by Edward and George Neale Driver.

45. 1827 Isle of Sheppey, estate of Sir Edward Banks surrounding Mile Town with property belonging to Board of Ordnance, surveyed by Messrs. Driver.

46. 1835 Bosham, Sussex, surveyed for Enclosure Award by Edward Driver.

Letter from Robert Driver to his eldest brother Charles

The Grange, Highbury
November 3rd, 1854

My dear Charles,

As you know, our daughter is being christened next month and it would greatly please Maria and myself if you would agree to stand as one of her godfathers. She is to be named 'Maria' though her mother insists on calling her 'Cissie'! We hope you will be able to be with us in church and at the little celebration here afterwards. We hope little Charles, even though he is only one, will take part in the service, even if his contribution is confined to bawling his lungs out, but Nanny Hodder assures us that she will keep him well under control. I am afraid we shall have to have a proxy for the other godfather Arnold Carpenter who, as you know, was our Best Man but is now in the Crimea with his regiment, poor chap. Clara was going out with him but was persuaded to remain at Somerton where she heard last week he had taken part in the siege of Sebastopol. There are rumours of disastrous charges by the Heavy and Light Brigades as part of a battle at Balaclava – you know they have an Electric Telegraph from London to Crimea now. Let's hope Arnold managed to avoid becoming that ass Cardigan's cannon fodder on what seems to have been another romantic fracas of the kind we are now used to associating with his name. I suppose it is my Quaker ancestry which prevents me from sharing the enthusiasm for this war which seems to have gripped so many of my fellow Englishmen. Are the Turks really worth it? It is all so costly – more and more taxes, direct and indirect. I suppose not having had to go to war since 1815 has made us 'soft'. But no sooner did they abolish the Window Tax in 1851 than they revived the Inhabited House Duty. And now Mr Gladstone has extended the legacy duties which amounts to taxing real and settled property equally with personal. Where will it end – when we have driven the Russians into the Black Sea? You can bet your life it will not. I suppose it is something we ought officially to protest about at the Land Surveyors Club, but I am afraid lethargy is so deeply entrenched in that once hopeful society that it will be difficult to arouse members to action of that or any kind. At least the Government are repealing the Usury Laws. I suppose we should be thankful for small mercies.

Maria and your potential god-daughter Cissie send their love,

Your affectionate brother

Robert

P.S. I believe you knew Willy Brooks once, who owned a number of estates in North and South London. He died this summer and we are up to the eyes in sorting out his property – Karslakes his solicitors have asked us to collect outstanding rents. Hercules Sharpe – remember? – is one of the executors.

Memorandum

To : R. C. Driver   *Date :* 5th August 1854
From : Mr Singleton

LATE WM BROOKS ESQ

The late Mr Brooks's sundry estates number ten, and the total rent amounts to some £265. The most valuable property is in Stoke Newington – nos 8 & 9 Nelson Terrace at £67 and £70 a year respectively with a Mr Lowe as lessee and a Mr Rose as tenant; and no. 1 Vittoria Place at £32 where a Miss Unwin is tenant. They have paid their rent to Mr Hindle up to Christmas 1853. I also understand, though it does not appear on Karslake's list, that Mr Brooks owned the Old Coach and Horses Inn on Stoke Newington Green – I will investigate this.

No. 4 Rodney Street, Borough, is let to weekly tenants who together pay £15 a year. A ground rent of £4 a year is payable here to the trustees of the late John Spiller Esq. Last February Mr Sharpe received of Mr Whittel of Long Lane, Bermondsey, the year's rent of £15 due to Christmas 1853 less outgoings of £6.14.4. We may have trouble here also over the property known as King's Head Court, Shoreditch, the two top floors of which and the cellar are occupied by a Mr William Chambers, cabinet maker, as tenant at £20 a year. The lower part of the building was lately let to the Revd Mr Evans as a Ragged School, but is at present unoccupied. The leasehold ground rent due from two of the three separate lessees who have let to separate tenants at Stamford Hill (Yeardley and Redknapp) is £10.16s and £5, and they have been paid in full to Lady-day 1853, but only half of the £22 due has been paid by the third, Miss Kemp, and that only to Michaelmas 1852.

Letter from Messrs. Driver to Miss Unwin

5 Whitehall, London
5 October 1854

Madam,

The House you occupy was left to Mr Hindle for his life and at his decease, which as you know has just occurred, goes to the parties for whom we are agents. We will settle with Mr Hindle's executors for the proportion of the rent due to them. We shall therefore be obliged by your forwarding us the ¾ yr's rent due at Michaelmas last, less Property Tax and Sewers Rate. Your early attention will oblige as we have shortly to render an account to the executors of the late Mr Brooks – you will please send the Property Tax and Sewers Rate receipt when you forward the money.

We remain Madam
Your Obedt. Servants
Samuel & Robert C. Driver

Letter from Miss Unwin to S. & R. C. Driver (undated)

Miss Unwin is surprised by the Executors of the late Mr Brooks applying to her for the rent from Christmas. Mr Hindle was her landlord (as he informed her) from that time, therefore Miss Unwin thinks she ought to pay the late Mr Hindle's Executors – an answer will oblige.

Your Obedient Servant

M. Unwin

N.B. there is the Sewer Rate and the Property-tax off of the £16.

S. & R. C. Driver

Letter from Miss Kemp to Messrs. Driver

Miss Kemp presents compliments to the Executors of the late Mr Brooks and begs to say that severe indisposition has prevented her going to London to receive her dividend. She is in hope either this or next week to be able to remit the $\frac{3}{4}$ year Rent due. The distance is so very inconvenient for Miss Kemp – could any place in town be nam'd for the future – it would oblige.

Spring Cottage

Grove Road,

Stamf. Hill

Oct 16th

Memorandum

To: Mr Singleton   *Date:* 7 November 1854
From: R. C. Driver

At to-day's sale the Old Coach & Horses, Stoke Newington Green was sold to a Mr and Mrs Rawlinson of Bristol, and their solicitors, Messrs Brooke Smith & Vassall have asked us to receive the rents on their behalf. There are seven tenants paying weekly rents here, and the total rent due from them in annual rent amounts to £8-1-3 less tax and expenses of £5-5-9 making a balance of £2-15-6. It is the responsibility of Mr Pearson in the Old Building to collect these.

Letter from W. Pearson to Messrs. Driver [see Plate 14]

Old Coach & Horses
Stoke Newington Green
November 22, 1854

Gentlemen,

I received yours dated 21st inst and herewith send you some of the vouchers I have paid for Taxes and Water and also for some repairs done on the Premises and have applied for other accounts which I will forward, with my Account, but I have only a small balance in hand on account of the bad Debts on the Premises.

I am Gentlemen,
Yours respectfully
W. Pearson

Messrs. Samuel & Robert Driver

Letter from Messrs. Driver to Messrs. Brooke Smith & Vassall

5 Whitehall,
Dec. 30, 1854

Dear Sir,

Mrs. Rawlinson's Stoke Newington Property

In compliance with your favour of the 27th we now have pleasure of forwarding you our Account relating to the Sale of the above property deducing a balance of £153-7-6 in favour of Mrs Rawlinson which amount we have this day directed our bankers (Messrs Drummond) to pay to Messrs Prescott & Co (as directed by you) to the credit of the Bristol Old Bank with Mr Brooke Smith, all of which we trust will find correct. You will observe that we have given credit for such Rents as we have already received. We have applied to Messrs Reid & Co. for the quarter due at Xmas and to Mr Forder for the half year due at the same time, and so soon as we receive these we will pay the amount to Messrs Prescott & Co.

With respect to the weekly rate of the premises comprised in Lot 6, we have applied several times to Mr Pearson who has the charge of the collection thereof, but he is very dilatory in responding thereto; indeed all we have been able to obtain from him hitherto is a short account of the Rates, Taxes and Repairs which he has paid – allegedly he has a very small balance in hand, but be this as it may he ought to render in his Account. We were thinking whether a letter from you desiring him to do so would not have some good effect or, if your names are not familiar to him, perhaps one from Messrs Karslake & Co., would be better. His address is Mr Pearson, Old Coach & Horses, Stoke Newington Green, Middx.

Wishing you both the Compliments of the Season,

We beg to remain Dear Sir,

Your faithful and obliged Servants

S. & R. C. Driver

Messrs. Brooke Smith & Vassall

Letter from Messrs. Brooke Smith & Vassall to Mr Pearson

Bristol,

2 January 1855

Sir,

We are informed by Messrs S. & R. C. Driver of 5 Whitehall, London that they are unable to get an Account from you of the weekly rents of the tenements at Stoke Newington belonging to the late William Brooks, Esquire and which have been collected by you – We are concerned for Mr and Mrs Rawlinson to whom Mr Brooks' Stoke Newington property was demised; and we beg to inform you that, unless you furnish Messrs Driver with a proper account within one week from the date hereof, we shall take immediate legal proceedings against you.

We are,

Your Obedient Servants

Brooke Smith & Vassall

Mr Pearson, Old Coach & Horses,
Stoke Newington Green, Middlesex.

Letter from Messrs. Driver to Messrs. Brooke Smith & Vassall

5 Whitehall,

January 15, 1855

Dear Sirs,

Mr Pearson not having taken any notice (at least to us) of your letter to him desiring him to settle his account with us for the weekly rents received by him for Mrs Rawlinson's property at Stoke Newington

Green, we sent a Clerk there principally this morning for the purpose of finding him out and make some arrangement with him as to settling his account, but we regret to say we fear there is not much hope of recovering anything from him, for he appears to be as much poverty stricken as the tenants themselves, some of whom it seems have decamped. On the other side is the account given by Pearson to our Clerk of his doings. We are at a loss how to proceed further in the matter under such untoward circumstances, for Pearson himself is now only a daily labourer at 15/6 a week; it would be useless to sue him even if he has any balance in hand which he says he has not. And as to recovery of the Rents from the runaway tenants this we fear would be equally fruitless. All together it seems one of those unfortunate cases for which no satisfactory remedy is to be found.

We are, Dear Sirs,
Yours faithfully,
S. & R. C. Driver

Messrs. Brooke Smith & Vassall

ENCLOSURE

Jan. 15th, 1855

Mr Pearson left the Old Coach & Horses about a week before Christmas and now lives No. 7 Prince Edward Street Back Road, Stoke Newington. He says that a short time before Christmas he sent all the tax receipts and bills and receipts for repairs to Messrs Driver and that last week he sent a letter on to Messrs B. S. & V. Bristol for writing which 2 letters he paid Mr Tadman (Shakespeare Road) 5/-, as he can not write himself. He says he has no money in hand as he did not receive much, the tenants refusing to pay him as he had no authority to receive them. He states that he got a gentleman (a Mr Fry) to write to Messrs Brooke Smith & Vassall for an authority but has never received it. He could not distrain because he could not get Mrs Rawlinson's signature and therefore the tenants refused to pay him. There is an amount of £15 or £16 owing from tenants who have gone away but he does not know where to. One owes £3-18-0, another £2-0-6 &c &c. He says he has had nothing but abuse and ill treatment from the tenants, and that even his life was threatened. He was thus obliged to leave, and now has a situation which occupies him from 5 a.m. to 6 and 7 p.m. for which he receives 15/- a week. He therefore cannot come here. I did not see him at home but at his place of employment.

Letter from Messrs. Driver to Hercules Sharpe, Esq.

5 Whitehall,
April 24, 1855

Dear Sir,

Premises, King's Head Court, Shoreditch

Mr Chambers the tenant of a portion of the above premises at £20 per annum (landlord pays taxes) is in difficulties, and a meeting of his creditors was called yesterday when a statement of his affairs was laid before them. There were only about 9 creditors and his debts are about £230, and a proposal was made to pay 7/- in the pound which all the creditors agreed to accept. One of our clerks attended the meeting (at Mr Karslake's request) to make a claim for the quarter rent due last Lady-day which the solicitor said he hoped to be allowed to pay out of the first funds that came to hand but he could not promise. They are also willing to give up possession of the premises at once. We have consulted with Mr Karslake this morning hereon, who quite thinks we had better accept possession of the premises, and if we cannot obtain the full quarter rent we must then take the offer of 7/- in the pound, but Mr Karslake wishes us to advise with you and take your opinion thereon. We would just observe that Chambers was in the habit of underletting the premises and his sub-tenants quitted before last quarter day and left nothing to distrain upon, otherwise we should have levied a distress for the rent due.

We are, Dear Sir,
Yours faithfully,
S. & R. C. Driver

Hercules Sharpe, Esq.

1857–1878

Journal of Robert Driver

February 6th, 1857

'What I say is customs – ways of doing things – are introduced for the benefit of the community.'

'But "the community" is all the time widening. The whole of Britain is fast becoming "the community", what with our modern roads, the waterways, the railways and the electric telegraph. No longer the counties and villages, no longer separate communities with local and differing customs. We really must come into the eighteen fifties – *all* of us.'

'Bah! What is it to us in Cambridgeshire what they do in Northumberland? It is the custom hereabouts with landlords when putting off their farms to *let* the straw and chaff with the land, and the tenant benefits from such a custom.'

'But the landlord loses?'

'He does; but he elects to do so in order to provide food for the land.'

I had been invited by Mr Samuel Jonas, whom I had met in London at the Great Exhibition, to attend with him a meeting of valuers in Cambridge to debate this controversial subject of the transfer of straw and chaff on change of occupants. William Nash of Royston was arguing his case with Mr Jonas, and I felt myself very ill equipped to offer an opinion one way or the other.

'We have to fall back on custom' explained Mr Nash without a suspicion of patronage, 'particularly where parties have made no provision for the terms of quitting either oral or written, and a valuer is called in to settle their rights.'

'I have always understood it to be a universal custom' said Mr Jonas puffing away at his pipe, 'that a man must go out as he came in.'

'By our custom the outgoing tenant may sell his straw and chaff at a market price.'

'And what may that be?'

'A sum that includes binding and delivery – 18s a ton net value in the barn, but 27s in the nearest market.'

'It is Essex custom I believe to sell by the *quarter*, is it not?'

'True, Essex custom by the quarter gives upon an average 8s 6d *a ton* consuming value.'

'So a third of the quoted market value is the fodder value?'

'Yes – and that's what the incoming tenant expects to pay.'

'If every farmer sold straw, the market value would descend to the fodder and dung value.'

Mr Jonas looked round at the men assembling for the meeting, and asked Mr Nash how many he thought would be coming. A couple of dozen he said, and for the most of them the Essex plan of computing value was nearer the truth than the acreage plan of Bedfordshire. I thought fit to ask Mr Nash what they did here in Cambridgeshire.

'The Essex plan more than any other' he said. 'It represents the value in most cases, that is where *average* crops of wheat and barley grow on *average* quality land; but on a farm where the crop is abundant as to straw but unyielding as to corn, as we have so often on the Fen land here, or t'other way round as happens on our chalk hills and heath lands, then it is way off course.'

'How did this Essex plan originate?'

'It came from Essex farmers agreeing that the incomer should pay the cost of threshing the corn and carrying it to market, he having the entire use of the straw and chaff.'

'So if the straw is abundant over corn, the cost of threshing is increased?'

'Quite so. And if corn is abundant over straw, it is diminished.'

'Forming a slide in the right direction?'

'As I have said, the valuation by the quarter can only be correct in the *average* of cases.'

At the meeting itself they discussed such niceties as the difference in price between machined and flailed straw; and finally agreed on the main question that the value of wheat straw and chaff, for instance, at 3s 6d per quarter of 8 cwt was equal to 8s 1½d per *ton*, and that one bushel of wheat gave 112 lb of straw and chaff or 8 cwt per quarter. That was something achieved at any rate, and one step towards establishing a standard applicable eventually, I presume, throughout the kingdom.

It was all a refreshing change from the squabbles of landlords complaining of under-compensation by the railway companies and the repetitive chores of the auction room. This attempt to rationalise the customs of East Anglia at least might well be emulated in the case of Poor Rate assessment. A uniform system throughout London would greatly reduce the type of work on which we are so frequently engaged – as for instance our recent activities on behalf of the executors of the late William Brooks.

Letter from Robert Driver to his Aunt Jane,
the second Mrs Samuel Driver (née Dudley)

The Grange, Highbury
April 21st, 1857

Dear Aunt Jane,

I am writing a formal note to express the condolences of Maria and myself on the death of Uncle Samuel, who, as you know, has been of such great support to me in these years at the firm since 1852 when we were deprived of the services of both Uncle Edward and Uncle George. The latter's death in 1855, we must all admit was a blessed relief, and to no one more than dear Aunt Mary, but at 71 Uncle Samuel, except at the end, was in such robust health both in mind and body. I greatly mourn his passing.

So I really am now 'at the helm' – and only 41! God willing, my ambition is to develop the business, particularly as land agents and auctioneers, to the very utmost. I do not see why over the next twenty years or so we should not push up our property sales to something in the region of a million pounds worth a year. And building on the reputation established by Uncle Edward, I am also sanguine of being engaged in land purchase for the new boom in railway construction on which I learn the companies are now about to embark. There are more than 5,000 miles of line now open in this country, which represents 85,000 acres of land which someone has purchased for the railway companies; but they will soon be buying many acres more – and I intend to get my share of the business. But this time of course the landowners will be more wary. They are determined to get their pound of flesh, even if it means stooping so low as to accuse us surveyors of 'conspiring' with our employers, the companies, to keep their compensation low!

If, as it seems, the flow of Driver-surveyors has temporarily dried up, I must either acquire a partner from outside the family, which will need the greatest care in selection, or 'paddle my own canoe' as they say. I think the latter for the time being, though of course I am only the helmsman of a great ship manned by as loyal and able a crew as any captain would find anywhere, headed by the redoubtable Elisha Singleton – long life to him! – and our staff of surveyors, valuers, rent collectors, clerks, cashiers and apprentices trained by Uncle Samuel and his brothers who have built up the business I now find myself sole heir to.

All our sympathies,

Your loving nephew,

Robert

Journal of Robert Driver

July 25th, 1859

'Farewell For Ever' spelt out the device that terminated the magnificent firework display that marked the end of the long life of Vauxhall Gardens tonight – a sparkling but melancholy evening. The last entertainment! What gaiety and romance this place has seen! The dancing and feasting, the bustle and laughter, the colour and the music! And now the famous Pleasure Gardens which Canaletto painted and the famous patronised are to be sold – to meet the demand for more houses, more bricks and mortar and smoking chimneys in place of this fine open space with arbours and walks and shrubberies; and mine will be the hammer under which it falls! How great-grandfather Samuel Driver the South London market gardener, who will have known and loved the gardens, would curse me! Down comes the curtain on tonight's familiar scene of movement and noise, and Vauxhall Gardens becomes just another 'property' to be auctioned by Messrs. Driver – and I don't mind betting that within five years the whole site will be built over and all that remains to remind us and future generations of the bright life that once filled this space is a street called Vauxhall Walk and Mr Canaletto's beautiful but dead pictures.

They say a Mr Jonathan Tyers leased the gardens for 30 years at £250 in 1728; and in 1821 they were sold for £30,000 to the three gentlemen who traded under the name of the London Wine Company, Mr T. Bish, Mr F. Gye and Mr R. Hughes. I wonder what the land will cost the building speculator who comes to kill the fun and the games when I auction them next month?

made and entered into this second day of May one thousand eight hundred and sixty Between Samuel Jonas of Chrishall Grange in the County of Essex Farmer and Henry Jonas of the same place (son of the said Samuel Jonas) of the one part and Charles Frederick Adams of Barkway in the County of Herts Land Agent and Surveyors of the other part in the manner following that is to say The said Henry Jonas . . . Doth hereby put place and bind himself Clerk to the said Charles Adams to serve him in the practice of a Land Agent and Surveyor for the Term of Three Years to be computed from the First day of May now last past and to be thence next ensuing. And He Samuel Jonas Doth agree with Charles Adams That Henry Jonas shall faithfully and diligently serve Charles Adams as his Clerk and shall provide for Henry Jonas suitable board and lodging also suitable clothes and wearing apparel and washing and also medicine and attendance in case of sickness, and that Henry Jonas shall not cancel obliterate spoil destroy waste embezzle spend or make away with any of the books papers writings monies models plans drawings or other property of Charles Adams or any of his employers which may be deposited in his hands, And that Henry Jonas shall keep the secrets of Charles Adams and readily and cheerfully obey and execute his lawful commands and not absent himself from the service of Charles Adams without his consent first obtained but conduct himself as a faithful Clerk ought to do with all due diligence honesty and sobriety.

In consideration whereof and of the sum of one hundred and ninety nine pounds nineteen shillings of lawful British money in hand paid by Samuel Jonas at or immediately before the execution of these Presents Charles Adams Doth agree with Samuel Jonas that he shall accept Henry Jonas as his Clerk in the practice profession or business of a Land Agent and Surveyor and to the utmost of his skill and knowledge teach Henry Jonas and provide all such instruments as may be necessary for his duties as Clerk and pay all travelling and other expenses, And at expiration of the term provided Henry Jonas shall have served him faithfully according to the hue intent and meaning of these Presents furnish him with such Certificate as may be necessary to enable him to practise or engage in the profession or business aforesaid either in his own account or otherwise.

Letter from Henry Jonas to his father Samuel Jonas

Barkway, Herts
14th March, 1861

Dear Father,

You remember in January J. Carter Jonas, your Cambridge cousin (?) and Tom Franklin of Thaxted, being appointed valuers to assess the amount that John Francis had to pay the executors of Mr Frederick Nash who died last month for the straw and chaff he took when the executors quitted Bury Farm at Foulmire? Well, Mr Carter Jonas and Mr Franklin appointed my Mr Charles Adams to be their umpire, should any question arise between them over the matter, and they agreed to accept his decision as final and binding, and to pay each of them a moiety of Mr Adam's charges.

There was in fact a dispute over the amount, and it was referred to Mr Adams who heard the evidence, considered the various papers submitted to him and decided what amount Mr Francis had to pay. As part of my duties as Apprentice-Clerk I was closely involved in the affair, and I penned a fine Award document in my best hand on a sheet of blue foolscap – and Mr Adams greatly praised the excellence of my script! He is most considerate to me at all times, and I am flattered that he should take so much interest in what I do. He is certainly an assiduous instructor, and I feel sure that by May 1863 when my term is finished I shall be well equipped to make my way in the surveying profession – but where to start? Perhaps before I engage myself I might make a small Grand Tour of the continent – I am obsessed at the moment with the idea of climbing mountains, say, the Swiss or Bavarian Alps? What about those German friends who came to stay at Saffron Walden showing their gratitude by returning your hospitality to your son – in their chalet amid the snows? I feel I shall be wanting by then an outlet for my energies of this kind. And when I get back, if I still have steam enough left in me, I will walk to London to seek my fortune in true Dick Whittington style, what do you say? – and see what's going. I may not find the streets paved with gold, but there can be no harm in knocking on one of the doors of one of those fine firms around St James's Park and Whitehall – you never know, someone might like my face and invite me in!

By the way, what relation *is* J. Carter Jonas?

Your ever loving son,
Henry

May 4th, 1864

Samuel Jonas, as one of the biggest corn producers in Britain, always made a point of looking in at The Baltic Coffee House in Threadneedle Street – it moved from its original premises at Monger's to the more pre-possessing South Sea House seven years ago. Here he could expect to meet the leading grain dealers and keep in touch with the latest state of the market. I had been viewing property nearby with a Mr J. Simms Clarke, a director of Credit Immobilier & Company who were interested in purchasing it, and we ran into Mr Jonas just as we were leaving. He persuaded us to turn about and join him in a glass of brandy.

'Here's something to interest you' I said to Mr Jonas as soon as we were seated and our cognac served; 'the land which Mr Simms Clarke and I have just been visiting once belonged to the monks of Bury in *your* Suffolk.'

'They have buried St Edmund long since' beamed Farmer Jonas, 'but they had other uses for their money. Property investment in London, eh? Whereabouts?'

'Jeffery's Square in St Mary Axe off Leadenhall Street. One of the lanes behind it is called Bury Street in fact. It is quite small. It was a very fashionable place of residence in Queen Anne's day.'

'Who was Jeffery?' asked our host.

I told him it was a mystery. 'There was once a coat of arms in the square, and as far as it could be deciphered the motto under it read "Je ferai". But there was no such arms or motto registered at the College of Arms and it is now assumed that Jeffery Square is a corruption of the French "Je ferai".'

Mr Simms Clarke observed that in the church of St Andrew Under-shaft at the corner of St Mary Axe and Leadenhall Street there were monuments to a family called Jefferys, but I told him they had no con-nection with the square. Credit Immobilier had plans for purchasing the freehold of the square with a view to building on it. We had been asked to make a survey of the site and make recommendations on how best to develop it, if we considered they could get it for a fair price. The houses on the north, south and east sides of the square were for sale, and the square itself, entrance to which was through an arched entrance carriageway on the west side facing St Mary Axe. Being at least a hundred years old the houses were in indifferent repair; the site had potential only as a building ground within six minutes walk of the Bank of England and the Royal Exchange. The vendors were asking £40,000 for the 19,500 sq ft – £2 per foot superl. I told Mr Simms Clarke that with regard to the present and future probable value of land in the City, this was fair and reasonable. It compared favourably with a much smaller piece lately sold at the corner of St Mary Axe of 2000 ft which fetched £18,000 or £9 per foot superl. Credit Immobilier were considering either erecting offices for merchants and public companies on the site, or bonded warehouses.

I told Mr Simms Clarke I thought the office building idea presented many manifest disadvantages. It would for instance be blocked by the old buildings on the west side not in the sale; and competition must arise from the speculation shortly to be expected in office property in main thoroughfares. On the other hand in the City proper the erection of superior bonded warehouses of improved construction (which reduced insurance premiums to a minimum) had not progressed in ratio with the vast increase of trade in London itself; and for this reason difficulty of procuring hitherto large freehold areas near the Royal Exchange, the Bank, the Corn Exchange, The Baltic & c at any moderate price was almost insurmountable. This then was the recommended project. The supply of warehouse accommodation was very limited, and the rents being obtained were very high. I gave him as an example the plain warehouse for colonial and other foreign produce in Crutched Friars, Minories, now in the course of erection – basement, ground floor and five storeys covering an area of 9,450 superficial feet, or about 94 squares. These premises had been taken, I told Mr Simms Clarke, by the most respectable parties at a rental of £3,200 per annum with a premium of £10,000 for the lease of 88 years. The lessees were given the option to purchase the freehold for £53,000. I said I thought one could add £500 to the rent to represent the £10,000 premium, so this gross rent of £3,700 a year divided by 94 squares equally produced £39.7 per square the whole height of seven floors, or £5.12 per square for each floor. A fair average rent would be £5 per square of flooring.

As far as Jeffery's Square was concerned I set out an Estimate as a basis for discussion as follows:

Outgoings

Cost of 19,478 superficial feet	£40,000
Less value of old materials of buildings	£1,500
	£38,500

Add cost of repayment to the Commissioners of Sewers of
    paving the square & c   £150

Add expenses, law charges, surveyors & c   £1,000

                                      £39,600

                       say,   £40,000

One or two blocks of warehouses with a cellarage under
    entire area built on two heights to obviate injury from
    adjoining lights averaging with basement, 5 stories and
    containing 1031 square of floors estimated to cost   £32,000

                   Total outlay £72,000

Returns

To gross rent on 1031 squares of warehouse floor including
    cellarage at £5 per square per annum   £5,055

Worth 20 years purchase   ×   20

                             £103,100

Shewing a profit of £31,100

I outlined the project briefly for the benefit of Mr Jonas who then asked me if I thought there would be many in rivalry with Mr Simms Clarke for the site, and if so what their plans for it would be likely to be. When I said I had no information on this point, Mr Jonas said it had occurred to him just then, while they were talking, that the Baltic Committee, which had the running of the Coffee House and was already finding South Sea House too small for their requirements, could hardly do better than make a bid for the site themselves and build on it a Wheat Exchange on the lines of Edward Moxhay's Hall of Commerce down the street. When Mr Simms Clarke showed alarm at such a happening, Mr Jonas assured him there was little possibility of The Baltic Company which had been set up to handle the property side of the coffee house would risk its capital at this juncture. But one day, he said, draining his brandy, who knows? Mr Simms Clarke sighed a sigh of relief, and we passed to other topics.

I told Mr Jonas that since I had seen him last we had moved our offices from no 5 to no 4 Whitehall last year – no great upset, but a move with all that is involved nonetheless. He said his son Henry last year too had completed his apprenticeship with Mr Adams at Barkway, and that after a holiday in the Alps he would be seeking an appointment suited to his undoubted talents — an observation in which I could not fail to remark a hint? But himself perhaps all too aware of the unintended impression he had made, he quickly switched to an account of a visit he had had at Saffron Walden last month by an American writer called Elihu Burritt founder of the Universal Brotherhood who was writing, à la Daniel Defoe, an account of a Whole Tour of Great Britain which he was entitling *A Walk to John O'Groats*. Mr Jonas could not affirm whether or not Mr Burritt had walked to that extremity, but he assured us he had certainly tramped every one of the three thousand acres of his five farms in East Anglia, and had insisted on being shown the inventory of his livestock which he had taken at Michaelmas last which revealed his sheep were worth £6,481, his horses £2,487, his bullocks £2,218 and his pigs £452, making a grand total of £11,638. He spent £4,000 a year on the oil cake and corn purchased for feeding them, and £17,000 a year for artificial fertilisers of guano and blood-manure – he was the director of a company formed for the manufacture of the latter. Mr Simms Clarke's eyes boggled at all this. His income, continued Mr Jonas, came solely from the sale of meat and grain. Not a pound of hay, straw or roots was sold off the estate. It was indeed impressive, and both Mr Simms Clarke and myself said we looked forward to reading a copy of Mr Burritt's book when it was published.

Memorandum

From: R. C. Driver   Date: March 3rd, 1865

For the Information of All Staff

Our business is expanding so rapidly, I shall from time to time circulate a few notes on areas of our practice with which certain members of the staff may be less familiar. Below is the first of these, set out for the purpose of reading, marking *and learning*, on the subject of

VALUATION OF ADVOWSONS AND NEXT
PRESENTATIONS

In valuing such properties in London, adopt the following mode:

Take the annual value which is the income derivable from land. (let);

Estimated annual value of parsonage house and premises; Tithe Commutation Rent Charges or Corn Rent and Surplice Fees – from which are deducted, 1st Curate's stipend, 2nd Repairs and Insurance on the parsonage house and buildings on Glebe and to Chancel generally taken at from 8 to 10 per cent on the annual value, 3rd Land Tax, 4th Rates on the Tithe Rent Charge for difference between it and the averages. The next annual value is then multiplied by the number of years purchase that an Advowson or Next Presentation is worth according to the age of life in possession. The Rate of Interest varies according to circumstances from £5 to £7, but £6 is the rate generally received.

Mr N. values these on a system quite different to the above general practice. He takes the value of the Glebe lands and Tithe Rent Charge, putting down nothing for the Rent of Parsonage and deducting nothing for repairs of same nor the curate's stipend. Then multiplies the net annual value by 16 years purchase (the value of a living if immediate possession could be given) and deducts therefrom the value of the life in possession according to the 6 pc Tables.

Journal of Robert Driver

May 14th, 1866

1866? a year of transition indeed! I have just left a little celebration given by my professional colleagues, fellow members of the Land Surveyors Club and hob-knobbers in the Westminster Palace Hotel where all the railway business is hammered out, to mark my 50th birthday – among them John Clutton, Walter Watney, Edward Ryde, Francis Vigers, Charles Adams and that assiduous recorder of passing time, Henry Allnutt, who founded the *Estates Gazette* eight years ago and is making such a success of it. How kind and good-hearted of them! We met at Garraway's, scene of so many auctions – alas for the last time! It is to be demolished next month, one of the last survivors of the old coffee houses and the provider of sale rooms in the days when there was nowhere else. And not before our Auction Mart, late of Bartholomew Lane, in which I have been asked to take £5,000 worth of debentures at five per cent (and will do so), rises in a new guise at Tokenhouse Yard.

They were good enough to congratulate me on the small contribution I have made towards the campaign for freeing the bridges over the

Thames from the tolls which have been proving so great a restraint on internal trade in the City, and was crowned with an initial success with the payment by the Corporation of London last year to the proprietors of Southwark Bridge the sum of £200,000 in compensation for the compulsory cessation of tolls. I hope it will pave the way to the withdrawal of these burdensome and unnecessary tolls from the rest of London's bridges.

An Act of Parliament in 1811 gave a company of proprietors the right to build a bridge from Bankside to Three Cranes Wharf after Mr John Rennie had pronounced that, after one hard frost, London Bridge might not last another year. Uncle Edward told me his father told the story of how the gentlemen of the committee of management partook of a cold collation on a temporary bridge erected on the works after the first stone pier was laid in May 1815 – and I suppose they have had to levy a toll for the champagne ever since! The next step is for the Corporation to purchase the bridge outright, and this I understand they intend to do within the next three years.

Not really a very jubilant moment for a jubilee, with the shock of the failure of the Overend Gurney bank still reverberating in nearby Lombard Street – and indeed far beyond. May 11th will for long be remembered as Black Friday. The Gurneys of course are a Norwich family – I did not dare ask Mr Adams, who hails from those parts and had the young Henry Jonas as his apprentice clerk up to five years ago, whether he was affected. The whole of the banking world seems disturbed just now. I must confess figures are not my forte; I have neither a liking nor a talent for them. I should never have taken on the position of Secretary *and Treasurer* of the Land Surveyors Club. In June last year I invested £142 in Consols in my name at 91⅜ through my stockbrokers Hutchinson & Son, producing stock valued at £155. *This belongs to the Land Surveyors Club*, and unfortunately it has got mixed up with my own money. It will have to be accounted for one of these days, with interest at 3 per cent, and paid to the future secretary or in charitable donations as the Society may direct. I really must be more attentive to such matters. I must consult Harry Rumsey our cashier more than I do at present – strictly in confidence of course, but he can thoroughly be relied on to keep these purely private matters to himself. I shall certainly steer clear of accepting any such office in the new 'Institution' which I and Clutton and others have been talking about recently. We must get a lawyer like John Horatio Lloyd, say, who is so hot on all that intricate railway compensation stuff, to draw up a constitution.

Mr. ROBERT
COLLIER
DRIVER

23 May, 1878

2204. You have had to consider questions, I do not say of tolls of a Bridge exactly like Waterloo Bridge, but questions of Bridge Tolls, and other securities that have come forward for sale or for purchase in the market?—I have. I have had a very large experience in the sales of all properties including tolls, houses, and land in all its varieties.

2205. Have you considered the question of what the value of Waterloo Bridge is?—I have.

2206. How do you deal with it?—I consider that this Bridge is not only substantial, but in all probability will last for all time.

2207. Of course with the works done to it which have been suggested?—Of course all necessary works being done to keep the piers from sinking, and the Bridge repaired from time to time with its approaches. That being done I consider that in all human probability it will last for all time. I also look upon it as a very unique Bridge being constructed of granite, with excellent approaches, one being nearly level, that is the Strand side, and on the Surrey side there being a very slight incline. I also take this Bridge, being in the centre of London, as in as good a situation as it is possible for any Bridge to be placed. Looking to the surroundings for traffic; and looking to the fact that there has been an increase in the tolls for very many years, and that there is a probable and possible increase of those tolls, I am of opinion that the multiplier of those tolls should be at 20 years' purchase, taking those tolls as the average of the last 10 years, which is the period that I generally adopt, and deducting from that gross amount the average of the net outgoings. On that basis I have proceeded in estimating the compensation.

2208. That brings out the figure, taking the actual tolls for 10 years from 1867 to 1877, deducting the actual expenses for the same six years, £70,000, in round figures, to £358,000, or 20 years' purchase?—There are some fractions. It is £358,000 in round figures.

2209. If the property were not what it is, after making full allowance for all disturbing causes, would you put such a multiplier as 20 years?—Certainly not, most assuredly not.

2210. If this property could be realised in the open market, either in whole or in parts, do you think it would fetch such a price?—Nothing like it.

2211. Less?—Very much less. The public would estimate it in a very different way.

2212. We heard something about a White Elephant; if the whole bridge were to be put up now, assume that the individual interests were to be put up and sold, do you think that these would command anything like 20 years' purchase?—No. That opinion is borne out by the fact that when these shares or annuities, £7 or £8 annuities, come into the market, they do not realise 20 years' purchase.

[Mr. Miller conferred with the Umpire.]

Mr. PHILLBRICK: I do not say that that is the proper principle to value it upon, I am merely using it as an illustration. In the absence of my learned friend, Sir Henry James, I should not for a moment say that we were to pay for it as if it were to be put up for auction to-day or to-morrow, but still that is an element to be taken into account.

Mr. MILLER: Certainly.

2213. Mr. PHILBRICK: I will not go through this valuation in detail because I do not think it necessary to do so, as it will appear upon the notes. I will just ask you this, just to explain your principle; you take the vaults all at five per cent., where they are rack rental,

March 23rd, 1868

This afternoon some twenty of us met at the Westminster Palace Hotel with John Clutton in chair and resolved to establish an 'Institution of Surveyors'. We formed ourselves into a provisional association and appointed a sub-committee to draft resolutions and regulations to enable us to found a permanent organisation. We are to meet again in June to elect a first Council, and we hope to persuade John Penfold to act as Hon. Sec. – he is an architect – and to allow us to use his premises in Parliament Street as temporary offices, while we look around for permanent headquarters, somewhere near the Houses of Parliament if possible – Great George Street, for instance, would be ideal.

We have all been talking about taking such a step for some time, but last month at a meeting of the Land Surveyors Club we appointed a committee 'for the purpose of considering how the club can elevate and improve the profession of the surveyors of England, especially having reference to the formation of an association or institute'. Eleven of us twenty who met to-day to launch the new institution are members of the LSC – a notable exception being my friend Edward Ryde, the great railway valuer who has helped to plan the extension of the South Eastern Railway from London Bridge to Charing Cross and brought coals of fire on his head from the entire medical profession for his insisting that there was no way he could take the line other than slap through the ancient St. Thomas's Hospital which has occupied the site for 400 years (it had to be demolished and rebuilt beside the Thames at Westminster Bridge). He was the prime mover of the new institution with Clutton. All previous attempts to institutionalise our profession have failed – unqualified impostors are still engaged by gullible clients who rightly protest they have been given no clue how to recognise a qualified surveyor when one presents himself. It is up to us to provide this clue – membership of an authoritative and widely recognised body to which entrance is controlled by examination and other qualifications. *We must not fail this time.* Most of us are Londoners, but our new body must become thoroughly representative of *every* aspect of our work in *every* part of the kingdom. The engineers and architects have their associations; it is time our profession caught up with them. The editor of *Building News* has much justification for upbraiding us for our inertia. At last perhaps – if we have the *will* to do other than dine and drink –

we can establish uniform standards for our charges – why even the government is progressing in this regard by setting up a Select Committee to investigate the possibility of introducing a system of poor rate assessment applicable to the whole of London, for which we have been rooting for so long.

November 6th, 1869

To-day attended the opening by Queen Victoria of the Holborn Viaduct which has at last relieved the long haul up the sides of the unhappy Holborn Valley which drivers and horses found so arduous. (On the same day the Queen opened the new Blackfriars Bridge.)

Our firm has given its services as surveyors in the construction of Holborn Viaduct since Messrs Hill & Keddell the contractors began work in June 1867: in fact we have been working with Mr William Haywood, the Engineer to the Commissioners of Sewers – and indeed the virtual architect of the project – from the early planning stages. The eventual cost of it all, including purchases of the land and premises with which we have been so closely concerned, and the goodwill, was £2,552,406 (the cost of Blackfriars Bridge was only £401,131). I understand the cost will fall mainly on Corporation of London revenues owing to the refusal of Parliament to grant a renewal of coal dues. Our firm helped to settle some 700 or so claims for compensation on behalf of the Holborn Viaduct Improvement Committee, but they did much of the work themselves without employing the services of outsiders like ourselves. Indeed, I was told that if the ground had been cleared by a staff of surveyors and valuers, the commission on the amount paid, £1,565,000, would have formed one of the largest items in the cost of the improvement.

I am informed that Leopold, King of the Belgians, is visiting the Queen at Windsor the week after next, and that he is interested in acquiring property in this country and that his steward is anxious to meet me to discuss ways and means.

Letter of Robert Driver to his eldest son, Charles

The Grange, Highbury
May 25th, 1871

My dear Charles,

As you know, I am very much looking forward, when you leave

school this summer, to your joining the firm as a 'pupil' to learn what this surveying and auctioneering is all about, and eventually of course to assume responsibility with me as a partner – a junior partner – for the Messrs Driver operation (when you attain your majority in 1874, say) along with your younger brothers Robert and James when they too come of age.

I am writing to you now, to avoid any future misunderstanding, to say that I have seen fit to take into partnership a Mr N. A. Bowlen whom I have known a number of years, with a view to helping us with an aspect of business which is fast growing, namely mortgages. I shall welcome his judgement in valuing properties for insurance companies and these so-called building societies which are generating more and more work these days. The point I want to make is that Mr Bowlen's appointment in no way affects your position or eventual seniority as my eldest son, and, I hope, successor as *senior* partner. Mr Bowlen fully understands this; his being made a partner is more to give him status and authority in his dealings. He is in any case already senior in another sense – in age.

We are consolidating our position on our office premises at no. 4 Whitehall by purchasing the leasehold from Messrs Beazley for £6,000 – the unexpired portion, that is, of about 50 years. As this stabilises, so to speak, the location of my place of business, I think it is time we as a family came closer to central London than Highbury, and I have been looking at some of the houses in the Cromwell Road area of South Kensington which I have always admired. There is a place called Melrose House which particularly takes my fancy, and I understand it is likely to come on the market either next year or the year after. So be prepared for an upheaval!

You will be sad to hear of the death of Mr Samuel Jonas whom you will remember we visited on his vast 3,000 acre farm in Essex in the Easter holidays a couple of years ago. He had certainly reduced agriculture to a fine art. Unlike so many enthusiasts of his type he was no crank, but put his theories into practice on the ground and *made them work*. Unlike the other personage, exalted in an altogether different sphere, who has just swum into our ken, no other than His ex-Imperial Majesty Napoleon III, son of Louis Bonaparte the great Napoleon's brother. As a 36 year old idealist during his four year imprisonment in the Fortress of Ham he wrote a book called *De L'Extinction du Pauperisme* which was published in 1844. In it he advocated the planned resettlement of the urban poor under the auspices of the government on land which had been allowed to pass out of cultivation. He, no doubt, would have encouraged the squatters on the America Ground at Hastings instead of turning them out like we did! But he was too preoccupied with dynastic ambitions to put his plan into action.

As you will have read in your papers, the erstwhile Louis Napoleon, who for the last 18 years has ruled France as the Emperor Napoleon III and given her a 'Second Empire' (!), turned up at Dover last week, and the Mr Strode whom he had met in the eighteen forties during his first exile in England once again put at his disposal his property Camden House at Chislehurst. The ex-Empress Eugenie came over in November last year after the defeat of the French at Sedan to make the arrangements. As the ex-Emperor's defeat looks like making his return to France an extremely unlikely eventuality, Mr Strode has asked us to draw up a lease which would give the fallen emperor a greater sense of security and remove any feeling of dependence or charity. I suppose the two of them will spend the rest of their lives here. Whether our Queen will allow them to be naturalised remains to be seen – I doubt it – but otherwise I suppose Her ex-Imperial Majesty will not be able to benefit from our latest step in the emancipation of women, the Married Women's Property Act passed last August, in the event of her illustrious husband predeceasing her.

I trust you will be leading the Football XI to victory this term in true Driver fashion – your Mother and I will try and come down at half term.

Ever, your loving
Father

Letter from Robert Driver to his wife Maria

Woodford, Essex
18th September 1871

My dear Maria,

This has been a most extraordinary experience. Someone in the solicitor's office of the Corporation of London discovered there was once something called the 'Court of Verderers' which had been constituted back in the past and never abolished, empowered to act as the Judicial Officers of the Forest Courts and to deal with unlawful enclosures of Epping Forest. The lords of the manor surrounding the forest have bit by bit been encroaching on the forest, felling timber and destroying its natural beauty, and no one, they thought, had the power or the inclination to stop them. But they had failed to reckon on the ingenuity of the bright lad in the City Solicitor's Office who unearthed the 'Court of Verderers'. All right, but what right had the Corporation of *London* to interfere with Epping Forest in Essex? they said. The answer was the Corporation had a foot under the door by reason of their ownership of Ilford Cemetery which gave them Rights of Common; and on the strength of this the City Solicitor instituted a suit in Chancery before the Master of the Rolls in August this year by direction of the Corporation in the name of the Commissioners of Sewers against the lords of the manors for a stay of all further illegal enclosures, and to obtain a declaration that all owners and occupiers within regard of the forest were entitled to rights of common over the whole of the waste lands. Well, that put the cat among the pigeons as you can imagine, and you remember I came down and made a number of surveys of the parts of the forest in question. This was followed by the meeting to-day of this ancient 'court' – last meeting 1848! – as a result of a writ addressed by the Lord Chancellor to the Sherriff of Essex directing the Three Verderers to sit and consider the long list of unlawful enclosures read to them by the City Solicitor and I had helped to prepare. You should have seen the faces of some of these local land agents and solicitors! They never thought such a thing could happen!

Yours ever,

Robert

Memorandum

From: R. C. Driver   *Date:* April 3rd 1872

For the Information of All Staff

The following notes are circulated for the information of all staff on the subject of

VALUATION OF MINES

The value of mines are calculated upon a certain number of Years Purchase on the Income derivable from Royalty Rent, and not upon the proceeds or net income received from them when worked by the owner. Mr Beale takes the years purchase at from 10 to 15 years on the royalty rent variable according to the certainty of a continuance of supply and demand of the article produced. The latter is very high and only used in extreme cases; 10 years were taken in the instance of the Clay Mines and Brick and Pottery works at Branksea. The royalty paid for some mines in this locality is about a 1/- per ton, but it is worth about 3/- per ton for working. Two estates called Clough Hall and White Hill Estates are worth a minimum rent for mineral purposes of £8 per acre. Property is frequently sold at surface value reserving minerals, and it may be done here. It is stated that under Clough Hall there is Coal 23 yards thick and the usual value as a mine for rent is £100 per acre for a yard thick; this calculation looks to the ultimate exhaustion of the minerals, an event no one can anticipate. As to rating, the only minerals rateable are coals. Ironstone is not rateable – the mode of rating coal mines is to ascertain the price and quantity of coal sold from the mine. Take $\frac{1}{8}$th as royalty and deducting $\frac{1}{6}$th you arrive at the rateable value.

Example: say 1000 tons @ 8/- per ton   £400
$\frac{1}{8}$th of £400 — £50 gross value
deduct $\frac{1}{16}$th of £50   £8-6-8
£41-13-4 rateable value

Letter from Charles Driver to Miss Florence Kingdon

Bala, Merionethshire
May 21st, 1872

Dear Miss Kingdon,

I am on a jaunt in Darkest Wales with father to have a look at a monster estate hereabouts, the sale of which the firm has been asked to undertake – and my goodness what a job that means, I had no idea! That's why I am here and seeking consolation in writing to you from the centre of this No Man's Land where Englishmen never set foot before except in pursuit of woodcock and other gentlemanly game of that sort. I am being indoctrinated. Your people being in the same line of business you are doubtless more familiar than I am with what selling an estate means. I told father I would ferret out any historical information about the property we could put in the advertisements which might appeal to Americans and other bidders likely to be impressed by Romantic Britain. I was rather hot at history at school.

The place in question is a 'freehold domain' – you see I am getting the hang of the jargon already – of more than 11,000 acres in the heart of

Merionethshire, and if you don't know where that is go and look for it on a map. It is called the Aber-Hirnant Estate. We came up by train last Tuesday as far as Shrewsbury, and then changed to a branch line with a single track and a fine little Puffing Billy of an engine to pull us up to Bala. We are staying at the only inn and very comfortable it is in a crude kind of way. Good wholesome food, don't you know! On Wednesday I visited the place in a wagonette the owners sent for us, and in the evening in front of a blazing log fire I wrestled with father over the fine descriptive prose I had drafted for what we call 'the Particular'; you know, this sort of thing:

> 'This important domain possesses valleys, gorges and passes of great beauty and extent. It is specially selected by tourists for their grandeur and picturesque character, the scenery being equal to the Cumberland and Westmorland Lake District.'

You see I had been to the Lake District one hols and thought this place strikingly like it. I had an argument with father over whether you spelt Westmorland with an 'e' or not; he thought there should be, I said not. He'll have the final word I suppose, and I bet he mis-spells it. More important he said was to get the Welsh spelling right – you know, a foreign language really –

> Among principal valleys are the Ystradgroes, Cwm Gwyn, the Hirnant where there is the confluence of the two rivers above which is a large pool the Nant-y-Sarn, the Hirnant-Corms, the Rhos-y-Gwaliau (the Plain of the Wounded where a great battle was fought).

Father said you could not put just 'a great battle', you must say what battle it was, who it was between and when it took place. I said Nonsense – Americans aren't going to worry about details like that. Besides, the native I talked to had no idea himself; there was just a local tradition that some kind of fighting took place here. It is probably all in some folk-lore book if anyone wants to look it up; but it is not the sort of thing you need to be Particular about.

I can tell you I have been adding to my knowledge of minerals in the last two days at an astonishing rate – which is not difficult seeing that up to last Wednesday it was nil. Father objected to my calling it a virgin estate on the grounds of indelicacy, but I thought as a description of an unravaged region it was very apt. It reads very well in my opinion:

> This domain may justly be termed a virgin estate, it having never yet been developed. It is known to contain most valuable beds of slate

156

besides Steatite, commonly known as Soapstone, limestone and red sandstone, and underlying it beds of coal.

Too many references to beds, did I hear you say? Mineralogically speaking I can assure you, dear Florrie, it is the only correct term, so stop interrupting. For there is greater excitement to come:

Indication of lead and *silver* and numerous quartz lodes containing faces of *gold*. Should these be hereafter worked, the results could be easily conveyed by overhead railway or wire through the valleys to the Bala Railway.

Who said there was no romance in being a Land Agent! I went all over this land myself, and talked with some of the men who had prospected there. I took away bits of quartz with gold in it in my pocket, and father says to write into the Particular the fact that specimens of the minerals can be inspected by would-be purchasers at our offices – to prove we are not making it all up.

Minerals below, and on the surface alive with game. The Grousing Moors extend for 7,577 acres; partridges abound. The house at the centre of all this is planned exclusively for slaughter – what we describe as a Shooting Box. Describing what the purchaser is going to get for his money, and how he can set about it, is a major operation, involving all kinds of bits of paper – I have managed to get hold of a railway map of the area showing how the lines converge on Bala to enable the army of shooters to find the place.

Last month I was engaged on a somewhat more civilised estate at Twickenham – Fulwell Lodge it was called, a 'comfortable mansion' with a pleasure ground and park, only 41 acres. I have arranged for an artist to make two lithograph drawings of the house, front and back, and from the rough sketches he has done I think they should be quite delightful. Some of the others in the office think this 'photography' is going to be much better – and quicker. Maybe, but it loses much of the charm. I also arranged for Fulwell a 'Plan of the Estate' showing the position of the house in the park, and a 'Ground Plan' showing all the rooms of the house, and of course the Particular and Conditions of Sale. I have been seeing they are all done properly by Richard Clay the printers, reading proofs, approving layouts and all that. You see what a busy young man I have become! But there is still plenty of time for Florrie

Your devoted,
Charles Driver

Fulwell Lodge, litho drawing for catalogue of 1820

July 7th, 1874

'But surely land has no value apart from what is, or is not, grown on it?'

'According to last year's Rating Act it has!'

'Surely I can increase the value of a plot by growing a crop of larch on it?'

'Not according to the Rating Act.'

'Two adjoining plots; one tenant grows corn, the other flax. Does not one become more valuable than the other and thus liable to be rated higher?'

'If it did, good, so-called 'intellectual', farming would be penalised. You do not make land good or bad by growing good or bad things on it.'

'Don't you, by George! Look here, my woodlands and the surrounding land which I've put under grass is only worth half a crown an acre. Do you mean to say that if I raised a paying crop on part of it, it would not be rated higher than the uncultivated part?'

'So our Liberal governors have decreed. The crop, which includes timber, is not rateable, only the land it is grown on, in its natural and unimproved condition. All sorts of circumstances determine its value, but what is grown on it is not one of them.'

'How is one rated when the trees are cut down and the ground is full of stumps? The value of the land must be diminished, since it is very difficult to raise *anything* on it.'

'In that case, as I see it, the rate would hardly be more than the rent it would fetch from a tenant for grazing purposes.'

'What about sporting rights?'

'Depends on size. When farms are put together for a shoot the sporting rights may have some value, but nothing when the same farms are rated separately.'

The discussion was between two gentlemen in the railway carriage in which I was travelling back home to Essex for the weekend after attending the Coming of Age Celebration of Charles Driver, Mr Robert's eldest son, and his becoming a partner in the firm. I was greatly honoured to be asked to this gathering along with a host of relations and other senior members of the staff. I had only been one of them a few months, having tired of the almost exclusively agricultural aspect of the work I found in East Anglia on completing my term with Mr Adams, and, having impetuously elected to uproot and journey on foot to the metropolis to see where my qualifications and experience could best be employed. Armed with a letter of introduction from my father, I knocked on the door of no. 4 Whitehall. That Mr Robert Driver finally agreed to add me to his staff as a surveyor was due more, I hope, to my estimated worth than any sense of obligation.

At the Coming of Age Celebration in their new house in Cromwell Road I met Maria Driver, Mr Robert's daughter whom they all call Cissie, and I must say she was very sympathetic. It was a gay evening. We were received in the hall which was beautifully decorated with evergreens and lights. We left our hats and coats in the billiard room similarly disguised; there was supper in the dining room – Mr John Searcy who did the catering told me that the silver had been given him by the Duke of Northumberland whose confectioner he had once been at Alnwick Castle – tea and coffee in the library. There was dancing in the drawing room to a pianoforte and harp, and Mr Charles' brothers, Robert and James, and Cissie sang a congratulatory trio to the twenty-one year old which they had written themselves. I danced a quadrille with Mrs Singleton and the Lancers with Miss Driver who, when I mentioned how perfect the floor was, said it had been 'brought in' by Mr Tansley the ball furnisher and laid on top of their own! She also said the family had once been Quakers and would never have countenanced a rout of this kind a couple of generations ago. We also danced several waltzes. I found her very diverting.

My companions in the train the day after had turned to the subject of the General Election in February which had resulted in the defeat of the Liberal Party after 40 years in spite of Mr Gladstone promising to abolish Income Tax *altogether*, and the return of Mr Disraeli and the Tories who were last in power in 1830. It was the first election held under this secret ballot of which my travelling friends were highly suspicious. They talked too of the strike of agricultural labour in the part of England for which we were heading, Norfolk and Suffolk; they talked of the project to construct a tunnel between France and England proposed by M. Lavalley the French engineer who had done such wonders over the Suez Canal; and they had just embarked on a dissection of the Tichborne Case which finally ended with Arthur Orton the would-be Duke of Portland receiving 14 years for perjury, when the train shuddered to a halt with a screeching of brakes and a hissing of steam, and we were pitched into one another's arms, our top hats descending on us from the racks above. I picked myself up and scrambled to the window to see what had occurred. Slowly settling on the line only a few yards in front of the locomotive was the garishly coloured envelope of a balloon! There was much shouting, and I opened the carriage door and jumped to the ground. Several men were running up to the front and I followed them. The basket of the balloon had fallen to one side and was halfway down the embankment. In it I saw a man curled up on the floor as if dead. The fireman from the engine was first beside him and was attempting to lift him out as the huge balloon, its air fast expelling, finally sprawled itself across the railway track.

The man in the basket turned out to be Jo Simmons who had gone up in his balloon from Cremorne Gardens that afternoon with Vincent de Groof 'The Flying Man' on board who, when the balloon had risen to a considerable height, had leapt as intended from the basket, spread the bat-like wings which were meant, but failed, to support him in the air, and fallen to his death in front of the crowd who had gathered to witness his much-advertised feat. Jo Simmons was so shocked by this unexpected turn of events that he fainted and fell to the floor of the basket where he remained unconscious while his balloon sailed with the wind across the Thames into Essex and then, gradually losing height, came down, as chance would have it, on the railway line right in front of our train which luckily was able to stop just in time. Perhaps I will live to see the day when man really *does* fly.

What a week-end! Something at least to put in my bread-and-butter thank you letter to Mr Driver – and perhaps warrant a brief billet doux to Miss Driver whom I am afraid I bored with my plans for a holiday in Switzerland, though she was polite enough to feign what seemed a considerable interest.

Letter of Henry Jonas to Miss Maria (Cissie) Driver

Hotel du Monte Rosa,
Zermatt, Switzerland
12 September, 1875

Dear Miss Driver,

As you take the greatest interest in Switzerland I send you a few details of my trip which promises to be a most successful one if the weather does but hold fine. I left Holborn Viaduct on Saturday morning the 26th August with a knapsack and ice axe as my only companions, and slept at Lauterbrunnen on Sunday night. Before reaching Thun I could see that snow had recently fallen heavily on the mountains and I met no less than 52 carriages full of people returning from Murren and Grundelwald on account of the bad weather. 150 English people attended service at Murren that morning and they intend soon to commence building an English church there. After 5 days patiently waiting for fine weather at Grundelwald I was able to start for the Strehlegg pass to the Grinsel Hospice on Saturday at 3 am. Facing the Grundelwald Glacier the way lies up the Eismeer and turns to the left. On reaching the rocky looking mountain which stops further view from Grundelwald I had intended to have turned to the right on reaching the same mountain and so cross the Monch Joch Pass to the Eggishorn; but the weather decided for the Strehlegg and I am very glad I took it. It certainly is by far the grandest pass across the Oberland and although it takes 14 hours active walking – 11 hours of which are on snow and ice – it repays for the trouble more than any other pass. My guide was delighted at my pulling through without any sign of fatigue and we at once planned a formidable sojourn of 3 consecutive days in the heart of the Bernese Alps.

We accordingly started Monday morning from the Eggishorn (near the Rhone Valley) myself and 2 guides carrying fire wood and provisions for the 2 first days, and travelled towards Grundelwald, our object being to cross the Monch Joch Pass and sleep at a hut built for suchlike purpose on the Bergli Rocks, a small ridge of rocks in the centre of a large and highly crevassed snow field about 8 hours from Grundelwald to the right of the Eismeer. We did not reach this hut till 7. The sun had set; the moon began to rise as we came up to the hut which is the oddest place I have ever slept in. The door was blocked up with 4 ft of snow and enormous icicles hung from the roof. These we had to cut and clear away with our ice axes and the guides turned in to light the fire, and prepared table d'hote of chocolate, cold meat and hard boiled eggs, while I turned out to contemplate the Alps by moonlight, which I have not had an opportunity of doing before. The moon had risen in a cloudless sky and bathed the whole scene in a livid blue, the rivulets created by the melting of the surface snows had all been hushed in the icy grip of an Alpine night, and the Eiger and Wetterhorn and some minor peaks towered over us in a silent and most solemn grandeur about the yawning crevasses. Below our rock had a most grim and forbidding aspect. But thrilling as the scene was, it did not protect me from the freezing atmosphere and I had to turn in. There was but one step from the beautiful to the wretched – a hut built of loose stone 8 ft sq contained a raised bench 5 ft 6 in wide full of wet straw, the other 2 ft 6 in wide formed a passage, at one end of which was a stone; a few cooking utensils and some coarse damp blankets completed the 'furniture'. The wood is damp, the chimney refuses to pass the smoke which ultimately finds its way first into the hut and then into our eyes and lungs producing the utmost discomfort. I laid as much of myself on the 5 ft bench as I could, wrapped myself up first in my plaid then in a damp blanket. But more than one hour's broken sleep was out of the question and I envied my two companions till they roused themselves at 1.30 and after more chocolate and bread and butter we started at 3 am to ascend the Monch.

.   .   .   .   .   .

I fear I have given you too much talk about myself and little or nothing of other topics. My only apology is that I am at present so wrapped up in my own pleasure I can't devote much thought to others, but I sincerely hope you have all been enjoying yourselves in Scotland and having less rain than I hear in Cambridgeshire.

With kind regards to all,

I remain, yours most sincerely,

Henry Jonas

Note in the Private Ledger of Robert Driver

28 September, 1875

Ealing Property – about 14 acres – part of the Castle Hill Estate which has cost me by purchase of the Metropolitan Assurance Office, £10,000. The reason of my purchase of this is consequent on my late partner (never to be forgotten by me but forgiven – N. A. Bowlen) having advised a considerable loan on a property at Ealing which afterwards turned out not to be the value advised by him to be lent, and hence I felt called upon to purchase about 14 acres in order to relieve the Metropolitan Assurance Office of the whole responsibility and burthen of the estate. It is at present let to a Mr Priest as yearly tenant at the snap rent of £40 a year, the landlord paying all the rates, tithes and taxes.

Note in blue chalk over the page which was pinned up

Note: This is the only Transaction after 40 years practice where I have been in any way troubled or asked a question after the valuation and mortgage have been settled; and this was *not* my fault but that of my *articled* partner in whom for 5 years (N. A. Bowlen) never to be forgiven by me as a *Principal* – a good valuer he MIGHT have been once but a long time ago.   RCD 1875

Note: I hope my residuary will not be in a hurry to sell or realise this property. It will turn up all right one of these days I fully believe.
                                                                      RCD Nov 1877

Minutes of Partners' Meeting, October 4th, 1875

Present: Robert Collier Driver
Charles William Driver
Robert Manning Driver

Mr R. C. Driver briefly explained the circumstances which had led to Mr Bowlen no longer being a partner, and welcomed his second son Robert who had celebrated his 21st birthday the previous month to the meeting – his first as a partner. He did not wish to dwell on his regret at the failure of his attempt to introduce outside blood into the family firm, but rather to express his gratification at having as his counsellors and true partners, in this the 150th anniversary of the founding of the business, sons on whom he could rely for sound judgement and balanced opinions, able to act, above all, as link men, as he and his father and grandfather had done, with the new generation and the new attitudes and techniques they heralded. This was no occasion, he said, for romantic speculation on what the future might bring, but he hazarded the guess that, God willing, they would still be in business in 1975 though God knew it would be a very different world from the Victorian age which, to all who lived in it, seemed so deeply entrenched, so solid, so 'permanent', it was difficult ever to see it changing. Yet change it would – and Messrs Driver with it. But integrity, good faith, honest dealing, energy and good humour however, he would like to wager, would still underly the conduct of successful professional men such as they. He looked to his sons Charles and Robert to maintain such standards into the twentieth century he doubted he would ever live to see, and never devalue the *service* every client of theirs had for so long been led to expect, and should be entitled to go on expecting.

Letter from Robert Driver to his younger brother James

The Swan With Two Necks, Broadgate
12th October 1875

Dear James,

You should have heard father at the Partners' Meeting last week – the first I had attended. He preached a *sermon*. He's been affected by this Bowlen business more than I thought. I believe he had to fork out *thousands* from his own pocket to put things right. He told us briefly about it, but not the whole story. Mother says he writes it all down in a little book which he keeps in his desk at the office. No wonder he's rattled. I know you are studying law and opting out of becoming involved in Surveying – sensible chap! – but I hope you will be able to help us with our legal problems and keep us from getting into the kind of trouble father found himself in. You can draw up our partnership deeds for us too.

I am down here on the south coast – on business for the firm, you know. The local baron is opposing the South Eastern Railway's plan to extend the line over his land – that's enlightened 1875 for you! I thought that kind of attitude had gone out in our great-uncle Edward's day. 'I will study the scheme' his lordship is reported as saying, 'but on a Cursory View it looks all rubbish as far as I am concerned. I do not think it would do a pennyworth of good to the estate as a building area.' That is his lordship's yardstick. What price the Public Good? Reaction is the order of the day in southern England in 1875 – marching doggedly backwards.

A Bill has been set on its course through Parliament by the railway company, and his lordship has been advised to resist it alone and not ally himself with other opponents. In this way he is free to close with the company on any proposal he considers advantageous to *him* but might not suit others. Rather the Bill go through than defeat it in cohoots with those damned outsiders! Self-interest reigns supreme.

It is apparently a question of the railway either coming to an 'arrangement' with the landowner to whom they make concessions but pay less, or making no accommodation and the landowner receiving the highest compensation for every inch of land the railway requires.

His lordship's legal adviser had hoped to submit a petition against the Bill, but the parliamentary agents he consulted told him he had missed the bus. The old rule for receiving petitions in the Commons after the second reading did not apply to the House of Lords, where it was after the first. But apparently he managed to get this procedural oversight waived, and got some kind of petition presented after all.

I attended a public meeting to protest against the Bill held in a village hall down here last Wednesday. I do not know if those who had organised it, expected it, but opinion was divided for and against. The main point of the opposers was the unsightliness of the arches which would have to span the High Street, and the amount of property which would be destroyed. Damage to their aesthetic suceptibilities vied with thoughts of pecuniary gain, and many sided in favour of the Bill when it appeared that it might well involve considerable financial compensation.

High spot of the evening was the lowering of a back-drop curtain, as they say in the theatre, on which was painted a scene of the High Street as it is now. Then at a wave of the wicked railway company's wand another curtain was dropped in front of the first one. This showed how it would look with the dark shadow of the railway bridge firmly across the old village street, its picturesqueness, so the speaker claimed, utterly destroyed. Contrary again, I imagine, to expectation, the dramatic lowering of the second curtain resulted not in a gasp of horror but several titters which then gave way to blatant, embarrassed laughter. We might have been watching the Fol-de-Rols! I must admit I couldn't help laughing myself. But, in the teeth of the evidence, Mr Ridley, his lordship's counsel who was conducting this part of the proceedings, defiantly nodded his head at us and declared he could assume the Bill was as good as dead. An unjust presumption, but a brave one.

The gentleman who was sitting next to me leant over and said that the speaker's optimism was no doubt derived from his knowledge that the Local Board was packed with anti-railway members. The Borough Council however, he confided, who were the real representatives of the people, supported the Bill. Sir Edward Watkins MP, who was a director of the S.E. Railway, had met the town council and pointed out how improved harbour accommodation would increase the port's continental traffic, and extension of the railway line was part of this improvement. His lordship had publicly declared he did not see the value to the town of continental traffic.

On giving me this last piece of information, my neighbour made a gesture of despair and returned his attention to the platform where Mr

Ridley was explaining that one of his lordship's main objections was not knowing the company's plans in their entirety. Mr Ridley was waving a letter in his hand. 'I have here' he said, 'a letter from his lordship in which he says "I have not that faith in railway directors to give them Carte Blanche over my property." ' And at this he paused to look over the top of the letter at us for approbation that never came. ' "If the Bill is committed" ', he continued reading from the letter, ' "I presume you are prepared on my behalf. Otherwise I strongly object to their having compulsory powers." ' At this there was some applause, though scant.

And what, said Mr Ridley, encouraged by this rare demonstration of sympathy, of the steam? 'The prevailing wind from the sea will blow steam across the road causing considerable risk of accident to the occupants of carriages. Nothing alarms a nervous horse more than a cloud of steam coming suddenly across his head.' We pondered this one, but could not be roused to any positive reaction.

I suppose the day will come when railway building has reached saturation point, and those who ride on them will take them for granted; when all the palaver over whether the line takes a left turn here, or stops short there, will have been forgotten – though I suspect they will go on talking about that Channel Tunnel idea of Monsieur Lavalley's for another 100 years, and village hall meetings of the kind I have just been attending will be held all over Kent to protest once more against the 'desecration' of the countryside. But while we are living through it, the costly business of opposing Parliamentary Bills, with witnesses and plans and computations, is good grist to the mill of surveyors like us – and long may it last! – to say nothing of solicitors whose company you propose to join.

I do not see an awful lot of Charles these days – his time outside the office is all taken up with Florrie Kingdon. But this Henry Jonas chap is good fun – you've met him haven't you? Mad on going for long walks and climbing hills – and, of course, Cissie.

See you at Christmas,

Your loving brother,
Robert

Minutes of Partners' Meeting, 5th January, 1875

Present: Mr R. C. Driver
Mr C. W. Driver
Mr R. M. Driver

Mr R. C. Driver said all partners should be fully apprised of the situation regarding the Holland Estate as a result of Lady Holland's objections to the development plan which the firm had formulated at the end of last year in conjunction with the Earl of Ilchester, whose agent he (RCD) now was. The 4th Lord Holland, Mr Driver reminded the meeting, had died in 1859; and what was left of the Holland estate had been left to his widow, whose style of life involved expenditure well beyond the income she could hope to derive from the estate, now greatly reduced in size.

When it had been bought by Henry Fox, the first Lord Holland, in 1768 from the Mr William Edwardes, who was to become the first Lord Kensington, for £17,000, it had consisted of at least 200 acres. It had once been as large as 500 acres. At the time of the sale the land had yielded Mr Edwardes £470 a year. The estate should have been inherited by Edwardes's son the second Lord Kensington, but Edwardes had obtained an Act of Parliament setting aside the entail imposed by the will of his father, Edward Henry Edwardes. The young Lord Kensington disputed his disinheritance and the Lord Holland of 1823 had settled the matter out of court by agreeing to pay Lord K £4,000 for confirmation of his title – which he could ill afford. For the Hollands of 50 years ago, as to-day, household expenses exceeded their revenue from rents to an embarrassing extent. There was nothing else for it but let some of the land for *building*. So in 1824 the works which were to save him from penury if not from bankruptcy were reluctantly put in hand. The leases he granted, initially to those ready to provide financial backing, were for 80 years from June 24th, 1824.

When the scheme ran into difficulties Lady Holland deplored the family's improvident reliance on building as a source of income. It was humiliating, but a sign of the changing times. As the operation became more protracted, the obtaining of money to finance the project became more and more complicated. In 1826 William Woods the builder was advanced money for building Addison Road and the sewer, and Lord Holland indemnified him from it by abating part of the rent payable to himself from others. Remote posterity might gain, but the only hope of betterment which those engaged in the operation could expect was from higher mortgage rates and the greater ease with which they could obtain them. But soon even they were not enough, and Lord Holland had to obtain a loan of £6,000 from Coutts Bank.

When the building had stopped in 1826 'in consequence of all the failures and panicks' Lady Holland bemoaned the fact that people had no money to spend on villas 'and keep closely what they have in the bank'. She regretted they had ever agreed to desert the traditional and safer use of land – 'it has been unlucky that we have cut up the land for building, as it might otherwise have been productive as pasture grounds'. Less income, but at least security. Letting for building was hardly improvement, if you could put neither houses nor cows on it. She thought of selling outright – 'in these times one must live from day to day and not, like our ancestors, think of an unknown posterity'.

By 1833 she considered the speculation to have failed totally, and sold 4¼ acres for the 'West London Railway' for £5,000 – the line closed after six months for lack of traffic. When her husband died in 1840, she was left Holland House and the Kensington Estate for her lifetime, reverting to her son the 4th Lord Holland, husband of the present Lady Holland, on her death, which occurred in 1845. This Lord Holland was determined to keep Holland House intact and to this end entered on the development of Holland Park and Kensington on a bigger scale and with greater determination than any of his predecessors. In 1849 he reached an agreement with George H. Goddard to build 863 houses on 70 acres at a ground rent equivalent to £20 an acre. That June he mortgaged Holland House. Like those before him he was unable to benefit from his projects; Goddard's scheme had only just been completed (1874); and Lord Holland died, as related, in 1859.

The present Lady Holland, with no son to turn to for advice, or indeed any children at all, was in desperate straits. She had been less concerned than her husband about keeping the estate intact; and to meet the demands of her creditors she sold off parts of the estate for £100,000. When James McHenry offered her £400,000 for the whole of what remained in her hands she sought the advice of her friends and of her husband's relations. Among the latter was a descendent of the elder brother of the first Lord Holland. This was Edward Fox-Strangways, 5th Earl of Ilchester, who persuaded her to resist pressures to sell Holland House outside the family. Although it was subject to a mortgage debt of £49,000, Lord Ilchester, who consulted his agent Mr Driver on the matter, agreed to take the estate, and not only allowed Lady Holland to live in Holland House for the rest of her life but gave her an annuity of £6,000. This arrangement which he had been instrumental in drawing up, said Mr Driver, had been completed in January of last year (1874).

C.W.D.   What annual income comes from the Holland Estate to-day?

R.C.D.   £3,227

R.M.D.   What interest does Lord Ilchester have to pay on the mortgage?

R.C.D.   Five per cent.

C.W.D.   What is the reversionary value of the estate?

R.C.D.   Very considerable. But the first building leases are not due to fall in till 1904 – 80 years from 1824.

C.W.D.   How does Lord I. plan to manage?

R.C.D.   He intends to underwrite the development of Holland Park and Kensington – and Lady Holland – from the very large income he enjoys from his well-managed and extensive properties in Dorset. It will be many years – not, I suspect, till the 20th century – before the London property becomes really profitable. But its potential is very great. It is a long-term *investment*. And Lord Ilchester is one of the lucky ones who can afford to wait.

R.M.D.   What is Lady Holland objecting to?

R.C.D.   Our failure to bring immediate prosperity, to set a vast project in motion overnight at a single stroke. Our plan is to go slowly and surely. I drafted a letter to Lady Holland for his lordship's signature which he sent her last month. In it I said we – that is Lord Ilchester and I – had decided not to consider at present any part of the estate beyond the Little Holland House portion, and that as we could not touch even that till after Christmas, we were determined not to be in a hurry to dispose of it, in the expectation of receiving offers for a large-sized class of house.

C.W.D.   Have you managed to dispose of any of it so far?

R.C.D.   The only piece we have offered is a plot to Mr Prinseps to build a studio and house for the artist Watts, and that is not settled yet. We have had no dealings with builders.

R.M.D.   Any plans for £70 a year houses?

R.C.D.   I have only drawn up one plan and that is designed to get the value of the land. It is for villas with gardens at £200 a year and over. These are the smallest we should think of, but of course we hope to get others for even larger tenancies.

I do not know if either of you are on Lady Holland's invitation lists for receptions at Holland House, or are likely to meet her on any other occasion – I do not believe any of us move in such exalted circles – but I thought it as well that you should be armed, in the event of such an encounter, with the facts that form the background to this interesting and responsible assignment of ours, and show a firm but polite resolution in the face of any attempt to undermine our loyalty to our client, or woo you away from considered plans evolved, in our belief, in her best interests as well as those of Lord Ilchester. A hundred and fifty years of service which 'Messrs Driver' will have achieved this October will have been of little avail if it has not cultivated, in those of us who have constituted the firm through six generations, a sense of objectivity and singleness of mind which enables us to dispense professional advice which instinct and experience tells us is fit and proper. Integrity – *sine qua non.*

Letter from James Driver to his father Robert Driver

10th April, 1875

Dear Father,

As the lawyer member of the family I was particularly gratified to learn that your efforts in purchasing the land for the new Courts of Justice in the Strand have at last borne fruit with a start on the building of the foundations. I passed the site yesterday. You will be relieved that construction is finally under way, though I presume you are no longer directly concerned. I know what a long and frustrating business it has all been, what with having to pass an Act of Parliament to buy and clear the land. And to think all those architects submitted their plans as long ago as 1866! I think the site between Temple Bar and Clements Inn an admirable one, but I imagine Mr Street must have been upset at having to reduce his plans for the original seven acre site to the 5½ acres they finally settled for. If you have 'economised' by paying £1,450,000 for the latter area, what on earth was the seven acre site going to cost! I realise of course that the sum includes the cost of clearing it. I am glad they have reduced the size – I think more than 500 ft frontage of Street's 'early continental Gothic' would be more than any of us could stand! Why can't our 19th century English architects develop a style of their own without aping 15th century France? I suppose it is contrived to awe litigants with the majesty of the law. Westminster Hall certainly does that, but without any 'contriving'; though latterly the noise and the untidiness of it all has become rather undignified (apart from the roof being liable to fall on our heads any moment!); the move to Fleet Street will come none too soon. But I suppose it will be a long time before we move in. On my first visit as an Officer of the High Court in its new home, I will raise my hat to you, father, for the contribution which 'Messrs Driver' has made to bringing the exercise to fruition.

Yours ever,
James

Memorandum

To: R. C. Driver   *Date:* March 14th, 1876
From: Robert Manning Driver

You asked me to gather information for the Particulars of the letting by auction at the Auction Mart on May 30th of the Tolls, Rents and Stallages at Greenwich Market. The authorisation for their collection is an Act of 1847 of which I obtained the detail from Mr William Bristow the market's solicitor at Greenwich which I visited yesterday. He also gave me the list of current tolls & c which we shall be letting, a full list of which I append. They are exacted from every 'stall, bulk, block, tressel or station' used in the market by anyone who sells meat, fish, live or dead victuals, fruit, china, glass, earthenware or other goods, rated according to the stall's size and to whether it is in the covered or uncovered market – 4s a square foot covered, 2s uncovered, a year; a penny a day or a halfpenny a day. For a one-horse cart the toll is ninepence a day. Anyone who sells his goods by placing them on the ground in front of him has to pay a farthing a day uncovered, a halfpenny covered. If you stand and sell chestnuts from a basket within the covered market you pay a penny halfpenny. If you bring a horse to sell, you pay sixpence; an ox, twopence; a calf, a halfpenny; and threepence for every

20 sheep, and a penny for a pig or half a dozen chickens or rabbits. The toll keeper also collects for weighing and measuring things like hide, tallow or a flitch of bacon. What the tollkeeper has to do in return is not quite clear, but Mr J. C. Loughborough, Clerk of the Works at the Royal Naval College, whom I saw, told me whoever gains the collection of the tolls always makes a considerable profit each year; so you can bring that in to your 'patter' when you do the auction. What you will be offering is the renting of the tolls for a term of one year from June 24th, 1876, with the option of renting for a further term of two years. The purchaser can also rent the No 1 Weighing Room in the market and the dwelling house at no 6 Clarence Street at £26 a year.

I visited the Wheatsheaf and Victory public houses at Greenwich as you told me, also the Crown and Sceptre at Deptford, and arranged with the landlords to hold and display copies of the Particulars when they are available.

Mr and Mrs Robert C. Driver
request the pleasure of your company
at the
WEDDING
of their daughter
Maria
to
Henry Jonas
son of the late Mr Samuel Jonas and Mrs Jonas
at Holy Trinity, Brompton
2.30 o'clock, Thursday June 24th, 1878
and afterwards at Melrose House, Cromwell Road

R.S.V.P.

METROPOLIS TOLL BRIDGES ACT, 1877.

FRIDAY, 12TH JULY, 1878.

BEFORE

ARTHUR CATES, Esq. - - - Umpire.

THE SOUTH-EASTERN RAILWAY COMPANY

v.

THE METROPOLITAN BOARD OF WORKS.

THIRD DAY.

[*Printed from the Shorthand notes of Messrs. Hodges and Son, 50, Chancery Lane.*]

Mr. ROBERT COLLIER DRIVER, *Sworn.*

Examined by Mr. FREEMAN.

1343. You have had a large experience for many years in valuing property of all sorts in London, and you have been largely concerned in bridge property?—I have.

1344. You have already been concerned lately with other bridges?—. Yes.

1345. I believe you were concerned with Waterloo Bridge?—Yes.

1346. And also with Lambeth Bridge?—Yes.

1347. Those are the two bridges which have been at present dealt with under this Act, and whose affairs have been inquired into?—Yes, I have gone into the matter fully.

1348. Before coming to your actual report upon this bridge I want to ask you something about what Mr. Ryde said the other day. I do not know whether you heard Mr. Ryde say that he found that 2½ per cent. per annum was the increase which all similar incomes had gone up to within the last few years?—I heard him say that.

Mr. ROBERT
COLLIER DRIVER.

12 July, 1878.

A

in a better position, and I think much more likely from the growth of population and other causes to increase in traffic. It is much more central.

1411. I understand you from your evidence that £9,580 a year net profit which you have deduced from the average of the last 10 years may be considered to be a permanent income without any fluctuation or without any prospective increase or otherwise?—There are great chances that it may be less. It has passed through my mind that it may happen again.

1412. What do you think the probabilities are? What would you say if you had to decide this yourself as to the probability of this income being maintained in perpetuity as you put it?—The probability is, it met with ups and down; the average amount I have taken it at.

1413. At £9,586?—About that.

1414. If I had to buy the bridge I might rely on getting an income of £9,580 per annum?—I think you might fairly consider so.

Mr. ROBERT COLLIER DRIVER, *sworn.*

Examined by Mr. PHILBRICK,

1415. I shall not ask you who you are. Have you had the figures which have been arrived at in this enquiry, and considered them with regard to the value of the Vauxhall Bridge property?—I have.

1416. Mr. Reid and you practically agree, I see. There is only one difference between you. You take off £50 for the manager's house, and he takes off £60?—Yes, I took the gas company the same.

1417. That is to say you took the gross income for ten years?—I have taken the gross income for ten years, which I believe to be the proper number of years for striking an average. That comes to £12,287 17s. 6d. The various outgoings are dealt with as detailed in the list which Sir Henry Hunt has before him, making the net sum of £9,527. Those outgoings are also on the ten years average. I consider that this is 6 per cent. security on 16¾ years' purchase, which gives £159,576. I take the gas company as £003 a year for the unexpired term on the 6 per cent. table. I took Dard's letting on the 6 per cent. table. I deduct the cost of the immediate repairs required to the bridge, which I apprehend the Engineers will be prepared to give you. Then after that I add ten per cent. for forced sale.

1418. I notice that you allow for Dard's letting, that is, for the license to moor barges in perpetuity 6 per cent., but the gas company's main you only value at nine year's purchase?—That is so.

1419. Because why?—Because there is a tendency now to let the Thames be the division between the various gas companies; in fact, the north of the Thames will be under one management, and the south of the Thames over another.

1420. That is to say, in 13 years do you think that which has happened in regard to Waterloo Bridge will happen with regard to Vauxhall Bridge?—Yes, having reference to what has taken place in Parliament.

1421. It would not be safe to capitalise that?—No, I should think before 13 years expired, the same thing that has happened with regard to the mains across Waterloo Bridge will happen with regard to Vauxhall Bridge; they will be disunited.

1422. Do you think that these tolls are going to increase?—I think

Minutes of Partners' Meeting, September 27th, 1878

                    Present: Robert C. Driver
                             Charles W. Driver
                             Robert M. Driver
                             Henry Jonas

Mr R. C. Driver welcomed his son-in-law Mr Henry Jonas as a partner in the firm, remarking on the satisfaction it gave him as senior partner that after so many years as the only partner, Messrs Driver should once again be in the hands of four. Mr Jonas informed partners he was coming up for election to The Surveyors' Association next year; Mr R. C. Driver said he had been a member since 1867.

A review of auctions due to be conducted by the firm over the coming six months was circulated and discussed.

Mr Jonas called the attention of the meeting to the reports of Professor Bell's 'telephone' which he had demonstrated to the Queen at Osborne last year, and said he hoped the firm would be among the first to adopt this obviously revolutionary and time-saving means of communication as soon as the invention was perfected and equipment made generally available.

Enter Jonases, Bishops – and the Twentieth Century

———————◆———————

NEW LANDLORDS

Many Partners and Sizable Staff

ST. MARY, ISLINGTON.

No.

1854.

Received from Mr.

	Rental At per £36 Pound.		£	s.	d.
The first portion of the Poor Rate, (including Police & County Rates,) made and dated on the 15th June, 1854, up to Midsummer, 1854	..	5d	0	15	0
The half of the Lamp Rate, made and dated on the 15th June, 1854, up to Midsummer, 1854	..	1¼d	0	3	9
The first portion of the Highway Rate, made and dated on the 15th June, 1854, up to Midsummer, 1854	..	3d	0	9	0
The Churchwarden's Rate, made and dated 15th June, 1854	..	½d	0	1	6
			1	9	3

Collector.

The Trustees request that the Inhabitants will not take any but a printed receipt for the Rate stamped and issued by them.

REGISTRARS OF BIRTHS AND DEATHS.

West District—*John Watts*, 2, *Albion Place, Upper Barnsbury Street.*
East District—*William Henry Butterfield*, 6, *Old Paradise Row, Islington Green.*
The road from the Angel along the Upper Street and Holloway Road to Highgate divides the districts.

J. and I. Trebeck, Steam Printers, Monkwell St., City, and Islington.

No. 2658

Received of Mr. Brooks 15 Sept 1854.

the Sum of fourteen Shillings for Two
Quarters Rent for Water, due to the NEW RIVER COMPANY, at Midsummer 1854.

£ : 14 :

J. Hay COLLECTOR. [14]

The COLLECTOR attends to hear complaints, and receive rents, at 3, High Street, Kingsland, on Tuesdays and Fridays, from 2 till 3 o'clock.

The NEW RIVER BOARD meet every *Thursday*, at their Office, New River Head, Clerkenwell, at 11 o'clock, and hear Appeals till 1 o'clock.

In case of Fire, or deficient supply, send to

FOREMEN.
S. Thimbleby, 11, Forest row, Dalston
A. Wood, Newington Reservoir

TURNCOCKS.
R. Goodbody, 19, Forest row, Dalston
C. Sortwell, 2, Dunn's place, John street, Shacklewell
J. Pike, 33, Sheperton street, New North road
J. Salisbury, Garden place, Coach and Horses lane

15. & 16. Two of the receipts which accompanied Mr. Pearson's letter of 1854

Old Coach & Horses
Stoke Newington Green

Nov 22. 1854

Gent⁵

I received yours dated 21 Jan⁵ and herewith send you one of the Vouchers have Paid for Tayed and Water and also for some repairs done on the Premises and have Afected for other Accounts which I will forward with my Account but I have only a small balance in Transst on Account of the Premises   I am Gentⁿ [...]

bad Debts on the Premises [...]

[signature]

14. The letter Mr. Pearson of the Old Coach and Horses inn at Stoke Newington paid a letter-writer to pen for him in 1854 explaining his inability to pay his debt to the estate of the late William Brooks, being handled by Messrs. Driver (*see page 133*).

ELEGANT

FREEHOLD VILLAS,

AND

Building Ground, Clapham Common.

Particulars

AND CONDITIONS OF SALE,

Of a most Desirable and Valuable

FREEHOLD ESTATE,

SITUATE ON

Clapham Common,

COMPRISING

Two Capacious Substantial Dwelling Houses,

WITH APPROPRIATE

OFFICES OF EVERY DESCRIPTION,

ELEGANT

GREEN-HOUSES, HOT-HOUSES, CONSERVATORIES,

Flower Gardens, and extensive Pleasure Grounds,

TOGETHER WITH SEVERAL OTHER

DWELLING HOUSES

Of smaller Dimensions, and a considerable Frontage of 664 Feet for Building on, next CLAPHAM
COMMON, with from Twenty to Thirty Acres of other

BUILDING GROUND,

IN A SUPERIOR SITUATION,

INCLUDING IN THE WHOLE UPWARDS OF

Sixty Acres of the most Fertile Land,

Which will be Sold by Auction,

By Messrs. DRIVER,

AT THE AUCTION MART,

On WEDNESDAY, the 25th of JULY, 1810,

At TWELVE o'CLOCK, IN NINETEEN LOTS,

(Unless previously Disposed of by Private Contract.)

To be viewed with Tickets only, which with printed Particulars and Plan annexed, may be had of Mr. WM. FRANKS, Clapham
Common; of Mr. STOCKDALE, Bookseller, Piccadilly, and of Messrs. DRIVER, Surveyors and Land Agents, Kent Road, or
at their Office, No. 5, in the Auction Mart.

17. Particulars of a property sale conducted by Messrs. Driver in 1810 at the
Auction Mart in Bartholomew Lane, London, of which they were one of the
promoters.

18. The classical façade of the Auction Mart in Bartholomew Lane, scene of considerable activity by Messrs. Driver, auctioneers, in the second half of the nineteenth century.

19. A property auction in full swing at the Auction Mart of the kind R. C. Driver conducted to the tune of a million pounds a year in value between 1860 and 1890.

MESSRS. DRIVER & CO.,

Surveyors, Valuers, Land Agents, and Auctioneers,

4, WHITEHALL, LONDON, S.W.

1866.

SCALE OF FEES

In Railway and other Compensation Cases, and to be Regulated on the Award or Verdict.

Award or Verdict.	Fee Guineas	Award or Verdict.	Fee Guineas	Award or Verdict.	Fee Guineas
£100	5	£3,600	31	£8,000	53
200	7	3,800	32	8,200	54
300	9	4,000	33	8,400	55
400	11	4,200	34	8,600	56
500	13	4,400	35	8,800	57
600	14	4,600	36	9,000	58
700	15	4,800	37	9,200	59
800	16	5,000	38	9,400	60
900	17	5,200	39	9,600	61
1,000	18	5,400	40	9,800	62
1,200	19	5,600	41	10,000	63
1,400	20	5,800	42	11,000	68
1,600	21	6,000	43	12,000	73
1,800	22	6,200	44	13,000	78
2,000	23	6,400	45	14,000	83
2,200	24	6,600	46	15,000	88
2,400	25	6,800	47	16,000	93
2,600	26	7,000	48	17,000	98
2,800	27	7,200	49	18,000	103
3,000	28	7,400	50	19,000	108
3,200	29	7,600	51	20,000	113
3,400	30	7,800	52	Above this, Special Arrangement.	

In addition to the above, £3 3s. per day for attending before an Arbitrator, Umpire, or Jury in London, £5 5s. per day if in the Country. Plans and Travelling Expenses extra.

1878–1928

Journal of Robert Driver

24th May, 1879

'I suppose' I said, 'there is something of the crusader in all of us.'
I was enjoying a glass of madeira with Mr Phillbrick QC at the club, to
which we had repaired after attending the opening by the Prince and
Princess of Wales of Lambeth, Vauxhall and other Thames bridges, on
their being freed of their tolls.

'I must confess that I find it difficult to resist fighting for any cause
that seeks to remove obstruction in any department of life,' I continued
'though far be it from me to admit that any such personal feelings would
ever colour my professional conduct as a surveyor or valuer. As counsel,
you, Phillbrick, will plead any case for which you are briefed and paid.
I too am at the service of any client with a job to be done – whether it is
'against' the authorities or involves acting on behalf of them – though
of course if the axe my client is grinding happens to be one with which
I find myself in sympathy, the work is more congenial and perhaps,
though not necessarily, more efficiently executed.'

Lord knows life is complicated and slow enough these days without
keeping alive archaic and artificial barriers to the easy flow of traffic in
and out of the metropolis where the management of trade and commerce, so greatly enlarged since the bridge companies were formed, is
necessarily seated. I find it distasteful that little enclaves of tollkeepers
should have hung on to their outdated contracts which clamp down on
these vital arteries and so effectively slow the City's pulse, until the
representatives of the people, the Government, have to pass an Act of
Parliament to shift them. But I suppose they have shareholders to
satisfy, who look to the tolls to provide an income just as to any other
commercial enterprise. To such the Common Good must needs be
secondary.

The Corporation of London acted ten years ago regarding Southwark

Bridge, and last year Charing Cross footbridge and Waterloo Bridge were freed of tolls; to-day marks the liberation of five more. By this time next year Hammersmith, Putney and Wandsworth bridges will be without tolls, the latter serving the one-time Surrey village where the worthy founder of our firm Samuel Driver tended the nursery and market garden from which 150 years ago our business sprang. As Samuel well knew, the land all about Wandsworth is liable to flood, for it is very low. This is why the soil was so favourable for the growing of fruit and vegetables, timber shoots and vines. Wandsworth Bridge is a road leading from King's Road to York Road, that is to say from nowhere to nowhere. The whole of the district which is open about Wandsworth Bridge will be years and years before it is at all built upon, and when I appear before an umpire next January on instructions from the Metropolitan Board of Works in the arbitration between the Board and the Wandsworth Bridge Company, I shall tell him so.

I invited Mr Phillbrick, doughty counsel for the Board in so many of the arbitrations at which I have appeared, to drink with me to the part we both have played in the minor but worthwhile crusade, to which we have conscientiously devoted so much time and effort in making sure that the bridge companies, with whom we have little sympathy, are compensated with all the fairness and justice to which they are entitled.

Had I in fact lifted a finger to hasten the passing of the Metropolis Toll Bridges Act of 1877 which empowered the Metropolitan Board of Works to acquire the bridges by forced sale and abolish the tolls? asked Mr Phillbrick. I told him that in November 1875 I had received an invitation from Mr Applegarth and Mr Edwards, the joint secretaries of the Metropolitan Free Bridge Association, formed to campaign against the tolls, to attend a meeting in the school room in John Street off Waterloo Road at which the Board's decision to introduce such a Bill was to come up for approval, and out of curiosity I had gone. Otherwise I had little time for public demonstration of my private sympathies. The Board were the body to conduct the campaign at the official level, and 'extra-parliamentary agitation' was unlikely greatly to affect the issue, though it indicated the extent of public feeling. When the Board was set up as the local government of London in 1855 there were only three 'free' bridges over the Thames – London, Blackfriars, and Westminster. Next year all would be toll-free. Following each Act of Parliament, compensation to the bridge companies, mostly formed in the first decade of the century, was determined by arbitration, and it was to the arbitrations held under the 1877 Act between February and July last year that I gave expert evidence on valuation and other matters. They took place not in a formal courtroom, but in places like the Westminster Palace Hotel and the Surveyors Institution. A major concern in arriving at a just compensation was probable increment in tolls in future years, of which the companies were to be deprived. This was largely a matter of conjecture and opinion, and I put my views, when I had any, as forcibly as I could. I crossed swords with Mr Bidder QC who appeared for the Vauxhall Bridge Company by asserting I considered there was greater possibility of increment in Waterloo Bridge than Vauxhall. (The Waterloo Company got £474,000; the Vauxhall Company £255,000.) He annoyed *me* by saying I had 'followed' Edward Ryde in taking an average of 10 years over Waterloo. I never 'follow' anyone; at 63, I have come to reach my own conclusions – I hope!

Robert Driver's Private Ledger

The East Street Estate (where Abraham and William Driver lived)
Rent

£8 0 0	J. Barton	
£12 0 0	Edward Barrow, 19 East Place, Kennington Rd	
£50 0 0	R. Kingdon	
£3 0 0	Mrs Barlow's executors	

Bell Alley & Swan Alley Properties

1880 28 June — By cheque Henry Jonas for £10,000 at present secured on his IOU but to be secured on Mortgage by deeds.
This has now been done and the Deeds are in my wine cellar at Melrose House. R.C.D. 15 July 1880

£1500 @ 5 per cent   £75 a year
£8500 @ 4 per cent   £340 a year
_____
£415 a year payable as interest

Metropolitan District Railway

1880 Jany — Bought £3000 shares @ £2,437 and sold them 28 Dec 1887 for £1087. The loss about £1380!!!
Sold at 36½ and bought at 81¼

Gibbs & Flew Ltd. Property Dealers

1883 30 June — Bought 500 shares for £4000 and in July another 100 at £1000 – so had £5000.

1884   5 months dividend on the above at £12 p c – £192-12-5
31 March   Oct half year   £118-11-5

Note: I do not believe these shares, £5000 paid, are worth the paper they are written on. My opinion is that the affair has been frightfully mismanaged from the beginning and that the facts etc of the management or mismanagement have eaten up the entire profits.
Moral: Don't be induced to invest in house property &c of this sort except under one's own control.

R.C.D. Dec 1885

Journal of Robert Driver

August 14th, 1884

I do not consider it helpful when newspapers talk of 'complete panic' as to sales of real estate. Agriculture is dependent on the whims of nature, and no farmer conducts his affairs unaware that his fortunes rise and fall with good and bad harvests. One thing at least the Government cannot legislate for is the Weather – thank God. What squabbles there would be as to what constituted 'good' weather – what was 'good' for one section of the community would be far from good for another. The terrible harvest of 1879 caused many to relinquish their farms in Cambridgeshire and Suffolk where Henry Jonas's father once leased 3,000 acres; but they will come to regret a step taken in the depths of despair. The Government is doing what it can to bring the farmer security but it all takes so long; Lord Beaconsfield outlined an Agricultural Holdings Bill on the wave of the disasters of 1879, but it was only passed last year – we are likely to derive work from carrying out arbitrations under it for unexhausted improvements. And of course there was the inevitable Royal Commission the year before last. But what the country needs is a *permanent* commission in the form of a Department of Agriculture – we must be the only country in Europe not to have one. Instead of periodic bites at the problems as they intensify, we want continuous chewing over of all matters *before* they become crises. Only then will everyone concerned – landowner, land agent, tenant – regard the Government as taking agriculture with the seriousness it deserves. In the meantime landowners themselves are taking the initiative to seek solutions out of their own experiences – I was impressed by the model lease proposed by the Earl of Fife who inherited 250,000 acres some short time ago; it contained a number of innovations of an original and helpful character.

One crisis at least has been averted by the gesture of my friend Mr J. Whittaker Ellis (as he then was) of Farebrother, Ellis & Co, who, on hearing that the running of the Derby at Epsom where it had taken place for a hundred years in succession might be removed to Gravesend, offered estates at Walton-on-the-Hill for the purpose. Whereupon the authorities had second thoughts and granted leases to Mr J. W. Monnery and others for training horses on the Downs and the traditional site of the great race was reprieved. And who shall ever turn their noses up at us surveyors again now that Alderman Ellis has served his term as Lord Mayor of London and received the traditional baronetcy – and this year entered Parliament as the member for mid-Surrey. Sir Whittaker we salute you!

Robert Driver's Private Ledger

Brompton Cemetery
1888 Bought a freehold site at Brompton Cemetery for a Family Grave – our darling only daughter first buried there (Mrs Jonas) in March 1888. This grave to hold six coffins.
Purchase money £57-3-6.

Robert Driver Conducts a Sale for the Ecclesiastical Commissioners (A Magazine Article of 1889)

There is an air of decorum about one of these functions which contrasts strangely with the usual push and bustle of a sale at the Auction Mart. Here there are no seedy-looking gentlemen on the look out for bargains, no sharp lawyerlike persons who dash like comets into the room, make a few hasty bids, and disappear with the air of being really too busy to wait to hear who the successful purchaser is. Nor does the overdressed and passée female, who decorates the other rooms at the Mart with her presence, assist in 'making a price' at this sale. Her object in coming to Tokenhouse Yard is, as she may be heard informing the dapper elderly man who accompanies her, to invest the savings of a well-spent youth in the purchase of a few houses which, by reason of neighbourhood or repute, may be going below their real value, and she knows that such properties are not likely to be found among the wares offered for sale by the Ecclesiastical Commission. On the other hand, there are plenty of countrified solid-looking gentlemen who have evidently come with the intention of buying, and a sprinkling of fat coachmen, who, having apparently driven their masters up to town, are now regarding the proceedings with the intelligent interest that a footman may sometimes be seen to exhibit under similar circumstances in the gallery of the opera, or the pit at the French plays.

The range of desks out of the centre of which the auctioneer's pulpit rises, shows signs of that careful provision against overwork which forms one of the proudest traditions of the English Civil Service. On each side of the auctioneer stand two stalwart clerks, destined, like Aaron and Hur, to upstay the hands of their master when wearied with exhortation. By the side of one of them is a dark man of Macchiavellian appearance, who is announced to the audience as 'a gentleman from the office' of the solicitors to the Commission. He in turn is supported by his clerk, and two other satellites, apparently of the auctioneer, are to be found on the other side. Under these circumstances, the platform at the end of the room is so well filled as to suggest the stage of a music-hall during a ventriloquial performance, or, to use a more decent simile in consideration of the reverend nature of the proceedings, a family pew in a parish church.

Mr Robert Collier Driver, the gentleman who discharges the office of auctioneer on these occasions, rejoices in long white hair scrupulously brushed across a well-shaped forehead, pleasant dark eyes, a ring on the second finger of his left hand, and a manner which his detractors (if he has any) might call fussy, but which in the time of Cromwell and the Saints would probably have been described as 'painful'. Altogether, a kindly looking old man, whom one can fancy the centre of attraction to a large and affectionate circle of nephews and nieces.

Mr Driver's method is in marked contrast to that of the gentleman whom we noticed last week. Instead of refusing to read the particulars and conditions, he insists upon giving us every word of them. Nor is this accomplished without some difficulty. With a view to this contingency Mr Driver has provided himself with a pair of very large double eye-glasses, which require the most careful balancing to keep them on the bridge of a nose which is decidedly not aquiline. As long as Mr Driver sticks to his reading all goes well, but directly he begins to vary this exercise by interjecting remarks of his own, and glancing at his audience to see how they are received, the rebellious pince-nez takes the opportunity to slide to the extreme tip of Mr Driver's nose, and there to take

184

up a position as defiantly oblique as the cock of a Dragoon's forage cap. In this entrenchment it is evidently far beyond its wearer's ken, and when he wishes to resume his reading, it is only after a series of wild and nervous clutches at his waistcoat, his shoulder, and finally at his nose, that the offending glasses are seized, and forced to return to their duty.

These little difficulties happily got over (in the achievement of which result the Aaron and Hur-like clerks render yeoman's service), Mr Driver leans back in his chair with the satisfied expression of a good man who had done his work, and done it well; and here the beauty of the Government system for the division of labour becomes manifest. No sooner has a stout gentleman in the front benches risen with an inquiry as to 'what the Ecclesiastical Commissioners will do' with regard to the tithes on the property, than the Macchiavellian person by the auction-eer's side leaps to his feet. The stout purchaser is apparently anxious that their reverences should covenant that, in the event of his buying the property, he should not be exposed to the liability of maintaining at his own expense a parson, a chancel, and other luxuries which seem to be somehow connected with the estate. The Macchiavellian one, while willing to give some sort of promise to this effect, is equally insistent that his clients shall maintain the privilege of a Government office to do nothing which is asked of them. The contest waxes warmer and warmer, until the dark representative of the Commissioners clearly thinks it time to display the iron hand which has till now been concealed by the silken glove. With a heated air he suddenly produces a document of brieflike form, which from its decrepit and dirty appearance might have been one of the original title-deeds of Naboth's vineyard. 'This deed,' says the dark one, brandishing it in the manner in which Mr Punch wields his stick, 'represents all that we are willing to do in the matter. It has been to many sales' (he did not add, as seems to have been the case, that it has passed its intervals of 'resting' in the dust-heap) 'where the same questions have been asked, and we have always refused to vary it.' *Bos locuta est*; and the stout gentleman asks no further questions.

During this dispute Mr Driver's face is a study. Leaning slightly for-ward, with his hands clasped placidly in front of him, he gazes over his glasses (which have long since finished their toboggan-like course to the tip of his nose) in mild deprecation on the audience. 'I have nothing to do with this,' one expects to hear him say; 'I am only a benevolent old gentleman who is anxious that *all* of you, if it can be managed, shall buy the property at the price that suits you; but this gentleman has been sent here by the department to do the wrangling, and my hope and trust is that you will none of you be hurt.'

When the biddings begin, matters progress with great smoothness for some time. Put up at £5,150, the property is bid quickly up to £6,000 (which the auctioneer has half hinted that he is willing to take), on to £6,350, and here for a moment or two the biddings seem likely to stick.

And now a strange madness seizes Mr Driver. He has not been able to keep in his mind the amount of the last bid, and therefore while one of the two competitors has really bid £6,350 for the property, Mr Driver seems inclined to adjudge it to the other at £6,400. The mistake is pointed out, apologised for, and rectified, only to be repeated a few bids further on, until at last one of the two supporters (it might be Aaron, but we think it was Hur) seizes his master's hand, and writes down with his own gold pencil the amount of the bid.

It is pretty to see the effect which these mistakes have upon good Mr Driver's audience. It is obviously out of the question that so venerable a man should make them intentionally, and the bidders therefore rightly attribute them to their own indistinctness of utterance. Hence they raise their voices against each other with a clearness which seems almost defiant, and the property is bid up to £7,150, at which price the weaker of the two rivals is 'beaten off', and his opponent declared the purchaser.

As Mr Driver leaves the box, we reflect sadly how much better it is to be clever than to merely appear to be so; and we fancy that we have obtained some glimmering insight into the method by which Mr Driver has obtained the reputation of being able to get better prices from his audiences than some of his professional brethren.

Letter from Henry Jonas to his eldest son Harold Driver Jonas, aged 13

74 Redcliffe Gardens,
September 12th, 1892

Dear Harold,

I am so glad we were able to have such a cheery evening at the Gaiety last night before going off to school to-day – the first term can be a bit of an ordeal, but I hope Ta-ra-ra-boom-de-ay ringing in your ears à la Lottie Collins will help to cheer you in these first strange days while you settle in, along with the contents of that tuck box! But don't use them *all* to bribe the other new boys on to your side! I know Mr Lankester *looks* a bit gruff but everyone says he is a first-class housemaster and of course an ace slow bowler.

I got the train home all right. You remember we were talking about how the railway companies had adopted different gauges and a Royal Commission had been appointed to enquire into making them uniform as long ago as 1846? Well, their findings are at last to be put into operation – The Broad Gauge is dead. Looking through *Punch* in the train last night I came across this bit of verse which I think might amuse you:

> Lightly they'll talk of him now he is gone;
>   For the cheap "Narrow Gauge" has outstayed him;
> Yet BULL might have found, had he let it go on
>   That Brunel's Big Idea would have paid him.
>
> But the battle is ended, our task is done;
>   After forty year's fight he's retiring.
> This hour sees thy triumph, O Stephenson;
>   Old "Broad Gauge" no more will need tiring.

Great grandfather Driver had a lot to do with purchasing land for Brunel's Great Western Railway planned on the broad gauge, as we are always telling you. He would have had to buy less – and so made less commission! – if the line had been narrow gauge. But this lies mostly in the past now; our main preoccupation these days is the sale of property and the whole business of 'estate management' – the Duke of Beaufort's estates, for instance, we have been managing since 1854, and the Holland Park estate of the Ilchester family in London since 1874. And how land values have soared! A field we let in South London (near where your forebears used to live) in 1882 for £40 a year is now worth £800 in ground rents alone, and the houses on it bring in £9,300 a year. Land which the Commissioners for the Great Exhibition bought in 1852 for £3,000 an acre was sold in 1890 for £51,000 an acre! The distress of the countryside is driving people into London. British agriculture, after confounding the prophets by staying alive for 30 years after the withdrawal of protection by the repeal of the Corn Laws in 1846, suddenly collapsed twenty years ago – from 1875 it ceased to be an economic proposition. There are more than a million acres less under wheat now than then. Whole areas of corn land have been laid down to grass, but we see precious few more livestock around – it's *frozen* meat from Australia and South America now! A whole way of life is dis-

187

appearing before our eyes, and what it represents in terms of human relationships and spiritual values can never return. We surveyors can play a part, not in keeping alive a dying corpse, but in helping to retain its vital features and making the process of transition less bitter, more meaningful.

Agriculture is still run on the 'estate system', but the people who run the big estates keep them going not from the proceeds of agricultural rents but from their income as ground landlords of far-away town properties, from industry and investments. Our clients, the country gentlemen who run the big country houses of to-day, know less and less about their management and so come more and more to professionals like us to tell them how. Industry and 'business' is coming to the help of declining agriculture – and we must have our feet in both camps.

People from the country swarm into London and quickly find employment in its business houses. With these new season tickets on the railways they can live in the fast extending suburbs and come into the centre to work both swiftly and cheaply. Their need is being exploited by the 'developer' who pays an architect a single fee for a house design and reproduces it by the thousand in Edmonton, Walthamstow, Leyton, Lewisham, Catford and the rest. The market gardens of Walworth worked by the 18th century Drivers are filled with the foundations of close packed, identical houses; washing hangs out where the vines once climbed, telegraph poles overshadow timber plantations long since uprooted. Such development is no speculation; the developers are backing a 'dead cert'. Selling on the leasehold system, subject to a ground rent around £5, they have created for themselves a permanent annual income of something like twice the original value of the land from which it came.

I hope I do not sound 'holier-than-thou' if I emphasise that we at Whitehall are not concerned with any of this. It has just not been the traditional activity of the kind Grandfather Driver has spent his life building up, and none of us intend starting now. The latter is 76 and very deaf, and I think in two or three years time 'the Governor', as they all call him at the office, will be retiring altogether and handing over the business formally to your Uncles Charles and Robert Driver and me. We look forward to taking you into the firm – and your brother Robert for that matter – should you feel inclined; I can tell you we will welcome all the assistance we can get to cope with the work. Apart from the partners we only have two other qualified surveyors – Mr Harwood Yarred who looks after clients in the country and Mr Melrose for town work. The whole salaried staff at no 4 Whitehall only adds up to ten, you know! And that includes old Joe Simpson the commissionaire and caretaker who lives on the upper floor, and John Lodge the receptionist. At the head of it all is Hubert Rumsey, the Cashier, who occupies the basement, assisted by Mr Sellwood who also acts as Rent Collector. There are three shorthand clerks – Mr Bradley, Mr Hart and Mr Warne who also does the filing and presses copies of our outgoing letters in a letterpress, then sticks them into a letter book. A diminutive and rather pompous little man called Tommy Twigg is Drawing Office Clerk, and I am afraid he gets rather ragged on occasions which probably does him good, but is not very good for the efficiency of the office! But we are very up to date in the way we run things – I see to that! Gas light of course. Over ten years ago we had a letter from Arnold White, manager of the Edison Telephone Company, suggesting we rented a line to his exchange, but nothing was done; then in November 1883 we were written to by the London and Globe Telephone Company – the first letter we received incidentally written on one of these 'typewriters' – and we hummed and hawed again, but a couple of years ago I persuaded my fellow partners to subscribe.

Best of luck! I know your mother would have been very proud of you.

Your loving
Father

Diary of Mrs R. C. Driver

7th December 1893

After two years of dinners and ceremonies as President of the Surveyors Institution (he had been a Vice-President incidentally since 1883) – fatiguing for a man of 74 – I am glad to say that Robert finally told the other association, the Land Surveyors Club, that it was time he gave up office; and this afternoon they presented *me* with his portrait in oils inscribed 'in kindly recognition of her husband's service as Treasurer and Hon Secretary for over 40 years' [*see* Plate 3]. It is good of them, (Charles incidentally is following him as Secretary) and I must say I made a very inadequate speech of thanks of which I am glad to think Robert heard very little – I have told him to use that ear trumpet only at home and *never* in public. It is a fine picture – he was glad the seals on his watch chain came out so well – but it will take up a great deal of wall space, and the question now is Where? I know the colour and the gilt frame and the size is more befitting a presentation portrait, but I confess there is much to be said for that excellent little portrait of exact likeness the photographer took of Cissie as a girl of six that time we went to Ramsgate which stands, frame and all, on my mantelpiece [*see* Plate 5]. It could hardly take less room than that! I suppose The Portrait will eventually hang in the Partners' Room at the office, but until then –?

It seems to me on reflection that Robert has done more for the Institution than the Club. I was never very happy about his taking on the treasurership; he is better at giving than receiving and having to keep an account of it. He has always been keen on people entering the profession being properly qualified – and recognisably so by means of organised competition – and when they introduced compulsory professional qualifying examinations to admit to membership of the Institution in 1881, the year it received its charter of incorporation, he offered an annual prize of £25 to the non-student candidate who obtained the highest number of marks in the Associateship Exams. For some reason which I cannot recollect the Council asked him to *reduce* it to fifteen guineas a few years later, and he has given this amount every year ever since. I understand he intends to bequeath a sum of £500 in his will for its perpetual endowment. At Drivers there has always been a traditional recognition of the importance of professionalism and training, and he welcomed this confirmation of his own attitude by the leading body of surveyors, in spite of opposition of men like Edward Ryde and William Sturge who said it would be impossible to find suitable examiners and considered the subject matter of surveying incapable of being reduced to a set of fundamental principles and a basic body of knowledge. Robert dismissed all such talk as pompous nonsense. It was not the first time he disagreed with Mr Ryde.

Another gift for which the Institution has Robert to thank is the fine stone portico at the entrance of their premises at 12 Great George Street, which cost £140 [*see* Plate 9]. Last year, when he retired from the presidency, he presented them with a badge of office to be worn on all public and official occasions by his successors in the presidential chair. He asked my opinion about the various designs put forward and I like to think I had some hand in the selection of the magnificent badge finally chosen. [*See* Plates 11 & 12.]

I hope that Robert now feels able to relax more; he accedes much too readily to demands on his time. I suppose they'll be after him to give evidence before this latest of a long line of Royal Commissions on

Agriculture which opened last week – just as his Uncle Edward did. At least the railway mania has died down – but only to be replaced with *tram* mania!

Diary of Henry Jonas

19th November 1894

'What we are doing is forming a new company.'

'A clean sheet.'

'Prescribe ourselves a constitution.'

'Father would never have had the trouble with Bowlen if he had had a proper deed of partnership.'

'He didn't have a solicitor son to guide him then, did he?'

'We've got to create a harness for ourselves to direct and rule our paths, which gives us every latitude and every safeguard.'

'Businesslike and legal.'

'What do we call ourselves – "Drivers & Co"? "Messrs Driver"? "Driver Brothers, Henry Jonas & Co"? "C & R Driver, H Jonas & Co"? "Driver, Jonas & Partners"?'

'We are two Drivers and one Jonas. What about "Drivers, Jonas & Co"?'

James, the solicitor Driver brother of Victoria Street, was going over points for inclusion in the new deed of partnership for Charles Driver, Robert Driver and myself, consequent on the retirement of R.C.D., to start on January 1st, 1895. We quickly agreed to routine things like the lease of the office being the property of the partners who paid for the expense of running the business. But we argued about the need to have any capital. James thought there should be, but demurred to our thinking that in the circumstances there was no need for the new firm to pay capital into an already running business. He advised we inserted a clause which said 'if any sum is required' it should be contributed by the partners to whom the profits – and losses, interjected Charles – belonged in equal shares. Each partner, said James, should be able to draw out of the partnership account, say, £800 a year in equal monthly drawings; but if at the end of the year it was evident that this amount exceeded his share, he would have to repay the excess. He suggested the deed bound us not to engage in any business or become a director of another company, or subscribe to an insurance policy, negotiate an accommodation bill, enter into a time bargain, speculation, gambling or hazardous

191

transaction, or sign a cheque in our own favour – without the consent of our fellow partners.

If a partner made a breach of any of these stipulations or went bankrupt, the other partners could expel him, and he would be bound for five years not to take an appointment with any company with which the partnership had done business inside the previous three years.

'What about the right to appoint our sons?' I asked.

'Any partner, I think' said James, 'should be able to give his share to his son – any one son – and introduce him into the partnership, having given due notification, on his attaining the age of – what?'

'Twenty three.'

'Twenty five.'

It was Charles who opted for the latter, and urged some such proviso should also be added like 'and upon his acquiring a knowledge of the business.' He did not want a chap, just because he was the son of his father, walking in and taking over without taking the trouble to learn what it was all about. 'Hear, hear' I said.

'What happens if the father dies without having a son in the business, or before he has notified partners of his intention to introduce his son?' asked Robert.

'Or if a son who has been nominated refuses to take his partnership?' I interjected.

'In that case' said James, 'I suggest the business is carried on to the end of the current year as if the partner was living, and his executors become entitled to his profits till then, plus three times his average profits over the three preceding years.'

We all thought that fair enough, but we were not too happy about James's idea of making each partner able to nominate any of his sons in his will to become a partner at 25, and James noted not to include this in his draft.

'How do I retire?' asked Charles.

Any partner, said James, could do so after giving, say, six months notice in writing to the other partners, and retirement would always date from March 25th. If he had no son taking his place, then he took with him his share of the capital, less goodwill; otherwise his son succeeded to his father's share.

'And I think we should stipulate' I said, 'that the partner who does retire must not start up in business as a surveyor anywhere in our area, eh?'

'Within five miles of no. 4 Whitehall' suggested James.

'And if we fall out over interpretation of the deed?' – this from Charles.

'You go to arbitration' said lawyer James, 'under the Arbitration Act 1889. That will be written in.'

The conversation then turned to the controversial London Building Act which the new London County Council had just introduced, and on their plans to obtain powers to levy 'betterment' rates on landlords whose property values had been increased by the Council's improvements to Tower Bridge, the Strand and Tottenham Court Road, which Charles said he found thoroughly objectionable apart from being unworkable; but Robert and I were anxious to terminate the discussion as we had to get to the Garrick Theatre where we had tickets to see Henry Irving in his famous role of an 86 year old army corporal in a piece called *A Story of Waterloo* by a chap named Arthur Conan Doyle. To think what the old dodderer was reminiscing about – and what a performance! – took place only a year before R.C.D. was born! I love the theatre, but I must say I am intrigued by reading in the *Morning Post* this morning of the opening in New York by a Mr T. A. Edison of what he called a Kinetoscope Parlour. I wonder what *that* can be?

THIS INDENTURE

made the thirtieth day of January one thousand eight hundred and ninety five between Henry Jonas of 4 Whitehall, Arthur Charles Driver of 153 Sutherland Avenue, and Charles William Driver, his father, Witnesseth that Arthur Driver Doth put himself apprentice to Henry Jonas who accepts him for One year in manner as follows That he will teach him the profession of Surveyor and Land Agent And Charles and Arthur Driver do covenant that Arthur shall serve Henry Jonas diligently and attend to the said business at all times, his secrets keep and his lawful commands willingly obey.

Letter from Mr Thomas A. Jones to his fiancée Miss Unstead

197 Earls Court Road,
September 3rd, 1895

Dearest Martha,

I've got it! I told you I got old Wainwright to write me a letter of introduction to these Driver people in Whitehall. Well last month I had an appointment with Mr Robert Driver one of the partners – a very posh room on the first floor overlooking the Horseguards parade ground. A fine building it is right in the centre of things – the Houses of Parliament are only just down the street – people coming in and out of the rooms in their frock coats and silk hats – oh yes very top notch. And your Tom has landed himself right in it. You see, I had heard they were looking for someone, though not of course why. Well, it appears they had to discharge someone for taking commissions from a builder. A firm of this sort can't afford to employ a chap like *that*, so he was *out*. One of the first things Mr Robert asked me was my age and when he heard I was only 24 his face dropped and he said he thought I was rather young. *However* – I exercised my charm on him and he said Come for a month on trial, and now the month is up and I'm IN. I didn't write to you until I knew it was definite. In the circs I hope you can come up to London right away – stay with your sister Marge? – and we can get married just as soon as.

They are a good lot of fellows to work with here. The office hours are nine to six with an hour for luncheon which I generally take in a public house round the corner in New Scotland Yard where you get an excellent meal for a bob. You also pick up gossip from other firms in the same line like Cluttons of Whitehall Place whose clerks also go there. We have Saturday afternoons off of course; but for some reason they won't let us off before lunch, but have to come back to the office before 2 and then go off *at* 2. What a how-d'ye-do!

The routine is livened by the pranks of the 18 year old son of Mr Charles Driver, another of the partners, who joined the firm from school as a 'pupil'. His main target is a scrimpy little, self-opinionated character called Mr Twigg, the Drawing Office Clerk, who is always swanking of 'his' surveys in an effort to show off to us juniors. He is always reminding us of when he surveyed Epping Forest single-handed, though Mr Melrose, one of the proper surveyors, assures us Tommy did no more than turn out a few tracings! One day young Arthur – A.C.D. as everyone calls him – had had enough, removed the metal consumer from the gas bracket, put Twiggy's silk hat in its place, lit the gas and thoroughly enjoyed the conflagration. Twigg was furious of course, but he calmed down on A.C.D., who after all has all the money in the world, promising to buy him a new topper. It was much better than the one which had been swept up from the floor in charred, smelly pieces, so I suppose Mr T. really did rather well out of it.

High jinks with Twigg's hat are not confined to the junior ranks of the Driver family. One day not long after the burn up, Mr James

Hutchinson Driver, not one of the partners but the firm's solicitor, came to see one of his brothers. A few minutes before, Twigg had gone in to the same room and put his hat on the chair beside the desk. Seeing Twigg's hat, Mr James, a large bulky man, walked to the chair and deliberately sat down on it, crushing the hat completely flat. For Mr James it was an enormous joke, but Twigg, not unnaturally, was appalled, and said so, appealing to R.C.D. for justice. He ended the day with yet another, even finer hat by way of compensation.

The most brutal bullying of Tommy Twigg occurred when, after some chaffing of a more incisive and prolonged nature than usual, he declared it had gone too far and he would complain to the Governor. All right, said A.C.D., go ahead; complain away and see where it gets you. At this, little Tommy Twigg thought better of his threat and told us he was ready to give us another chance. But A.C.D. would have nothing of it, and insisted he reported us as he had so boldly announced. Then, carried away by the gathering momentum of his own enthusiasm, Mr Arthur ran at him and stripped off Twigg's clothes and, calling to one of the others to help, carried him bodily down stairs to outside the Governor's door, knocked on it and, when a voice from within said Come in, opened it and pushed the debagged Twigg into the presence of the All High.

There was hell to pay I can tell you. A.C.D. calmed down a bit after that escapade. I think he was told by both his father and his grand-father that the senior partner's office was not the place for a 'dormy rag', and the sooner he realised he had left school and grew up the better. But would you believe it, within days a stiff complaint came from a senior officer in the War Department offices on the other side of the road over the Horse Guard's arch, who alleged he was being seriously hindered in his work by someone flashing the sun at him from a mirror in the window on the 2nd Floor of no 4 Whitehall, and that it MUST STOP FORTHWITH. It was the irrepressible A.C.D. of course. He thought it was the greatest lark ever. But it stopped – forthwith.

In spite of his being such a silly ass on occasions like these, I get on with him all right, which is just as well, as most of what I do is with him. My first job however was on Lord Mansfield's Estate at Gospel Oak. I was told to go and supervise the contractors' men building a row of houses in Savenake Road. I found one of them making mortar with mould and lime.

'What are you doing there, my man?' I said.

'Mortar, chum' he said superciliously. 'That is what that is, mortar.'

'It is not, you know' I said. 'Not with mould and lime.'

'And how would you mix it, mister?' he said, pitching his cap on the back of his head and leaning on his spade.

'Sand. Not mould.'

'Not mould? I've been using mould on this 'ere site, mate – and on plenty others for that matter – for long before you were born, see? No one's ever complained before.'

'No one's ever seen you mixing it before – no one who knows what's what, like I do, that is.'

'You know what's what, eh?'

'I know the kind of mortar that's going to last when the frost comes, and that kind won't. And what's more I know the kind of mortar – made with sand and lime that is – that is going to get you the surveyor's certificate you can't do without. If you will insist on putting up these houses with mortar made of mould and lime, you'll have to pull them all down again. Drivers Jonas & Co don't sign certificates for builders who use the wrong materials.'

He spat heavily – not in my direction – and went off to seek some sand.

I told Mr Robert what had occurred and I think it impressed him that at 24 I could handle a man on a point like this who, as I pointed out, was old enough to be my father.

But what perhaps impressed him even more was my ascent of a 120 ft ladder up the side of the chimney shaft of Acton and Bonemann's Emery Works in Holloway Road, which was reported to be fractured after being hit by lightning. The remedy, it was decided, was to cut out and make good the brickwork and ring round at intervals with iron straps. Mr Robert and I managed to get on to the flat roof of the works, but you could not see the state the top of the stack was in from there. 'Are you going up?' said Mr Robert. What could I say? Up went muggins, rung by rung. Never again. Not only was it completely vertical, but at the top the chimney had a protruding cap and the ladder projected outwards to clear it. You could feel the stack swaying in the wind. Coming down was perhaps worse than going up – treading into space as it were. O Martha, what an intrepid fellow you are allying yourself in marriage to!

Cheerio, pip-pip!

Ever your loving
Tom

I, T. E. Twigg, hereby declare
that I will not wear my old
topper (by Springall etc Strand) up to
No 4. Whitehall ever again unless
it is a soaking wet morning
when I start from Fulham.
I also swear that I _will_ wear
my new Topper recently given
me at Whitehall every morning.
except under the above condition

Signed - T E Twigg

Witness - Artd Charles Dix.

Witness - Brigadier Buck Jones.

Dated this 16th day of November 1897.

Twigg and his Topper, joke affidavit of November 16th, 1897

Robt. C Darwin &c
1863

Letter from J. Harwood Yarred to Charles Driver

The Croft, Pine Avenue, Norwood
14th April, 1898

Dear Mr Driver,

I feel I must write to offer my condolences on the death yesterday of your revered father, whom I had the honour of serving for so long at Whitehall. I know the death of your mother in 1895 was a great blow to him, and I fear his last illness was both long and painful. It will have been a great comfort to him however to know that his sons would be carrying on the traditions of the family business which for 20 years he maintained – and indeed elevated – entirely on his own. He will be missed, I know, not only in the surveying world, but in local government in which he helped as a burgess of Westminster and Deputy Lieutenant of the City of London, and in charity work as vice-President of Charing Cross Hospital. It must have been gratifying for someone who was born in the reign of George III to have lived to see the great Diamond Jubilee of Queen Victoria last year. He has shown me many personal kindnesses, as he has many others of the staff at Whitehall, and I shall always remember them – and him. He was a great and kind man, and the profession of Surveyors suffers a great loss with his passing.

Yours very respectfully,

J. Harwood Yarred

Letter from Henry Jonas to Robert Manning Driver

74 Redcliffe Gardens
August 10th, 1898

My dear Bob,

I know the family's decision to insist on Charles leaving the country immediately was in all the circumstances the right one, but I must admit that as an outsider I am glad not to have been consulted or to have been party to his 'banishment'. I am writing merely to assure you of my loyalty of which I know you are not in doubt, and of my intention of adopting a policy of Business As Usual which I trust will be shared by everyone at Whitehall.

A personal crisis affecting one of the partners should not affect the professional reputation of a firm of our standing and long tradition; only those who wish us harm will stoop to take advantage of Charles's lapse, and I do not believe they will be many, if indeed any at all. As we said last night, we can never forgive, but we can forget. Time will heal all. I propose never referring to the matter again. What Charles does with the rest of his life in South Africa is his own affair. One cannot deny that his sudden and unexpected removal from our midst, quite apart from the reason, is a great loss to Drivers Jonas, but with RCD gone also, it behoves us to take the reins firmly into our hands as joint senior partners and be seen to be steering a straight and vigorous course which will recover what morale we may have lost through the sad events of the last months. I look forward to the day when Arthur (whom I am glad to see is not too badly affected by it all), and my boy Harold, can become junior partners – in seven years' time or so?

Symbolic, in a sense, of a new lease of life and a new regime, is our move from 4 Whitehall – which I hear they wish to demolish to make way for a new War Office building – to 23 Pall Mall on September 12th where I was hoping we could have had the new electric lighting, but I fear we shall have to wait. The lease with the Hollonds was signed on May 31st and it is effective from June 24th for the residue of a term of 21 years at a rent of £500 a year for the first seven years and £550 for the remainder of the term. You and I stand as trustees for the firm in this regard. I hope perhaps the move – and his father's removal – will have a sobering effect on young Arthur. I don't think there is much harm in all this Ananias Club nonsense – 'Gryphons Buck to!' and all that – in fact, it probably engenders a team spirit among our employees, but I think it has to be watched, specially in regard to old Tommy

Twigg. I hear they sent him to Coventry for a whole month last February. I regret to say my Harry was as much a ringleader as Arthur.

I am afraid it is brewing up to real trouble in South Africa. If President Kruger goes on as he has been doing lately it looks as if we shall be at war with the Boers by this time next year. And where will *that* put Charles?

My regards to Georgina,

Yours ever,
Henry

P.S. I hear Birkbeck Institution are proposing to the Surveyors Institution that one of their female students takes their exams. Good luck to her!

Minutes of Partners' Meeting, May 29th, 1902

Present: Henry Jonas
R. M. Driver
In attendance: A. C. Driver
H. Driver Jonas

Mr Henry Jonas said he considered the growth of the auctioneering side of the firm, both in number of sales and the size and value of the properties, had been so great in the first two years of the new century as to warrant serious thought being given to the desirability of increasing staff to meet the demands. The routine of producing the voluminous amount of printed material required for each sale was obviously becoming too much for the staff as at present organised; mistakes were creeping in to Particulars which, though a small matter in itself, reflected, albeit unfairly, on the efficiency and capabilities of Messrs Driver Jonas in general. Historical notes undoubtedly helped to sell buildings with a history; but only if they were correct. Better no notes than inaccurate ones.

Mr Jonas said that on the second day of the sale of the Usk Section of the Monmouthshire Estates of the Marquis of Worcester at Usk Town Hall in May 1899, for instance, a man came up to him, introduced himself as the local schoolmaster and asked him if he was responsible for the description given in the Particulars of Usk Castle, the 'well-preserved ruins' of which were Lot Eleven of the sale that afternoon. He read out to Mr Jonas the following paragraph:

Famous alike in peace and war, it held an important position in the Border Wars of the West, but is perhaps most renowned as being the birthplace of two of our kings, Richard III and Edward IV; on the death of the latter it passed to Henry VII and then to the first Earl of Pembroke and hitherto has always been owned by Royalty or a Peer of the Realm.

His interrogator had said he was sure there was no deliberate intention to give the castle greater importance than it in fact had, but most schoolboys knew that Richard III was born at Fotheringay and Edward IV at Rouen, both in the same year 1452; and that Usk Castle had been granted to the Earl of Pembroke by Edward VI. Mr Jonas thanked him for the information, which he noted, and assured him it was an error of ignorance rather than design.

Mr Jonas said that anyone disposed to take a less charitable view of the mistake than the friendly schoolmaster might have formally challenged it under the Conditions of Sale, and the firm could have suffered. He fully appreciated that for the staff of 1899 the Usk sale had been an arduous exercise: 61 lots on the first day (669 acres); 40 lots on the second embracing a large part of the town of Usk itself including the town hall and the Twyn Square, and the whole of the Monkswood Estate of 1,116 acres; 50 lots on the third day. The whole had been conducted with great expedition and flair, and he in no way wished to infer that the matter of the historical error had detracted from this success to any major degree. But they should all learn a lesson from it, and see that no occasion arose in future whereby the firm could be similarly criticised. The firm was gathering a reputation for its ability to handle these large scale auctions, and it was one they should build on.

A main purpose of calling the present meeting was to hold a 'post-mortem' on the extended operation which had begun in March last year and ended yesterday – the sale of the Duke of Beaufort's Monmouthshire Estates which the firm had been managing since 1854. The opening three day sale of 26th, 27th and 28th March 1901 had put a great strain upon all Drivers Jonas staff, who had however risen to the occasion admirably. The Rolls Hall at Monmouth was not the ideal location for an auction, but the arrangements could not be faulted. The 51 lots in the town of Monmouth and Dixton Hadnock were disposed of swiftly and profitably. Sale of the Troy House Estate, with its Inigo Jones mansion and 1,670 acres with trout fishing in the Trothy and salmon in the Wye, with its eight farms bringing in £2,000 a year in rents, had gone without a hitch. No one had questioned that Henry V, the hero of Agincourt, had been born at Monmouth Castle, the ruins of which constituted Lot 119. The 'several nice residences well suited to form the country seats of gentlemen', topped by The Garth with its 142 acres, had all fallen at good prices. The Old Schools by Chepstow Railway Station had been filled for the second series of auctions on July 30th and 31st last year, in which 1,180 acres around Chepstow changed hands – the second day had realised £20,133 alone – and there were plenty of bidders in Usk Town Hall on November 20th when Drivers Jonas sold the 1,094 acres of His Grace's North Western estates between Monmouth and Tintern in 78 lots. At the final session at the Westgate Hotel Newport yesterday, when the 2,650 acre Wentwood Section of the Duke of Beaufort's estates, including 'the largest wood in England' (the remnant of the Primeval Forest of the Gwent Tribe) came under the hammer (Lot 18), the Duke's agent personally congratulated Mr Jonas on the efficient manner in which the series of auctions had been conducted, and Mr Jonas said he hoped those at the meeting would convey these congratulations to all concerned.

Entrusting the sale of great estates of this kind to Drivers Jonas by leading landowners like the Duke of Beaufort reflected on the reliability and integrity of the staff, and, what was more, the firm's ability to obtain for their clients the highest prices the market would stand. He realised the actual auctioneering at the rostrum was only the tip of an iceberg; what the public did not see was the months of painstaking, and often tedious, preparation which led to the sale. Of this he was very appreciative, and of the high standard of design and presentation of their sale catalogues and advertisements. He hoped the quality of the photographs would gradually improve – his father, said Mr Jonas, had been a pioneer of photography in the early days and was one of the first to see the role it could play in the work of a surveyor and estate agent. The firm's Tathwell Estate catalogue had used photography with conspicuous success; it was a field in which he believed Drivers Jonas was once more an innovator.

The breaking up of the big family estates was a process he believed would continue throughout this 'Edwardian' era on which they had just embarked; they were only just seeing the beginning of it. It was indicative of the change in the social structure and the redistribution of wealth – and of political power – which the Driver partners had watched taking place down the years, but at a pace then slow and now accelerating. It was not for the firm to challenge the inevitable – that was for their clients to do if they had the time and the temperament; the role of Drivers Jonas was to make the transition easy and profitable for those who came to them with their business and sought their advice on the technicalities. As his father-in-law, the late Mr R. C. Driver, had observed over the freeing of the Thames bridges of their tolls, it was not for him to 'take sides' but provide a service. The firm had views on how best to manage whatever part of the estate a client decided to keep for himself, on ways of improvement and development, on how to turn it into an *investment* which would give him the return it merited, on how to comply with the law to his best advantage. In this way a client could benefit from the firm's century and a half of experience and share in their treasurehouse of knowledge.

Asked by Mr Jonas, Mr A. C. Driver said the valuation side of the firm's business was also accelerating. In 1901 they had carried out valuation for their clients, the Baker Street and Waterloo Railway Company, of no 280 Regent Street for compensation; for their clients Queen Anne's Bounty of Sir Robert Peel's Drayton Manor Estate for a loan; for the Duke of Beaufort of nos 1 to 11 Hay Hill and for the Duke of Norfolk of Albany Villa, Clun, for purchase; for Lord Grantley of his Surrey estates for mortgage – to select a few interesting valuations at random. They had carried out valuations for enfranchisement, new leases, insurance, partition; of timber, of tillages, of Streatham Town Hall, of the Oxford Music Hall. They had acted as umpire for disputed dilapidations at 22 Grosvenor Place; made a report on the prevention of floods at Thames Ditton; made a survey for road making at Ealing; prepared an improvement scheme for Earl Carrington's Spalding Estate; sold a freehold wharf on Regents Canal, the waterway which the firm had bought land for when it was being built at the beginning of the last century. These were some highlights only. The volume of work was very great.

Mr Harold Driver Jonas reported on the sale by private treaty, which he had handled, of the Chateau de Castell'nou near Perpignan in the French Pyrenees on behalf of the executors of Vicomte de Satgé de St Jean. Drivers Jonas's renown for organising the sale of big estates in England like those of the Duke of Beaufort would, he thought bring the firm commissions for the sale of properties abroad; and he looked forward to one of the firm's main activities in the 20th century they had now entered being the development of overseas business. Mr Henry Jonas concurred.

Office Diary of George Sellwood
23 Pall Mall

27th April, 1905

I have taken over as the firm's Chief Clerk and Cashier from Mr Rumsey – I come up each day from Clapham by motor bus; Mr Rumsey used to come from Baker Street on the Underground Railway. He was in reminiscent mood when we had a parting glass of ale at the Red Lion in Duke Street, expanding on the day he played truant to walk to the Mall to watch Queen Victoria's funeral in 1902 (so did I, but I didn't let on) and the occasion Mr Thomas Jones returned one afternoon from viewing dilapidations on the Melhuish Estate in Upper Street Islington, all covered, unbeknownst to him, till Rumsey pointed them out, in fleas. At no 239 Upper Street, Mr Jones had told Rumsey, he had met a Mr Marks to arrange a lease of the premises for a second Penny Bazaar following the success of his first venture with a Mr Spencer in a railway arch at Atlantic Road, Brixton. He had remarked on it, as he thought what a good idea it was, and wondered whether it would catch on.

Today I witnessed the signature of Mr Henry Jonas, Mr Robert Manning Driver, Mr Arthur C. Driver and Mr H. Driver Jonas to new Articles of Partnership admitting Mr A. C. Driver and Mr H. D. Jonas as junior partners, effective from January 1st, and entitling Mr Robert Collier Jonas, Mr Henry's second son, who is now 24, to become a junior partner at any time after December 31st 1906. Mr Henry and Mr Robert established a capital of £2,000 carrying interest of 5 per cent; and as senior partners they are each entitled to four twelfths out of his share, so the others' shares are not upset, so long as Mr Robert Driver remains a partner. I understand he is likely to retire at the end of this year, and that probably R.C.J. will be not made a partner till 1907. H.J. and R.M.D. can each draw £600 a year in monthly drawings, and the junior partners £200. The main articles were in line with those drafted by Mr James Hutchinson Driver, the solicitor, in 1895.

It had been planned to make a ceremony of the signing of these new articles, and Mr Henry Jonas had sprung a surprise on everyone by arriving at the office in his beautiful new motor car – one of the first from a new company which was only formed last year. It attracted a crowd of admirers in Pall Mall. Handing over the document to me for safe keeping Mr Jonas was in a confidential mood – they had had a prolonged celebratory luncheon in the Board Room – and when I remarked on his new equipage we both moved to the window and looked down on it with what I can only describe as awe. He said the invention of the internal combustion engine would bring a social and economic revolution of a more durable kind than even the railways. It would lead, he said, to the development of the whole of the British Isles. It meant good business for surveyors, but unless the Government saw fit to control it, the countryside would be delivered over to the unprincipled building exploiter with results future generations would be unlikely to thank us for. Motor traction was giving us speed such as we had never known before; its consequences could not be left to chance. The 20 mile an hour limit introduced in 1903 would control the speed, but who would control the building? 'Town Planning' was now the talk of architects and so-called 'land economists', and being debated in every corner of the Institution in Great George Street. They seemed to fear it when they should be welcoming it. It was a public responsibility, and Drivers Jonas must play a part in it. He hoped the firm's role would not be one merely of defending private owners against the planning authorities when they were set up, and securing owners their due compensation, but actively contributing to decisions on the basic nature and purpose of planning. He asked me to start a file on the subject and a dossier of information to which any member of the staff could refer.

Mr Harold Driver Jonas came in after he had left, offered me a cigar, and said he thought I would like to know that his wedding to Miss Catherine Griffith had been fixed for next month. I offered him my congratulations, whereupon he turned, tripped on the mat and very nearly fell flat on his face. He pulled himself up, beamed at me, asked me what I thought of his father's motor, and before I had time to answer said he intended buying one of the cheaper vehicles Mr Herbert Austin had just started making at Birmingham. The telephone rang at that moment and when I had finished telling the caller to hold on as I had someone with me, I no longer had. H.D.J. had gone. But the fragrant fumes of Napoleon brandy lingered.

Letter from Henry Jonas to his daughter-in-law Mrs Harold Jonas

Builth Wells
11th October 1906

My dear Catherine,
We had just finished auctioneering the last of the lots of Lord

Glanusk's 1,200 acre estate here when I received the wire telling me the good news that I am now a grandfather. And a boy too – well done! Another Henry Jonas, eh? Congratulations my dear, and I am glad to hear that all went well. I cannot come home quick enough to catch a first glimpse of him. The speed of my return, I regret to say, is governed by the 20 mile an hour limit; I wish I could exceed it but I have no wish to fall into one of these police traps one reads about. Perhaps I should join this Automobile Association I hear has been formed to thwart over-eager country policemen having the time of their lives with their stop watches and measured furlongs, and the JPs gloating over the sudden influx of fine money. But now these two Wright brothers in America have put a petrol engine in an aeroplane and lifted into the air under their own power, I suppose we'll soon be able to escape the road traps by *flying over* them! How I long to get my hands at the controls of one of *those* machines! In the meantime my motor car goes remarkably well, if slowly, all things considered. But I took the train to York last week where we had to auction the 6,400 acre Seamer Estate at the Station Hotel, and to Hull the week before for our sale of the 6,900 acres of the Earl of Londesborough's estates in those parts. Motoring to Yorkshire and back would be beyond a joke.

In July last year you know we sold virtually the whole of the town of Selby for the Earl – the best portion of it at any rate: some 15 shops, three banks, a dozen of the town's nicest residences, the Londesborough Arms Hotel where we held the auction, and a complete ironworks (Ousegate). For some reason, at the last moment, his lordship withdrew the house in The Crescent used as the Conservative Club. Perhaps he thought it might be bought by the Liberals and used as headquarters for this year's General Election. What a landslide for the Liberals that was – an 84 majority over all other parties! To use a motoring metaphor, we have been moving in the same gear since the Reform Act of 1832, and it looks to me as if we have now changed gear for good – a new era has started. Mr Campbell-Bannerman is 'threatening' sweeping social reforms, and the pattern of property holding will be at the forefront, I'll be bound. It all heralds increased work for us surveyors, and I am glad to have such a tower of strength as Harry at my side to ease the burden. My brother-in-law Robert Driver, as you know, is going to retire next year, which will not make things easier, but of course Harry's brother Robert Jonas is now with us and learning fast. And before we know when we will have the assistance (I hope) of the eighth generation which you have been so clever in producing for us while I have been attending to milord of Glanusk's affairs in this remote region of Her Majesty's Welsh demesne. God's blessing on you, my dear, and on my young grandson.

With all my love,
your affectionate father-in-law
Grandad Henry Jonas

Diary of Harold Driver Jonas

15th July 1909

My brother Robert and I were coming back in the train from Cambridge where we had been for our sale of Madingley Hall, the Elizabethan mansion where the king had been made to stay (much to his disgust) instead of in rooms in college while an undergraduate at the university. Having both read the report in the *Times* of yesterday's mammoth meeting of the Land Taxes Protest Committee in the Queen's Hall, we fell into a general discussion about all that Mr Lloyd George was proposing and the likely effect of his 'revolutionary' proposals on us, our clients and the country as a whole.

The first 29 clauses of the Budget which the Chancellor of the Exchequer introduced on April 29th concerned the Land. His Finance Bill proposed putting a 20 per cent duty on 'unearned increment' payable on the sale of any piece of land, on the granting of a lease of more than 14 years, and on the passing of land on death. The tax would be both on undeveloped land and on the increment value of developed land. As soon as this became known there was an outcry from everyone affected. Spontaneous protest from the outraged swiftly gave way to organised agitation by groups calling themselves the Land Union, the Central Landowners Association etc, who lobbied and demonstrated for the dropping, or at least the modifying, of the hated land clauses, as the Irish did to air their sense of outrage at the Budget's proposed tax which was going to raise the price of a bottle of whiskey from 3s 6d to 4s. A body named the Budget Protest League met to protest at the Budget in general at the Cannon Street Hotel last week.

At the Queen's Hall meeting which father, I know, had proposed attending, a large banner was draped above the platform reading 'Nationalisation of the land. That must come, but you must proceed by easy stages – Mr Lloyd George, President of the Board of Trade, at Llanelly, October 1906.' Now he was Chancellor he presumably could take the bit between his teeth. Lord George Hamilton chaired the meeting which was composed, he said, of people whose business was connected with the valuation, sale, transfer and improvement of land. Among them were Mr Wood, President of the Land Agents Society (formed as recently as 1902), Mr Watney of the Auctioneers Institute, Mr Martin of the Surveyors Institution, Mr Trustram Eve, Secretary of the Farmers Club. So this was a meeting not of landowners but of their professional advisers. I remember father saying once it was not our business to 'take sides'; well, here it seems the profession were doing just this with a vengeance. Though perhaps not. They had met, declared Lord George Hamilton, for the purpose of *self*-defence (not, it seems, in defence of their clients, but of the existing, 'traditional' way of administering the land of the British Isles). The land clauses constituted a grave danger to their businesses, he said. They suggested legislation of a new and arbitrary character absolutely unknown in the fiscal history of Britain and not part of the fiscal system of any civilised country in any part of the world. Mr Lloyd George was proposing new taxes on one particular class of property, based on new and empirical forms of valuation and on ultimate assessment made by Government officials from whose decision there was no appeal. Law was being put on the statute book for closure. The legislation partook more of the edict of a Star Chamber than the sound legislation of a democratic assembly. Those affected would be everyone to whom land was a raw material for the purpose of improvement, development and of profit. On transfer, sale or inheritance 20 per cent of the increase of the site value over the original site value was to be forcibly extracted from the owner by the state. Neither Mr Lloyd George nor any member of the Government had yet been able to give an intelligent definition of 'original site value'. If anyone had an interest in more than one estate he was not going to be allowed to average his losses or his gains. All the decrement fell on him, and 20 per cent of the gains were taken by the state. What regulated the rate at which undeveloped land could be turned into developed land depended on the capacity of the public to occupy and take the houses thus created, which was limited. Only an infinitesimal proportion could annually be taken up by the public, yet everyone who happened to have land classified as 'undeveloped' might be taxed for many years though he wishes to, but could not, develop it. The scheme involved minute and detailed evaluation, and it was the owner who would have to pay for it. The cumulative taxes and the cost of valuation would put a heavy burden on land improvers.

Mr E. G. Pretyman MP moved that the land clauses were 'destructive of security, financially unsound, arbitrary in administration, unconstitutional in form, and unworkable in practice'. Unemployment would result which would arrest the movement to supply houses for the working classes. The Chancellor, after only a few months in office, was legislating about something of which he was completely ignorant. It was like a man who had read a book on engineering driving an express train.

Yesterday also the Central and Associated Chambers of Agriculture had held a protest meeting at which a surveyor called Anker Simmons said the valuation proposals in the Finance Bill were unworkable. They were based on a series of fallacies. Mr Simmons said he had told Mr Lloyd George that he did not realise the work which valuation would entail; whereupon the Chancellor had replied that he would send his office boy to do the work. If Mr Lloyd George's office boy was as clever as his expert adviser, he very much doubted his ability to make the necessary valuations (laughter).

'What I ask myself' said Robert rising to pull the window up by its strap to keep the smuts out as we passed through a tunnel, 'is whether their objections to the means – no appeal, legislation by closure, impracticable valuation – hide an emotional and instinctive objection to the end, the taxing of property, the principle of it. Once upon a time all land was "held" of the king in return for service. Is it still sacred and untouchable?'

'Many landowners' I said, 'many representatives of the families who once "ran England" doubtless resent the former source of their power and status being tampered with. In their death throes this dying race are bound to cry out in anguish. But if I were them, I would prefer a clean surgical operation that puts a swift end to their agony than a drawn out, lingering process which holds out hope of a return to their former glory but never realises it. There are times when ruthlessness is charitable, and I think Lloyd George's in 1909 is a case in point.'

'They have at first to get out of thinking in terms of "betraying my class", "betraying the past", "betraying my birthright" and then admit to themselves that Lloyd George represents a trend that has come to stay, a revolution and not just a fashion which like all fashions can change – back.'

'Talking of revolutions, the date of yesterday's Protest Meeting will not have escaped you – the Quatorze Juillet.'

'We manage things better than in France. Reform not revolution.'

'They are calling it "punitive legislation", "Star Chamber tactics" .'

'To any minority, legislation passed in the interests of the majority is "punitive". Emotive adjectives won't help them.'

'Lloyd George's speeches do not discourage them. "This is a War Budget" he says, "to raise money to wage implacable war against poverty and squalidness." '

'I always thought the word was "squalor". No statesman is going to carry through a reform of this magnitude with grey speeches. He has not disguised the fact that he has mounted an attack not only on the abstraction of Poverty but on the flesh and blood of landlords who reap the benefits of increased rents and sales derived from the labour or needs of others, without raising a finger themselves. "Unearned increments" is the parliamentary phrase. They have had it too good for too long. Lloyd George has spelt it out – land owned by the Duke of Northumberland wanted for a school, land needed to extend London docks, the renewal of a lease of land owned by the Duke of Westminster only on exhorbitant terms. Actual instances strike home more strongly than vague rhetorical flourishes. The consciences of the remnant of the landed aristocracy has been stirred and they resent having to admit it. That is why they are hitting back so fiercely. The Government's majority will see the Bill through the Commons but the landowners in the Lords will make sure it goes no further.'

'What's worse – for us – is they are going to keep land off the market and go slow on improvement and development. Even Lloyd George cannot stop them *not* selling. Which is a pity in view of this year's Town Planning Act which of course the Surveyors Institution helped to draft.'

'This is what we should be doing, going with the stream not continually battling against the current, not always appearing on the defensive. We should contribute to planning thinking, not obstruct it. All power to John Burns's elbow! That new Kingsway we saw carved through all those streets from the Strand to Holborn last year – the finest piece of town planning since the Fire of London.'

'*Town* planning is one thing; the wresting of the land from private ownership – Lloyd George's avowed "nationalisation" of the land – is another.'

'As surveyors, do we care? Should we care? Apart from any private views we may have on the subject.'

'As surveyors we should welcome any legislation which is going to bring us more work – the compulsory valuation the land clauses will

21. Arthur Charles
Driver, 1877–1943,
President of the
Auctioneers Institute
1924.

22. Robert Collier
Driver, grandfather
of ACD, President in
1892–93 of the
Surveyors Institution
– a photograph taken
in 1890.

23. Philip Jonas,
born in 1914,
who retired in
1974.

24. Christopher Jonas, born
in 1941, who became a
partner in 1969 –
representing the ninth
generation.

25. William Bishop, born in 1901, who became a partner in 1945 and retired in 1971.

26. Robin Bishop, born in 1931, who joined the firm in 1958 and became senior partner in 1974.

27. In 1975 the head office of Drivers Jonas occupied the whole of 18
Pall Mall, off Trafalgar Square, London (seen here) which the firm
moved to from near-by Charles II Street in 1969.

bring, for instance. But it is our duty to point out what we think is un-workable, and this is where I think the protesters are on surest ground. I think it is in this sphere that Lloyd George will become unstuck.'

'In yesterday's debate on the Finance Bill a Mr Faber attacked it on these very lines. Hitherto, he said, valuation of land and buildings had been as a going concern; under the Bill they had to value a hypothesis – an impossible task. Compared with it, said Mr Faber, the difficulties of a blind man placed in a dark room to look for a black cat which was not there was trifling.'

'The cost of valuation is estimated at £20 million – a sum, as someone has been quick to point out, which would provide the country with eight Dreadnoughts. The Chancellor conceded it was difficult to distinguish agricultural land and land with special value for building and industry, but not impossible. He also made the important amendment of exempt-ing small holders under £500. But I have an idea that when we come to get down to valuation, the sheer scale of it and the subsequent time lag, will bring the whole thing to a halt. Let's hope the Treasury will have paid out one Dreadnought's worth of fees to us all before that happens anyway.'

'But that's the point. It won't be in *fees*, but in temporary civil servants' salaries. The Government will have to set up some kind of Valuation Office, or whatever, to carry out the work. I suppose Lloyd George will first of all call on our office boys, and then, when the light dawns that the work is a little beyond their capabilities, our senior and most experienced valuers. How shall we carry on then?'

'I can't see it ever coming to that. In my view the twenty million pounds, added to the cost of collecting the tax, is unlikely to exceed what the Government will receive from it, and the Treasury boys will be quick to point this out. This is the real objection to the Land Tax, and the spokesmen of our profession will be well advised to keep away from all other arguments, particularly those with reactionary overtones which will only serve to label us all as old-fashioned and stick-in-the-mud, and concentrate on constructive and objective criticism demon-stratively free of bias and passion. It is no help to call Lloyd George a "robber gull" as Lord Lansdowne has done. If there are extreme members of the House of Lords who still believe the British constitu-tion exists to protect privilege and property, there is no reason why we should – we who are going to have to live the greater part of our lives in a twentieth century which socially is going to be very different from the nineteenth. Our clients – yours and mine, Robert – are going to look to us to fight their battles in the kind of new world Lloyd George is creating, not rearguard actions in defence of a world which is dying.'

With a hissing of steam and cries of 'Porter!' from the platform we jerked into Liverpool Street Station and clambered out.

Extract from the Memoir of Thomas A. Jones

In 1910 we had to value for mortgage a large portion of the Johnston Estate at Weymouth and Radipole, and A.C.D., R. C. Jonas and self went down and put up at the Royal Hotel where we stayed for three weeks. Mr Gray of James Gray & Son was with us part of the time.

We worked from 9 am to 11 pm for seven days a week except one Sunday afternoon when we went for a stroll along the beach eastwards under the cliff and being a hot day decided to rest and went into the sea in the nude and laid out to dry, not having towels. All was well.

That morning I got up early to go for a bathe before breakfast as there was a bathing jetty opposite the hotel, but did not notice the iron railings had recently been re-painted with red oxide, and I got smothered with paint and had a job to get it off. I had to cancel my dip.

In 1912 Capt J. V. Taylor gave instructions for the preparation of a development scheme for the whole of the Grovelands Estate at Southgate comprising about 250 acres. This was done and the scheme approved by the Urban District Council and added to their Town Planning Scheme. Broad Walk was constructed from Bowne Hill to the Green at Winchmore Hill and a section of land adjoining was reserved for a public park. The remainder of the land was sold to several speculating builders who constructed certain sections of the interior roads except Broad Walk which sold in single plots for good class dwelling houses.

At 23 Pall Mall I shared the 2nd floor back room with Yarred and Gardner. The three tables were close together, Yarred having his back to the door. One day I was interviewing Sir Luke Fildes a prominent artist and lessee of no 9 Melbury Road. He was sitting in Yarred's chair and had white hair (as had Yarred). A lady typist suddenly came into the room at the back of Sir Luke and mistaking him for Yarred exclaimed 'Hello darling!' and stroked his head. Realising she had dropped a brick, she fled. Sir Luke did not comment, but I found the position disconcerting.

Letter from Arthur Driver to Harold Driver Jonas

3rd October 1914

My dear Harold,

Congratulations to you both on the arrival of your second son –
Philip are you calling him? A glimmer of light in the gloom cast by the
outbreak of the war. However they're saying it will all be over by
Christmas, and let's hope they're right. It certainly looks as if the
Kaiser has bitten off more than he can chew this time. I suppose there
will be members of the staff at Pall Mall who feel it their duty to join
Kitchener's Army, but I hope not all at once! War or no war there's
still plenty of work for 'Surveyors, Valuers, Land Agents and Auctioneers' as we now style ourselves. Whatever else the Land Tax did, it has
not stopped property owners from selling as so many predicted, has it?
And what a good job the Surveyors Institution did with issuing a scale
of fees to be charged for valuation work under the 1910 Finance Act;
saved an awful lot of haggling and ill-feeling. But like the war, I don't
think the Land Tax will last long. The breaking up of the big estates
has, if anything, accelerated since Lord Howard de Walden sold part
of his Regents Park estate for half a million in 1911 and then the Duke of
Bedford shed his Covent Garden estate. Having to find money for Death
Duties is at the back of a lot of it of course. 'Real' owners transferring
their property to 'nominal' owners who are merely holders under
mortgages to banks – that is the pattern of things these days. And the
private treaty negotiations which have to take place are protracted and
complicated as we well know – and they can't do without us, or for
auctions. Tenant farmers are not coming out of it too well – I was glad
to see the President of the Board of Agriculture setting up that depart-
mental committee of enquiry into how the breaking up of the big
estates affected them.

The rush to sell certainly shows no sign of abating. Lord knows we
were busy enough last year, with another section of the Seamer Estate
at Scarborough (14 freehold farms covering 3,000 acres); another 3,600
acres of the Selby estate; the 2,300 acre Ashcombe Estate in South
Devon; the 1,300 acre Accommodation Lands of Sir Henry Dering on
Romney Marsh – these alone took up so much of our time and were a
fraction of the total. This year we have even more on our plate – the
auction I conducted of the 1,200 acre Brookman's Estate in the Peahen
Hotel, St Albans, last month was typical, and I know how busy you are.
And I'm glad to see how game your father still is. Seems set on joining

the Special Constables. He showed me a card he had had issued to him when he became one in 1887, and said he was awaiting a second Call to Duty any day now!

At least young Philip will avoid being caught up in anything like that, without the stigma of being pointed at as a 'shirker'! But mind he doesn't get hit by shrapnel. My love to Catherine, and again congratulations to both of you – another potential partner takes his place in the wings.

Yours ever,
Arthur

Memorandum

To: Mr Sellwood   *Date:* 17 December 1919
From: Mr A. C. Driver

Please send in the files on the following matters undertaken this year for my annual review:
1. Londonderry House – valuation for assessment for Marquis of Londonderry.
2. Seamer Estate, Yorks – 4th sale for Earl of Londesborough.
3. Holland House – valuation for Quinquennial Assessment for Mary, Countess of Ilchester.
4. 223 Regent Street – valuation for 'Madame Isobel', couturier.
5. 'Duke of Clarence' public house, 103 Holland Park Road – licence.
6. Betchworth – tithe redemption for Major Henry Goulburn (for whose family Drivers purchased the estate in 1809).
7. Stanhope Mews – conversion of stables to garage.

Minutes of Partners' Meeting, 22nd June 1920

Present: Henry Jonas
A. C. Driver
H. D. Jonas

Mr Henry Jonas said they all regretted the decision of his second son Robert Collier Jonas to retire from membership of the firm, and he knew it would be the wish of all present formally to express their thanks for the work and effort he had put into the partnership during the period he was a member. His retirement was effective from December 31st, 1919 and necessitated the addition of a Memorandum to their Articles of Partnership of April 27th, 1905 and the Deed of Covenant made to it on January 10th, 1907 when Robert had been introduced as a member of the firm. This was merely a statement of ten lines re-allocating the profits and liabilities of the remaining three partners in the proportion 28/72ths to Mr Henry Jonas, and 22/72ths each to Mr Arthur Charles Driver and Mr Harold Driver Jonas.

The three partners of the new firm then appended their signatures which were witnessed by Mr G. H. Sellwood.

Extract from Memoir of Thomas A. Jones

One day in 1920 A.C.D. and I had to go to Grantham for the Cust Estate sale. We decided to go up the day before to make ready and arrived at King's Cross station early. We gave our luggage containing all the auction papers to a porter with instructions to put it on the train to Grantham. We went on to the platform, and seeing a train at it, took it to be ours. So we boarded the Pullman Car to reserve places for luncheon. To our surprise it almost at once pulled out – it was the train before the Grantham one! All our luggage was left behind, but the porter had of course put it on the *right* train. By changing at Reading, which was our train's first stop, we managed to arrive eventually at Grantham where, however, we could find no trace of our lost cases. The stationmaster told us they had gone on to Hull. It was *Oh Mr Porter What Shall I Do?* in real life. Assured it would turn up in the morning, we went to our hotel. I told Mr Arthur I would mount guard at the station and seize our bags the moment they put in an appearance. I stayed there till two in the morning and still no sight of them. A lugubrious official told me they were arriving on a train due in at 4 a.m. So I returned to the hotel – to find I was locked out! I discovered a side door unlocked and stepped inside. Someone was lying on a bed by the wall opposite, with dark hair spread all over the pillow. But it was no girl but the Boots, who quickly woke when I shook him, and let me into the hotel. I snatched a couple of hours sleep and was back in the station by 4 a.m. What devotion to duty! It was rewarded to my relief by my seeing our cases with their precious contents stacked on a trolley beside the train just arrived from Hull. What we would have done at the sale without the papers I dare not think.

Minutes of Partners' Meeting, 16th May 1922

Present: Henry Jonas
A. C. Driver
H. D. Jonas

Mr Henry Jonas said he had called the meeting to discuss the implications of their having signed that morning the agreement appointing the firm Receivers and Agents of the so-called Northern Estates of the naval Greenwich Hospital. It involved becoming Local Managers and Superintendents of the hospital's estates at Langley Barony, Trockley, Scremerston, Tweedmouth and Spittall in Northumberland, and Alston in Cumberland; and acting as stewards and keepers. The commission was for three years from July 1st, on which date Mr Harold Driver Jonas, who would be personally responsible for conducting the business, would report to the Director of the Greenwich Hospital for briefing and instructions.

The agreement they had just signed entrusted Drivers Jonas with the 'general management and working and superintendence and improvement of the Northern Estates'. It included keeping accurate plans showing the surface of all mineral royalty areas, tenements and allotments; writing up the rent roll; making plans required for tenancies and leases; arranging terms and generally making suggestions as to management and improvement. The agreement did not cover the valuation of land intended to be purchased or offered for sale; that would be separately paid for. It did however require the keeping of Account and Cash books for everything else. Hiring and paying all labourers would be their responsibility and certifying the correctness of their pay sheets. The firm would collect all rents and royalties, fines, heriots, court fees etc due to the Admiralty, and levy any distress for rents in arrear.

Mr H. D. Jonas asked if that included taking proceedings in court, and the answer was that it did not. A final responsibility was advising on what fire insurance should be paid on the property, and seeing that the premiums were paid.

The remuneration would be £500 a year. Mr H. D. Jonas asked about expenses and was told the agreement provided for an inclusive allowance of £150 for travelling etc, plus £200 towards the salary of a resident bailiff at Alston who lived in the agent's house free of rent, rates and taxes, with free coal and light. This bailiff was purely an employee of Drivers Jonas acting on their instructions only; he had no executive power of his own.

Mr A. C. Driver said he thought the commission would necessitate the firm opening a branch office in the north. After some discussion it was decided that the most suitable location for this would be Chester. A qualified manager would have to be found, to be responsible to Mr H. D. Jonas.

Mr Driver said under 'Any Other Business' he would like to take the opportunity of formally congratulating Mr Henry Jonas on becoming the doyen of the Surveyors Association. He was himself hoping to be elected a member next year. Mr Jonas in thanking Mr Driver who, he noted, had followed the Driver tradition of becoming a member of the Clothworkers Company in 1917 though he was unable to see what they had to do with the Profession of the Land, observed that the 'honour', if it could be so termed, was not an achievement but merely a circumstance dictated by his date of birth which in turn had dictated his date of joining the Surveyors Association, and now he was the man who had been a member longest.

He admitted to being a member both of the Association and the Institution, but on the whole deplored the proliferation of societies for the Profession of the Land. It was a good sign that the Quantity Surveyors Association had just seen fit to amalgamate with the Surveyors Institution. He also welcomed the granting last month of a royal charter to the College of Estate Management which had been founded in 1919. He had for long been an advocate of proper training for the profession, as Mr R. C. Driver had been, and he was glad to hear the Surveyors Institution was at last contemplating giving it the support it merited.

Such sentiments he hoped showed that he was not unduly conservative (with a small C), but he could not but regret the substitution of the elegant Auction Mart in Tokenhouse Yard which the Bank of England had acquired at the end of the war, by the new and less elegant building opened by the Lord Mayor last April in Queen Victoria Street. They spent so much time in the Auction Mart – Robert Collier Driver had been a director of the company promoting Tokenhouse Yard in the eighteen sixties – it was a kind of second office, and one grew attached to it.

The first auctions he had conducted in the new building had been for farms, the demand for which he noted had increased considerably. They were, he thought, in the middle of a farm boom. They were fetching as much as £28 an acre. Even more were being sold by private treaty. The trend for landowners to sell their farms to current tenants derived from the Government's ruling that landowners could not increase rents just because arable production was increased. Most farmers these days were owner-occupiers as a result. Before long, he reckoned, a quarter of the tenants in England and Wales would have purchased their freeholds, though with the Government passing the Corn Production (Repeal) Act and withdrawing support, farmers were finding themselves exposed to overseas competition at low prices.

In the towns the picture was somewhat different. The immediate effect of Mr Lloyd George's Land Tax had been to check building and the bulk of house property was held for letting. With the growing scarcity it became more difficult for families to find accommodation, and owners began to develop restrictions as to the type of tenant they would accept. With the war, of course, came the entire cessation of building; the Land Conference held in 1916 to lobby for the repeal of the Land Tax was flogging a dying horse; the land clauses of the 1910 Finance Act had proved unworkable and unrewarding as so many had predicted, were never fully implemented, and were soon quietly dropped. But wartime Rent Restriction Acts had overlapped into the peace, and the greater cost of building materials and higher wages made it unprofitable for anyone to build houses as an investment. 'Homes for the People' were either those built before the war which survived the Zeppelin raids and were subject to rent restriction, those built by local authorities at uneconomic rents subsidised by rates, and those bought for occupation. The satellite towns of Letchworth and Welwyn represented an interesting industrial experiment which might have far reaching results on the life of the metropolis. They represented the new use of land as the old country houses with their armies of servants and retainers, now no longer available, represented a way of life now being smothered by heavy taxation and death duties.

Mr Jonas said he saw more and more work coming their way, as the 20th century progressed, from the new 'institutional' owners of land. The Church, the Crown, the colleges of Oxford and Cambridge, had for long invested in land, and their new client the Commissioners for the Greenwich Hospital similarly derived their income from estates. This ancient example was now being followed by other institutions, the growing forest of insurance companies and banks in particular. The accumulated experience of Drivers Jonas as Crown Estate Surveyors and agents for big families like the Ilchesters (Holland Park), the Goulburns (Betchworth), the Gunters (Earls Court and West Kensington) could now be brought to the aid of people highly qualified in the manipulation of statistics and abstruse actuarial computations, but unversed in the Profession of the Land.

Memorandum
to All Staff

October 1925

BI-CENTENARY OF DRIVERS JONAS

To mark the 200th anniversary of the founding of our firm by Mr Samuel Driver, great-great-great-great-grandfather of Mr A. C. Driver, in 1725, the partners are granting every employee a bonus which will be included in next week's wages. To celebrate the occasion it has been decided to hold a dance at the Wharncliffe Rooms in the week before Christmas; particulars will be circularised as soon as arrangements have been completed. It is very much hoped that every member of the staff will be able to attend and bring a guest.

Extract from the Memoir of Thomas A. Jones

In 1926 a large area of land between Embercourt Road, Ember Lane and Speer Road, Thames Ditton, was to be developed for building, but on surveying it was found it was not possible to connect with the adjacent sewers, as they were either to shallow or blocked by large water mains. Speer Road where the sewer was 30 feet deep was clear, but to obtain access to this our proposed sewer would have to be taken under the railway and under the new Kingston By-pass, the first of its kind in Britain.

Levels were taken and consents obtained from the railway company and the local authority. The job was carried out and miners laid an iron sewer with five 5 ft diameter manholes – luckily just before the General Strike. Unfortunately the weather was wet and most of the land flooded. The water came very near to the manholes but just failed to reach them. But I was very thankful when the rain stopped and the flood water subsided.

Minutes of Partners' Meeting, May 19th, 1928

Present: A. C. Driver

H. D. Jonas

With the death of Mr Henry Jonas who had joined Drivers Jonas exactly half a century ago, said Mr Driver, the firm had suffered a great blow. He was the first non-family partner to be admitted in the 200 year history of the firm, and the enthusiasm and good judgement he had brought to bear on all he had done for the partnership had inspired everyone who had come into contact with him; his contribution to their progress in so many new fields, and development in so many traditional ones, could not be over-estimated. He could never be replaced, and the firm would now be carried on by the two remaining partners, Mr A. C. Driver and Mr H. D. Jonas, with an equal share of the profits.

Mr Driver said in the circumstances he was glad he got his presidency of the Auctioneers Institute behind him (1924) as the duties had taken up a great deal of his time which, with only two partners to carry the burden, he would not now be able to afford.

1928–1975

Memoir of Harold Driver Jonas

Drivers Jonas have always tended to act on behalf of landowners rather than tenants, and the death of my father in 1928 occasioned no great or immediate change. Father had been an 'agricultural' man and I followed him in this, with Arthur Driver, two years older than me and coming up to his fiftieth year in 1927, entrenched behind the thickly padded door of his room at Charles Street, ensuring that the firm became more and more involved in urban work. He was an experienced auctioneer and had been President of the Auctioneers Institute in 1924. His right hand man was still Thomas A. Jones, now in his 23rd year of service.

I admit to being slower than I might have been in seeing where the future of the firm lay, but though Arthur and I did not always see eye to eye, we managed to steer a course many perhaps would describe as steady rather than inspired. The main body of our work at the end of the nineteen-twenties was for long-standing clients such as the Chamberlayne Settled Estates (around Southampton), Mary Countess of Ilchester and the Earl of Ilchester (the Holland Park estate), the Greenwich Hospital Department of the Admiralty, the Grosvenor Settled Estates Trustees (Belgravia and Mayfair), Speer Trustees, Portsmouth Estates Improvement Company, the London Permanent Benefit Building Society, Viscount Bertie of Thame, Lord Ebury, the Goulburn family, Conduit Mead Company, Colonel Abel Smith. It was fairly routine work – an encroachment at Winchmore Hill, agreement on footings at Esher, dilapidations in Euston Road, an inventory in Weymouth Street, a report on the sale of a disputed strip in New Bond Street, a wayleave in Thames Ditton, 'light and air' in Chelsea, valuation for mortgage in Chislehurst, for compensation in Surbiton, for a second loan on the Egerton Estate in Manchester, for fire insurance in Harley Street, for estate duty in Leatherhead, for probate in Hampton Wick, and the granting of leases and tenancies, and renewals, on estates which we managed. We drew up the schedule for a new lease of the Café de Paris in Coventry Street, so soon to be destroyed; we acted for the Arsenal Football Club over their property at Highbury; we settled the terms of an agreement for easement for electric cable across the Chamberlayne Estate at Chandlersford for the West Hampshire Electricity Company; we made a valuation for the purchase of Osea Island, Blackwater, by the Industrial Welfare Society, of ground rents by Peterhouse, Cambridge; we handled fire claims for the British Law Insurance Company; we advised St Thomas's Hospital on the policy of purchasing the Coughton Estate at Alcester.

Business was inevitably slack through the Economic Crisis of 1929–32 when I suppose activity at 7 Charles Street to which we had moved in 1919 from 23 Pall Mall reached an all-time low. We listened to the news on our wireless sets with growing depression, and sought refuge from reality in *The Good Companions* borrowed from Mudie's Library, *Bitter Sweet* at The Palace, the novelty of the all-talking, all-singing film at The Regal, Marble Arch, and the familiar hilarities of a silent Charlie Chaplin in *The Circus* at the New Gallery.

We came through The Crisis relatively unscathed, and in 1934–5–6 acquired additional landlord clients who were to remain with us for many a year – notably Sir Ronald Gunter Bart (Earls Court and West Kensington), Rev George Pollen's Trustees (Old Burlington Street, Savile Row etc), James Kent's Estates (The East End, City Road etc), the Earl of Radnor's London Estates (around Fleet Street). We handled the latter from January 1935 in association with G. J. Brown & Co. In 1935 too we conducted the sale of Lurgashall Park Farm at Petworth for Viscount Cowdray. I was also personally engaged to conduct land valuation for the Agricultural Mortgage Corporation which had been established by Act of Parliament in 1929 to provide long term credit to the agricultural community. I did a considerable amount of work for the A.M.C. throughout the nineteen thirties.

Robert Manning Driver, my brother-in-law, died in 1935, and we made a valuation for probate of his property at Horsell, Woking. I like to think it was a sign of our moving into a more modern world when in November 1935 we made a valuation and report for a proposed golf course on the Cadland Estate at Fawley in Hampshire for Major Cyril Drummond's trustees. We became further involved in the game, which was having such a boom just now, when we advised Lord Ilchester on the grant of a licence for alterations to be made to the indoor golf school of All Weather Golf Practice Ltd at Melbury Road, Kensington. We also arranged on behalf of Lord Ilchester the building of Abbotsbury Road, Kensington, thus joining Melbury Road to Holland Park and providing a link road to Bayswater Road. There was a harking back to the Old Days with our handling the Extinguishment of Manorial Incidents at East Betchworth Manor (Bellamy's Enfranchisement) for Capt E. H. Goulburn; but in the same month we knew we were firmly back in 1935 when we conducted the compulsory sale under the Housing Acts of a house in Hackney, prepared a case for the Apley Estate, Bridgnorth, against the Wolverhampton Corporation Water Bill, and conducted a Town Planning Appeal for the Manor Estate at Aldershot. The country was on the way back to recovery when in 1936 at the age of 22 my second son Philip Griffith Jonas joined us at Charles Street as a trainee-assistant, and the eighth generation of the family took up its position.

In 1936 we first became involved in an activity which was to become familiar in after years, the conversion of houses, mostly in Kensington, for Mr R. G. Gunter and Sir Ronald Gunter, into 'flats' and the stables into garages. Many a 'licence for user' we arranged for premises which had been residential becoming doctors and dentists' consulting rooms, architects studios and offices. But when in October 1938 we received instructions through Lord Ilchester's solicitors, Fladgate & Co, to arrange for the construction of an air-raid shelter at 83 Addison Road, we knew a curtain was about to descend, unlikely to rise on a scene which had any resemblance to the England we had known so far. We felt sure 'they' would extricate us from The Slump and things would return to normal; but there were few who could console themselves with any hope that the Munich Crisis could be other than the prologue to war with National Socialist Germany fought to an end which was bound to be bitter and demanded a new beginning. A last reminder of a life that would never return came with the arbitration we took part in that December of 1938 at the request of the President of the R.I.C.S. between the Borough of Barnes and the Ranelagh Club, the setting for so many enjoyable, lazy afternoon teas under the cypress trees listening to the band and watching the croquet. It was a world which was fast going out of focus.

The demand for licences to build air-raid shelters grew; we made ourselves familiar with the requirements of the Civil Defence Act and advised our clients, the James Kent Estate with its East End property, in particular, on something called A.R.P. – air raid precautions. After a preliminary few months with us in 1936, my son Philip went to serve his articles with Colonel Frank Trumper, Fellow of the Land Agents Society, and by the outbreak of war in 1939 had qualified as an associate of the Chartered Surveyors Institution. He rejoined us briefly to help with the kind of work which came to us in those first months of the war – valuation and inventory of effects of Bramshot Golf Club, Fleet, which had been requisitioned by the War Office, advice to Robert Gunter on underground rooms at Wetherby Gardens, the sales by auction, the licences for alterations, the timber valuations, the installation of lifts, the valuations for purchase and probate. But more and more prominent became valuations 'in respect of requisition by the War Department' or Air Ministry, and preparing schedules of 'Plight and Condition'. We arranged for the temporary requisition of Heathcote House, Epsom, for Lord Rosebery's trustees, the sale of Mrs E. R. Chamberlayne's land at Hamble and Netley to the War Office – and in August 1940 we were negotiating with the Sub-Area Quartering Commandant, West, for the *de-requisitioning* of Bramshot Golf Club!

Came the autumn of 1940 and General Goering's aerial blitzkrieg on London, and the bulk of our work moved into the category 'valuation of contents of flat for war damage in Eaton Place', 'surveying re Air Raid Damage at Burlington Fine Arts Club, Savile Row'. We reported on the damage done by the bomb which fell on the Chancery Lane Safe Deposit in September 1940 for the trustees of Viscount Folkestone; on the tragic wrecking of Holland House; on the repairs needed to rebuild the Arsenal Stadium. We advised the Gunter Estate on their rights regarding the requisition of railings (for melting into guns) and the proper compensation rent for emergency water supply tanks on bombed sites. We were kept busiest of all with the very extensive damage the German Luftwaffe had inflicted on the East End property of James Kent Estates, though we were also called on to count the cost of action by our own troops – surveying the 'Damage by Military Occupation' on the Betchworth House Estate for our client Major E. H. Goulburn.

Philip left us in 1940 to join the Royal Artillery and was formally made a partner before enlisting. Arthur's son Robert who was 19 in that year was called up shortly afterwards. The work slackened off, though as there were only a handful of us to do it we were all kept busy. When many firms decided to 'evacuate' from central London, we followed suit by moving to Harold D. Jonas's house in Limpsfield but returned to London and Charles Street after a few months.

Arthur Driver died in 1943 at the age of 66. As the urban specialist

A.C.D. had played a significant role in the development of Drivers Jonas in a period of accelerating transition. Although an able surveyor, he was not in the same class as his great forebears, R. C. Driver, Edward Driver, William Driver and Abraham Purshouse Driver, but in helping to bring the firm out of the Edwardian era into the motor and air age and the new social structure of Between the Wars, he equipped us to meet the demands of the post-war Britain he never lived to see; and I for one, though we disagreed on many matters, can never underestimate this contribution. In the event he was the last Driver in the firm – it was some time after the end of the war that his son Robert Driver decided to enter the surveying profession, and when he qualified he joined the staff of the Crown Estates Commissioners.

Concerned almost exclusively with the rural side of the business I had need of help to sustain our activities in urban work, and to this end I established a temporary working association with Fred Ragg of Alfred Savill & Sons. I was now the sole active partner, as Robert Collier Driver had once been. When the end of hostilities – and victory – came in sight in the winter of 1944, and I too had reached the age of 66, it was obvious that surveying and valuation work, especially on the urban side, would soon increase and our depleted staff would have to be built up if Drivers Jonas were to get their share. More important, someone younger and more broadly experienced than I would have to be persuaded to join us to direct their operations – someone above all with the contacts and reputation to enable us to gain the new business we needed, in conjunction with Philip when he returned.

Change was in the air once again – and we had to be part of it. There was nothing 'out-of-date' in being landlords' men. It was merely a question of serving the new landlords – the insurance companies, investment houses, banks, charities, developers, hospitals and schools which we lumped together and called 'institutions'.

Confidential

Memorandum

Subject: New Partner
Date: 3 March 1945

Last month I asked the Appointments Secretary of the Institution of Chartered Surveyors to notify me of any senior member of the profession, suitably qualified and experienced though probably not a partner, who he thought might welcome a move and the responsibilities of partnership. On Thursday he telephoned to say he had given my request considerable thought and that he had drawn up a 'short list' at the top of which was Mr William T. Bishop, a senior assistant at Cluttons, aged 44, who had intimated to him he was considering leaving. Did I know him and would I like to meet him? I said I knew of him, had never met him but would very much like to. William Bishop and I had lunch together to-day at the Junior Carlton and I took to him immediately.

He told me his father had been a civil engineer at the RAF Research Establishment at Farnborough, and that when he left school he too had ambitions to become an engineer. When he was 19 he obtained an interview however with Jimmy Merrett of Cluttons, who had joined the firm in 1865, and as a result was appointed a junior assistant, one of a staff which consisted then of about 50 to 60. This was in 1920 and he had been with the Great College Street firm a quarter of a century. He was a Fellow of the Surveyors' Institution (F.S.I.) which in 1930 became the Chartered Surveyors' Institution, and I understand next year is to become The Royal Institution of Chartered Surveyors when the qualifications will change to F.R.I.C.S. He had accumulated a wide range of experience in urban estate management and handling Crown Estate work. At Cluttons it was unusual for anyone who was not a Clutton or a Trumper to become a partner, and he had decided that with the coming of peace he should take the opportunity of a general post-war re-shuffle of staffs to make a break, or else he would be stuck at Great College Street for the rest of his life and with little chance of preferment. He had married in 1929 and his son Robin, born in 1931, was at Charterhouse.

I told him I was desperately in need of help, and there and then invited him to join us as a full partner as soon as Cluttons would release him. I said I would talk to William Trumper at once. I told him he would be only the second partner who had not been a member of the Driver family. He seemed greatly pleased at the prospect of joining a firm of our standing and tradition, and we drank to our future co-operation.

H. D. Jonas

Letter of Harold D. Jonas to his son Capt Philip Jonas, MC
(serving with the Royal Artillery in Italy)

Limpsfield,
9 May 1945

My dear Philip,

Victory in Europe – 'V-E Day' as the papers are calling it – was marked with riotous celebration in the village yesterday – a huge bonfire, fireworks, singing and drinking, and a church service at which we gave heartfelt thanks for it all at last being over. I wish you could have been with us, but we look forward to your being demobbed in September and taking up your reins here where you left off in 1940 – lucky to be able to start as a Professional Associate of the Surveyors' Institution and of the Auctioneers' Institute. At 31 you will be able to give us the impetus we need to carry us into the post-war world – new work is already coming in and we shall need all the help we can get.

William Bishop has been with us two months now and is proving a tower of strength. We came to a compromise with Cluttons who agreed that he should come to us at once part time. He has been spending three days at Great College Street, dealing mostly with war damage claims on the Crown Estate at Eltham which Drivers surveyed in 1806 and two at Charles II Street (as Charles Street has been re-named). He has renewed his acquaintance with Arthur Barton, the qualified urban surveyor who came to us from Cluttons previously, T. A. Jones, the urban auctioneer whom of course you know all about – he's been with us 50 years now! – and A. J. Challenor my agricultural assistant. We have only about a dozen staff here now, and we must build this up as soon as we can – but good men are not easy to come by. During the war most firms gave each other mutual assistance, and as you know G. J. Brown & Co. came to us for help over managing part of the Radnor Estate as well as the property of Sir John Pollock Bart. We are still co-operating.

Most of our 1939 clients are still on our books, names which will all be familiar to you – Ilchester, Gunter, Speer and Chamberlayne, through whom we earned our coveted reputation in both urban and rural work. We still manage the Greenwich Hospital's Northern Estates for the Admiralty, though I think we shall probably be selling the office we set up in Chester to handle this work. The Agricultural Mortgage Corporation still keeps us pretty busy, and this is something I hope you will be able to take over, with Challenor to help you.

Property sales either by auction or private treaty have dried up almost completely, though at the end of the year we are selling Queens Hoo on the Woodhall Park Estate for Tim Abel-Smith and a certain amount of work is coming our way from Davis Estates. The new landlords are beginning to take notice of us and use our services – Shell and Guardian Assurance for instance. And of course there is always the work generated by something – or someone – coming to an end; valuation for probate of the contents of Betchworth House on the death of Brigadier Goulburn stands at the end of a long line of services to this family dating back to the 18th century.

I expect to continue as senior partner for another five years or so, and then hand over to William Bishop who by then will have been able to bring Drivers Jonas into the forefront of urban work. We shall not of course allow ourselves to slip from the eminence we have achieved in the agricultural field, and I have an idea we would be well advised to appoint a fourth partner who is a specialist here – I have my eye on a man called Donald Whittaker who is a Fellow of the Land Agents Society and widely experienced. We will talk about that when you are back with us. In the meantime your mother and I send you our best wishes and congratulations on the distinguished part you have played in achieving the victory we civvies celebrated so gratefully at Limpsfield yesterday. And don't overdo the Lacrima Christi and the Strega!

Ever your affectionate
Father

7, Charles II Street,
St James's Square,
London, S.W.1.
27th February 1950

My dear

My partners and I will be so pleased if you can join us at a small Dinner Party of our professional friends at the Junior Carlton Club (Parliamentary Room) on Monday, 20th March, 1950 at 7 o'clock for 7.30 p.m. to celebrate the Two-hundred-and-Twenty-fifth Anniversary of the foundation of our Firm.

Yours sincerely

Dinner Jackets   *R.S.V.P.*

Notice to All Staff

2 April 1957

Our present offices, comprising three Georgian houses, nos 6, 7 and 8 Charles II Street, have come to the end of their useful life and they are soon to be demolished and a new building erected on the site, of which we will occupy the 3rd, 4th and 5th floors, the Canada Life Assurance Company being in the lower part. We anticipate being able to return to Charles II Street in 1958, and in the meantime we have accepted the kind offer of one of our clients Mr Tim Abel-Smith to use his house at no 32 Hertford Street as our offices while Charles II Street is being rebuilt, and we plan to move there on May 27.

W. T. Bishop

THE NATIONAL COAL BOARD
SURFACE ASSETS COMPENSATION
Report of a Meeting of Partners and Staff

In the chair: Mr W. T. Bishop

Mr Bishop said now the main valuation work for the National Coal Board had been completed, he thought it would be helpful for all those who had been in any way involved in it to review this comprehensive essay in consultancy to a nationalised industry, since it would set the pattern for future commissions of this sort. He hoped everyone would learn what they could from the report, and from the discussion which followed.

The Board had been established by Parliament (the Coal Industry Nationalisation Act, 1946) to manage the industry on behalf of the nation from January 1, 1947. In the months before the Board came into commission there was considerable activity by way of acquiring premises, and in 1946 Drivers Jonas were asked to advise on the price which should be paid for a building in Cheltenham required as a research laboratory. The following year the firm received an urgent request for similar advice over the offer the Board should make for the purchase of Himley Hall, the Worcestershire seat of the Earl of Dudley which they suddenly had an opportunity of buying as a North West Headquarters.

Mr Bishop, Mr Philip Jonas and Mr Donald Whittaker had made a hasty visit to the property, and in the afternoon discussed the matter with Mr Guy Bigwood FRICS who represented the noble owner. Their brief was only to advise, not actually to negotiate the purchase, which was carried out shortly afterwards by the Board's representative direct with Lord Dudley. These jobs led to Drivers Jonas being consulted on what rent the Board should pay for a group of ex-Government hostels in which they proposed housing foreign miners, and to the instructions which were the subject of the present meeting to act for the Board in the settlement of the compensation to be paid the colliery owners for the transfer of their surface assets under the 1946 Act. These were not the winding equipment at the pithead, nor the coal down under, but the houses (and let farms) in the vicinity of the coalfield which the companies owned and rented to their miners.

The period of this consultancy work was from 1951 to 1954, though the commission came in 1950. For the job of settling this compensation rate, said Mr Bishop, the Board engaged several firms of surveyors and divided the coalfields between them. Drivers Jonas were made responsible for the coalfields of South Wales, Forest of Dean (where a Driver had made a survey some 150 years back), Somerset and Kent. It was no 'desk research' operation; every area had to be visited. It was a gargantuan task, and the work was spread round the office in shifts, as it were. Mr Eric Real with Mr Peter Blowers, Mr Sandy Copland, Mr John Schilling and others took it in turns to spend a week in the field and then a fortnight at Charles II Street. On many of the visits he made, said Mr Bishop, he had been accompanied by Mr Rafe Clutton, son of Mr Robin Clutton, who had come to the firm to gain experience before going to the family firm.

Mr Eric Real told the meeting how the team had relied on the efficient, cheerful Elfrieda (Freddie) Browne i/c secretariat and transport, whose dogged driving and unerring map reading in Darkest Wales kept morale high and the programme on time. The natives were mostly friendly as members of the team knocked on doors and were allowed in to see the parlour, inspect the usual offices and note their answers to questions about the drains and the water supply. Mr Real reckoned they had put a value on 14,000 houses in South Wales alone, though of course two or three random visits to homes in a row of identical terrace houses often enabled them to calculate the value of the whole terrace. The problem was not so much getting the information as applying it on the basis intended by the Act.

Answering a question from the floor, Mr Bishop said in the case of most of the smaller owners they managed to settle a provisional value on the ground, which had only then to be approved by their clients the National Coal Board. But, along with their colleagues who were covering the other areas, they found there was a minority of the bigger coal owners who saw the wisdom of taking advice on the interpretation of the Act and the likelihood of their receiving more if they refused to settle on the ground direct with the surveyors. These could afford to wait for the Government to make the next move, and bided their time.

The Government agreed the drafting of the Act was obscure, said Mr Bishop, and set up an Arbitration Tribunal to decide just what it was Parliament had intended should be the basis of valuation of this surface property. It would have taken too long to investigate every coalfield remaining unsettled, so the tribunal took three test areas. The owners were represented by three counsel and three surveyors and the Coal Board likewise. The tribunal was chaired by Lord Silsoe QC (formerly Sir Malcolm Trustram Eve) and for ten days the surveyors on either side went into the witness box to give their professional views on what should be the basis of valuation and to be cross-examined by the other side's counsel.

The point came when Lord Silsoe, having heard all the witnesses, said he did not agree with any of them. He called Mr Bishop back into the witness box and said he wanted to ask him a question.

Lord S: If I shut you and Mr Brackett up in a room and asked you to settle it, what would happen?

Mr Bishop told the meeting there was a deathly silence at this question. He had his back to the court room and could not see the expressions on the faces of his friends or opponents. Mr William Brackett, he explained, was the chartered surveyor acting for the owners of the test coalfield in the Drivers Jonas area.

Lord S: Someone will have to give way. Who would do so first?

Mr B: It would not be me.

Lord S: Are you prepared to give way?

Mr B: (who had had no instructions): Yes sir. I am prepared to give way – a certain amount. Not very much.

Lord Silsoe then announced he would have to adjourn, but that he would ask Mr Brackett the same question when the tribunal assembled the next day.

The nub of the tribunal's report, said Mr Philip Jonas, was a formula setting out the property into categories – those built at certain periods with so much floor area, so much per foot super. The firm had then to send a team back to the field and prepare schedules which applied the formula to every part of these unsettled surface assets in agreement with the owners' surveyors. The firm's opinion was that the formula gave the people with the best estates too low a compensation and those in the lowest categories too much. When Mr Bishop came to apply the formula to one property, the owner could not resist reminding him that he had offered it to the Board at £50,000 *less*. It was not the only example of this kind. Under the tribunal's ruling, when the surveyors came to what they called 'buts and bends', the near-derelict property which came below the lowest category, they had to agree together on an arbitrary figure. This led to a certain amount of haggling among the terraces, but they had disposed of the matter as crisply and professionally as they could, given the tribunal's instructions.

Summing up, Mr Bishop said it had been an invigorating exercise of national importance and Drivers Jonas were grateful to the Coal Board for putting the firm's resources and stamina to the test. He thought staff had stood up to it extremely well in the circumstances, and the 'ordeal' would stand them in good stead. There were going to be more national-ised industries; Drivers Jonas would be ready to serve them.

TRINITY HOUSE
Letter from William Bishop to Philip Jonas

Oxshott,
21 May 1963

Dear Philip,

I am sure everyone at the office realises that Trinity House making me a Younger Brother is as much an honour to everyone at Drivers Jonas as to yours truly, but I thought I would just drop you a line for the record and hope that you will let it be known generally that I regard it as such, and fully recognise the teamwork which lies behind all the firm has done for T.H. over all these years – who was it by the way who came across a cairn on a cliff with 'T.H.' carved on it and took it for a memorial to Thomas Hardy?

'All the firm has done for T.H.'! Golly!

'These years' seem to stretch way back, but I suppose set beside the 450 years of the Corporation's existence – it was founded in 1514 – the time we have devoted to them is very little. In their four and a half centuries they have become the general lighthouse authority for England and Wales, the principal pilotage authority in the UK, and a charitable organisation assisting needy seafarers and their dependants. The money which enables Trinity House to act in the latter role comes from the property it owns in various parts of the country, much of it bequeathed by grateful master mariners. For long this was managed by a number of different surveyors, and around 1947 the Corporation thought the time had come for one firm only to advise upon and manage the whole of their property, which included an extensive estate in Southwark, premises in the City near to Trinity House by the Tower of London, and agricultural property in Essex and Lincolnshire.

In June 1947 I formally 'attended on' Sir Arthur Morrell the Deputy Master who was responsible for the day-to-day running of the Corporation, the Master being the Duke of Gloucester. Shortly afterwards we received the Corporation's formal instructions. That is how it all began. Our brief gave us considerable latitude but there was no forgetting Sir Arthur's admonition: 'Mr Bishop, we will not often give you a directive, but if we do please remember that we are seamen and have been used to giving orders from the bridge and having them carried out with alacrity.'

Trinity House had owned the large residential Southwark estate for some 300 years. A great part of it had been requisitioned in the war and damaged in the air raids. Our first commission was to reinstate the two well-known garden squares of Trinity Church Square (with the statue of King Alfred in the middle, said to be one of the oldest in London) and Merrick Square. Part of the job, which was a lengthy and extensive one, was preserving the buildings and gradually modernising the interiors, together with rehousing many of the existing tenants (some of whom had lived on the estate for several generations) and removing non-conforming 'business' users. This began with the lateral conversion, under Bernard Holland's supervision, of the three most severely damaged of the 68 houses in Trinity Church Square. In this we were acting as 'building surveyors', a role we had not played to any large extent up to this time. Eric Rowley, you will remember, undertook such building jobs as came our way, but when he left to go to Uganda the responsibility for developing this side of our business was passed to Bernard Holland who had been my urban estate management assistant for three and a half years at Cluttons and joined us in March 1947. He cut his teeth as a building surveyor on 48, 49 and 50 Trinity Church Square, and soon had a big operation on his hands which of course is still continuing on this estate.

233

Holy Trinity Church in the middle of Trinity Church Square, the site of which the Corporation had presented to the church authorities in 1821 for one of the Waterloo Churches, had a diminishing congregation, and as a result of its deteriorating structural condition was closed for worship some years ago. The future of the church building was the subject of much controversy, as you will remember, especially as its location in the middle of the Trinity House estate would have a considerable effect on the Corporation's tenants and the locality generally. When the Corporation regrettably but necessarily had to oppose a Parliamentary Bill designed to change its use to offices, I gave evidence on behalf of Trinity House before a House of Commons Committee which rejected the proposal.

We were directly involved too in settling the compensation for the fire and bomb damage to Trinity House itself on Tower Hill. The Corporation commissioned Sir Albert Richardson to restore the building with many additions for office purposes, and we advised on the arrangements for the new Trinity House, which Her Majesty Queen Elizabeth II opened in 1953. After this we investigated the possibility of restoring the historic Trinity House almshouses in Mile End Road which had also been very badly hit in the air raids; but we advised against doing this on economic grounds and they were sold to the former London County Council to add to their neighbouring housing developments. We were asked to find an alternative site on the south coast within reach of London where new almshouses could be built, and picked a fine plot of land at Walmer in Kent. We helped Mr Alan D. Reid FRIBA in the design and building of these new Trinity Homes which the Duchess of Gloucester opened in 1956. Subsequently we were concerned in the building of a Nursing Home Wing which Trinity House and the Dreadnought Seamen's Hospital built at Walmer as an integral but separate part of the Trinity Homes.

Work for the corporate side of Trinity House led us to being invited to advise on the pilotage and lighthouse aspects of the Corporation's activities, and this again enabled us to serve as building surveyors.

When Trinity House decided they wanted a land Pilot Station at Folkestone we were instructed to advise on how this could be achieved, and subsequently to secure its erection. John Hill, an architect, worked with us on the project – he being responsible for the overall design and we for the detailed specifying and supervision of the construction. This job came under Bernard Holland's immediate control. Waves, he was told, would be breaking over the two bottom storeys – thus it was necessary for glass in the windows to be three-quarters of an inch thick and as none of them could be opened air-conditioning had to be provided. Where to put the compressor for this latter when the roof, where you normally put it, had a radar tower on top, was a problem. It had to go inside the building and be cooled with water – sea water. It would have been no use laying pipes on the beach, the waves would have smashed them to pieces – so we had to sink a well. The drill at first found nothing but mud and then hit something they thought might be a second bomb, which made them run for the REs – who told them it was a rock!

The Elder Brethren explained that the operational staff using the Station needed to be able to scan three miles out to sea from their Pilot Station, and they asked us how high the building would have to be for them to do this. There seemed nothing for it but pushing Bernard Holland up a fire engine ladder with a cine and a Polaroid camera to photograph the view to seaward, over various intervening buildings, jetties and other obstacles, at various heights. All went well till Bernard got a message on the telephone at the top telling him a gale was blowing up and if he didn't come down at once their very expensive ladder which was already beginning to buckle would collapse.

From the pilotage to lighthouse activities – and the journey to Tater Du. The positioning of the 93 lighthouses and 27 light vessels to warn ships off unfriendly sections of England coast had been static for many a year when the cry was raised in the West Country that the absence of a light between Lands End and the Lizard was 'a scandal'. The agitation, engendered by a crusading local MP and probed by a BBC television programme, led Trinity House to bow to the storm and to pronounce the best position for such a light to be a quarter of an acre of land at Tater Du near Penzance. This was part of a small farm which an elderly Scot had bought for his retirement some years previously; and I was asked to go down to Cornwall to negotiate a suitable purchase price. Ken Clemens came with me. The site was the cliff edge looking out to sea, and taking our lives in our hands we climbed down to see the position from the beach. The would-be vendor was waiting for us as we clambered back to the top, and as we walked together up the lane between his scratchy potato fields I asked him what he thought the land was worth. His reply stopped me in my tracks. I had been thinking in terms of hundreds; he was asking for thousands. I explained to him my clients were trustees and did not have that kind of money.

'When the light comes on there up the road' he said, 'my heifers jump over the bank.'

235

'What light?'

'At The Lizard.'

'But that's 20 miles away.'

'It frightens them none the less.'

'But this light will face right out to sea, so they won't see it.'

'What about the foghorn?'

'We have new foghorns now. They look like egg boxes, not like megaphones any more. The sound goes right out to sea.'

'But the wind will blow it back.'

'There's no wind in a fog.'

'Hae ye no seen the Cornish Mist?'

He held out till four o'clock that afternoon, refusing to budge from his unreal demand, and back and forth our negotiation continued. He took my original offer in the end, and once it had been agreed he was very friendly and helpful. But I think he was surprised I dared show my face again at the opening of the fine lighthouse some 70 ft high, which they eventually built on his land. Light and foghorn were operated from Penzance so there was no keeper to trample his produce or frighten his heifers. Having people come and put a lighthouse at the bottom of your smallholding is not everyone's lot, but though my Scots friend's dream of riches was never realised, the payment which came to him from Trinity House out of the blue (or should I say out of the fog?) was, I like to think, a welcome windfall, even though tacitly acknowledged.

You will be relieved to hear that it was not part of the T.H. installation ceremony to present me with a flag, as I know, if that had been the case, you would all have felt obliged to buy me a boat to stick it on. They gave me a much-prized necktie and the assurance that I would never again have to serve on a jury, as I have sworn that within three hours of an emergency I will be aboard one of Her Majesty's ships.

I am afraid to-day's ceremony has opened a floodgate of reminiscence which I am in danger of swamping you with, and for this I apologise -- put it down to the Brethren's port. But the many facets of the service we have rendered Trinity House – and of course are still rendering – indicate the extent to which the work of the profession is broadening; I reckon that when the time comes for our successors to look back over a similar period of time, their experience will be even more diverse, though it could hardly be recollected with greater pleasure.

Yours ever,

William.

Discreet and Discrete Observations
from the window of a train going to Durham
BY ROBIN BISHOP

I am stepping out of the frame since we thought that at this stage you, the reader, deserved a few authentic particulars which, apart from being unquestionably authentic, were presented to you authentically. I consider it only fair that, having arrived at the relatively present (which is becoming the past as I write) you should hear about it direct from the senior partner, which is what I am, rather than via the author who can speak authoritatively (by virtue of his research) but not however authentically.

At the beginning of 1975 I took him as travelling companion on one of my last monthly train journeys to Durham City, and in between cups of expensive British Rail coffee, pointing out landmarks, reading of the latest drop in share prices and the newest outbreak of industrial unrest, stretching the legs along the corridor and consuming Inter-City breakfast and lunch, I surveyed activities since 1958 when I joined the firm. Beforehand I had spent 1949–50 at the old Charles II Street offices learning book-keeping and the like from the greatest of all teachers, personal experience, and then after Cambridge (Emmanuel) I was with Cluttons from 1955 to 1957.

I had read the Story So Far at the weekend, and in stepping into the train at King's Cross it was as if we were transferring to it for the next instalment on the conveyor belt along which the steady journey through time since 1725 continues.

The purpose of my journey was the start point of our conversation. This was to attend a meeting in Durham Town Hall of all those involved on behalf of the city and county councils and relevant central government authorities, 'to report progress' on the redevelopment of an outworn part of the historic core of the City of Durham for which we were estate and valuation consultants alongside William Whitfield, the eminent architect and member of the Royal Fine Arts Commission.

To-day's journey is all part of what we call Local Authority Consultancy. In the case of Durham it is certainly only a part of what we do for them. As well as advising the council on this particular redevelopment scheme which has been complicated by the relationship of the site to the historic setting of the cathedral and castle and has therefore been a fairly lengthy assignment, we've helped them on at least a dozen other problems, ranging from reservation of future public pedestrian rights of way, private enterprise city centre developments, disposal of a neighbourhood shopping centre on building agreement and lease, to being responsible for advising on and subsequently letting two modest-sized redevelopment schemes which the council itself carried out to provide much needed shop, office and residential accommodation on the edge of the central area suitable for traders displaced by the major through-road scheme.

Durham is one of those places where things really happen. A major road to relieve traffic congestion and remove motor cars from a large part of the city centre has not only been planned and argued over but practically built, including two fine new bridges over the river Wear.

Our work in Durham is really only an extension of our traditional role of acting for landowners. Here we are in 1975 acting for the new landlords the local authorities who after all have been consulting the profession ever since the first Town Planning Act of 1909 which the Surveyors Institution helped to draft. Even before this the firm was involved in the development of Letchworth, begun in 1903, in which had been worked out the principles expounded by Ebenezer Howard in his *Garden Cities of Tomorrow* published at the turn of the century. It may not be all that of a coincidence that, as well as valuing land to be purchased at Letchworth in the early nineteen hundreds, we also valued in 1958 the assets of First Garden City Limited, the company responsible for initiating the further development of this the first proper New Town.

The principles of Planning were kept alive in the nineteen-thirties by, among others, the Town and Country Planning Association. The reports of the Barlow Commission and the Uthwatt Committee which examined the subject in a depth which had hitherto been considered unnecessary, resulted in the Town and Country Planning Act of 1947, and Planning became an accepted profession. Many moved in on the act, not least ambitious engineers and, not surprisingly, we surveyors.

At Drivers Jonas we considered our skills particularly relevant. Eric Real, who came to us from Weatherall Green & Smith in September 1947 and assisted in the expansion of the firm which my father and Philip Jonas set in motion in this immediate post-war period, made himself fully acquainted with all aspects of the preparation and implementation of Development Plans. So when the Worcestershire County Council invited us to become their consultant surveyors in the early nineteen-sixties we were well placed to help them appraise schemes for the expanded towns of Droitwich, Halesowen, Kidderminster and Stour-bridge. Subsequently we were appointed by Wiltshire County Council to assist with the difficult and sensitive problems of development of part of the central area of Salisbury, another famous cathedral city of course. Appointments to act in a similar capacity at Durham, where we're going to now, and other places, followed.

In 1963 we felt we needed another partner to assist with this new work, and we were lucky to persuade Ken Clemens to join us, a forward thinking chartered surveyor and town planner whom we had met in the early Worcestershire days. Ken Clemens, who later came to be assisted by Rex Mercer from Kent County Council, was able to advise clients on planning, leaving Eric Real to advise on implementation. It was about this time incidentally that we closed our Southampton office where Derek Beauchamp had taken over from Kenneth Jenkin, so as to concentrate our efforts and financial resources in London.

Planning a dirty word? It dates from the days when 'planners' produced a plan which they presented as The Solution, and considered all that remained to be done was for others to come and make it work. To-day we insist that the chartered surveyor has a contribution to make to the planning process at *all* stages; that people who know about the economics of development should be brought in when the plan is being *prepared*, not merely when the time comes to implement it. You won't find many people these days accepting a plan on the grounds merely that it adheres to so-called 'planning principles' drawn up by the planners themselves and has been accepted by local politicians. 'Structural Planning Procedure' is what to-day's planners swear by, and by it they are sworn to examine all kinds of possible solution and make sure that a Planning Yes is accompanied by a Valuation and Investment Yes.

The pure planner rarely has the temperament for detail. For him the 'broad brush' approach. The architect can go to town with an artist's impression. But the surveyor who may have as lush or lusher ideas than either planner or architect can only indicate them with earthy figures which cannot paint a picture with the same panache and sweep as high sounding phrases or line and wash. However much of an idealist the surveyor may be, his feet have to be always on the ground. His dilemma is reconciling his aspirations with the earthy nature of his medium. But he can, and does, act as a bridge between planner and other specialists. What's more, he can interpret in a much more common sense way than either of them the social, political and aesthetic objections which are rightly made to every plan, and help to strike the balance between what is reasonable in planning terms, practical in financial terms and desirable in social terms. He can put weights on the various objectives postulated and thus eliminate emotional considerations in arriving at a solution of a conflict when it arises.

Our role is not in creating plans but in helping to see they make sense. This is what we have been doing at Durham; what we have done for Skelmersdale, Runcorn, Redditch, Warrington, Northampton, Wellingborough, Kidderminster in England; Livingstone in Scotland; and Ballymena in Northern Ireland. To give you an example, the Department of the Environment, the name given in 1970 to the former and much enlarged Ministry of Housing and Local Government, were not satisfied with the first plan presented to them for the new town of Skelmersdale. So we were asked to analyse on a common base the three new concepts subsequently submitted. Our job was to put price tags on the various features of each scheme so our clients could set aside areas of decision-making which were purely financial and say to themselves 'What kind of town centre do we want socially and aesthetically seeing there is very little difference in the costs and returns of the three plans?'

We're passing through Hatfield now, and over there is the one-time De Havilland airfield. Which reminds me of the exercise we undertook for the Roskill Commission which was enquiring into a possible site for a second – or was it third? – London Airport. Like at Skelmersdale we 'weighted' the points they should consider for selecting one out of 16 urbanisation schemes proposed as support for the four suggested new London Airports. Four schemes were submitted for each of the four airports, and we analysed the 16 of them on a common basis. Our report was fed back into the overall scheme; and when the necessary adjustments had been made in the light of it, the Commission had only one Preferred Design to consider for each proposed airport rather than four. Here again we were contributing to the useful activity of reducing the arena within which an eventual decision had to be made.

Look at that enormous marshalling yard! I suppose we could never have been considered a one-track profession. But to-day we're branching out more than ever. Local authorities, government inquiries, new towns, industry – all avail themselves of the professional services of the chartered surveyor to solve problems which would have been quite foreign to previous generations of surveyors. When an oil company asked us to find them a regional distribution centre to satisfy a long list of factors we found ten possible sites and recommended one at Kingsbury in Warwickshire, which they accepted. But as it was in the Green Belt there had to be a public inquiry, at the end of which the Secretary of State said he was not satisfied sufficient search had been made. We ringed round an area of 250 square miles and went over it kilometre square by kilometre square. Ken Clemens flew over it all in a helicopter. We came up with 54 possible sites, reduced them to 12, finally to four. The Department of the Environment reviewed these and, a quarter of a million pounds later – not all our fees I might add! – returned to square one by choosing – Kingsbury.

Our planning reputation has been built up with the help of a number of younger partners and associates who have been with us for varying periods of time, some leaving to go elsewhere, others still with us. The demand for our planning services has taken us as far as Canada and the United States. In Italy we were invited to advise on a major re-development project for Bologna, the Communist city state. Following this and similar experience in other foreign countries, we decided to be ready for Britain's proposed entry into the European Economic Community by opening a general practice office in Milan under the guidance of Hugh Rayner who learnt the language in the first year of his operation in Italy to which he moved en bloc with his family. The market place in Italy proved as different from the one we knew in England as we had anticipated – but considerably more difficult to penetrate. The bull point was that there was no indigenous profession comparable to the Chartered Surveyor, but the corollary was that the Italian race having survived nearly 2000 years without us had a good chance of continuing thus unless we were able to show the direct benefits we were able to bring to those we hoped would become our clients locally.

We concentrated our efforts on Valuations, Investment Advice and Commercial Property Lettings. I doubt whether Hugh Rayner will ever again experience the feelings of isolation he must have felt when he first arrived but gradually the contacts were made, mutual trust grew between other professional people and ourselves, and some local people and companies started us on our first commissions. Hugh was joined by

Peter Shapeero and – more recently – Derek Ames and the range of clients for whom we act in Italy is now looking healthy. Italy itself has started to pull through its economic problems – at least for the time being – and our Valuation and Investment services have been used by some well known names both Italian and British.

The problems of explaining to the English layman about the services of Chartered Surveyors are dwarfed beside the job of introducing ourselves to the Italian business world. The Chartered Surveyor's principle of only acting for one party in a transaction is becoming acknowledged – if not fully understood! – and we have established a bridgehead in a new and difficult market from which the range of the firm can expand over the years.

Those oil storage tanks? Yes, I see them. They *are* a blot on the landscape, I agree; but they've got to go somewhere. You can put the pipes underground but not the tanks. We've been involved in the siting of both. In 1955 a firm of civil engineers came to us to do what they call 'referencing' in connection with a Parliamentary Bill to authorise the laying of pipes for oil in South Wales. 'Referencing' is locating and recording the particulars of the owners of every 'interest' in the land reserved for the pipe, as well as of other pipes and ducts lying in the way of the proposed route. We allotted this country exercise to our agricultural section. We managed to do this comparatively small operation with our own staff, but when, on the strength of our success with this, Shell came to us for a much bigger operation, it was obvious we would have to recruit outsiders.

'Recruit' was the operative word. An appeal was made to retired services organisations and within no time our agricultural section had mobilised an Action Squad of some 15 to 20 retired majors, flight-lieutenants and naval commanders, used to the open air life in all weather, physically fit and mentally agile, able to treat with farm labourers and noble landlords with equal ease. Anthony Eden assembled them for a briefing meeting in a room in the Junior Carlton Club, and before giving them any instructions said he hoped they would all agree that from that moment on they shed their rank and everyone became Mister. Between them they covered literally thousands of miles, by car and on foot, and made many thousand enquiries person to person and by post, to ascertain the identity of the various owners and the nature of their interests, and plot the position of every water pipe, electricity cable, telegraph wire, sewer and the like which might obstruct a pipe-line due to run from the refineries on the Thames Estuary to the Mersey, to say nothing of innumerable 'spurs'.

A retired staff colonel was in charge and he organised the team on thoroughly military lines, with an Order of Battle chart which included a heading 'Casualties' which, considering one of them shortly after-wards suffered a coronary, showed considerable foresight. There was a strict target date for the deposit of the Reference Book, and all this was achieved with military precision. As a result we gathered a reputation for this tedious but important work which still brings us in commissions from all over the country from parliamentary agents, water under-takings, dock boards, local authorities, oil companies and the like. We've now given responsibility for this to our planning section.

The job does not always end with the delivery of a completed Book of Reference. When a Bill is passing through Parliament experts are often asked to give MPs evidence in the Committee stage on any aspect of the Bill on which they need guidance – remember Edward Driver doing this for the Great Western Railway Bill on compensation and R. C. Driver's evidence to the tribunals enquiring into the freeing of the Thames bridges from tolls. On one occasion my father was called upon to appear for Shell who were promoting a Bill through Parliament to establish machinery for the acquisition of easements for pipelines and a basis of compensation. He explained to the Committee that in his opinion an easement authorised by Parliament should be assessed under the provisions of the Acquisition of Land Act and not the Land Clauses Act of 1845. Though Shell was not a central government department or a local authority, he said, since they were authorised by Act of Parlia-ment they should be considered as such and given the benefit of the Acquisition of Land Act.

All rather familiar stuff; those of us who are carrying the torch in 1975 giving a contemporary twist to the theme of Transport which has brought so much work to the firm over these two and a half centuries – the turnpike roads, river navigation, canals, railways, toll bridges, air-ports, and now moving oil and other fluids through 'continuous cylin-ders' – pipelines to you.

Thank goodness the advertising men have never been allowed to get their hands on the green fields of England as they have in America where so many of the transport routes one drives along are lined with

243

flashing neon signs and blinking lights. Our train has been travelling for mile after mile now through rolling countryside, and how fresh and well cared for it seems! Think how many different surveyors are engaged in giving the owners advice on how to manage and farm it! But most of their time will be taken up with the work involved by the holdings, or parts of them, changing hands from one owner to another. And very few of them handling this work will be based in London, I reckon. The high cost of London rents, rates, staff and overheads generally will preclude it. I always remember Philip Jonas's father saying 'London overheads need London fees' and that is even truer to-day than 25 years ago.

With the change from a rural to an urban based population our practice has tended to specialise more and more in urban matters rather than rural. Indeed at the beginning of 1975 we decided, rather sadly, that in view of increasing overheads we must reduce our rural commitment, and Anthony Eden who took over the rural (or agricultural) section when Donald Whittaker went in 1958 has just left us to take up the important post of Resident Agent for the Ilchester Country Estates in Dorset and Somerset.

Happily, for some years we have had a working association with Smith-Woolley & Co., a well-known firm of rural chartered surveyors whose senior partner Martin Argles was President of the Royal Institution of Chartered Surveyors in 1972/3. We assist their clients with their urban problems, and they help us on the rural front. It is an arrangement which befits the day of the specialist in which we are now living.

Slowing down? A signal against us I suppose. At least you and I, sitting in this train, know where we're going. There's little chance of our being diverted, however often we may stop and restart. You can't be so certain in the work. Our agricultural activities were slowing down, but then along came this pipeline referencing and we were off again. And, more important, in 1961 we found ourselves once again in Crown Estate work. The clients we once had served for a century at a stretch, the Crown Estate Commissioners – Mr Fordyce, Mr Milne, Lord Carlisle et al – once again came knocking at our door.

The first approach was made earlier than that. In March 1957 they sought the independent advice of two chartered surveyors on the ground rent they should charge Vickers for the Crown Estate site on Millbank where this giant enterprise intended building a skyscraper for its head office. We were one of them, and this re-introductory exercise was the signal for us to return fully to the fold in 1962 as one of the Commissioners' advisory surveyors in respect of the part of the Crown Estate north of Piccadilly Circus comprising the whole length of Regent Street and parts of Soho. Cluttons of course are our opposite numbers in the Crown work south of Piccadilly, and it is interesting that it should be in the hands of Cecil (Sam) and Rafe Clutton both of whom at one time were pupils of my father.

Ah, we're moving on again. It looks a pretty straight stretch here. I wonder what held us up? Acquiring land for the railroad in open country like this would have been easier than for the construction of the new Regent Street which was driven through that conglomeration of small streets and houses which stood between Charing Cross and Regents Park. The Crown bought only the land immediately on either side to allow them to build a road roughly along the line of Swallow Street, of which the lower part still remains of course. Lord Foley, whose house and big garden stood where the Langham (now BBC offices) stands to-day, refused to budge, so the street had to take an abrupt left turn into the existing Portland Place, and to make up for the anti-climax of his grand processional way having to disappear round a corner John Nash built All Soul's church opposite Foley's house at the turning point – they celebrated the 150th anniversary of the church's consecration last year.

In the mid nineteen-sixties we got wind of some of the land on the east of Regent Street coming on the market, and persuaded the Crown to buy a narrow lane with an electric power station in it, and no one had heard of much, called Carnaby Street. We have since been responsible for the latest development of this emanation of what was once called Swinging London, the pedestrian precinct known as Carnaby Court. It was on the tip of my father's tongue, I understand, to ask Her Majesty the Queen, when he was presented with the CBE in 1971 for his services to the Crown Estate Commissioners, whether she knew that he had been responsible for buying a substantial part of Carnaby Street for the Crown Estate, but I regret to say his nerve failed him.

Will Piccadilly Circus *ever* be redeveloped? You may well ask. Your guess is as good as mine. It won't be for lack of trying. When Lord Perth and the Commissioners set up a special study into the future of the Circus and Regent Street, we helped Sir Hugh Wilson FRIBA, Harold

Samuel the estate developer (now Lord Samuel), Sir Frederick Gibberd and Professor Buchanan to prepare and evaluate a scheme for a covered pedestrian shopping street over Regent Street to allow traffic to flow freely beneath. However, when the Greater London Council proposed treating Piccadilly Circus in the same way this was not feasible, and after much detailed investigation the Regent Street proposals were abandoned. Sic non transit gloria.

Glory however came to a less exalted part of the Crown Estate, Hackney, where we have been acting as advisory surveyors since 1965, assisting the Commissioners and their local staff with the management of a substantial 'mixed use', but principally residential, estate centred on Victoria Park which itself was mainly laid out in the middle of the last century by the Commissioners' predecessors.

I was personally involved in this, and I must say it was an exercise in which I found great satisfaction, supervising the building as we did of some 250 new houses and flats on bomb sites and otherwise empty land. The work of rehabilitating and maintaining existing premises of course still continues at Victoria Park.

On top of this we have negotiated the sale of various outlying parts of the Hackney estate and purchased some eight acres from, I think, 12 different owners over the last few years, so the Crown Estate in these parts forms a very much more compact holding. We even helped to organise the building of a fine new estate office in the centre of it all, from which the Commissioners' local staff can more easily keep in touch with their tenants, which the Commissioners have always considered to be an essential part of good estate management.

And your good health too! What of the last days of Holland House, you were asking as we fought our way along the corridors to the restaurant car. Poor Holland House! scene of so much intrigue and gaiety! It was so badly bombed during the war that our client the sixth Earl of Ilchester no longer wished to return to live in it. He therefore instructed us to offer the house and grounds to the LCC for use as a public park. A long and difficult negotiation followed, which was complicated by the enactment halfway through of the Town and Country Planning Act which gave the LCC the opportunity to claim that the sale should be at 'existing use' value. On behalf of our client we strenuously opposed this last minute change in the basis of valuation, and after a private arbitration a special Act of Parliament was passed to enable the sale to go through on a basis acceptable to both sides. It's all a long time ago, and since that bitter wrangle the Ilchester Estate and the council, now the Greater London Council of course, have become firm friends. In recent years the two have collaborated closely on a number of projects with a feeling of mutual respect.

But of course the estate is very much larger than Holland House, as the Story So Far has shown. In a post-war world in which worthwhile domestic staff are almost non-existent most of the houses around Holland House, in St Mary Abbots Terrace, Addison Road and Melbury Road, for instance, are much too large for a single family to run. For those who wanted to live in Kensington in post-war style the Ilchester Estate, with our help, built some 700 houses and flats of a type more suited to the times. These were on the sites of buildings already half demolished by the bombing and on land in other parts of the estate which for various reasons had become available. The actual building work was arranged through 'developers' a generic term covering entre-preneurs, building contractors, institutional investors and others. But the sites were all let on building agreement and lease, most of which contained rent review provisions. This was a new departure for the residential field. It was something we initiated in 1960 as a bulwark against the day, discernible even then, when values would no longer be stable and looked like becoming even less so. We also organised the return of tenants to such buildings as were habitable. Rehabilitation went hand in hand with Improvement, the activity which has survived the whole of this story. The retaining and improving of all the property on the estate which we considered suitable for this purpose, together with careful phasing of the erection of new buildings, has enabled the social fabric of the area to continue and thrive – a good mix.

Estate Management. That's always been the heart of this business – and still is. Sandy Copland and I are the partners who now manage the considerable number of estates for which the firm are responsible. Our main task is not only overseeing day-to-day problems, but in particular looking to the future and endeavouring to ensure that the owner, be he or she an individual, a charity, a corporate body, a university college or an institution, is at all times properly looked after and that a good land-lord-tenant relationship exists.

Hurtling out of London like this reminds me of the increasing anxiety of so many firms in recent years to quit the metropolis for keeps in order to avoid high rents and minimise the effects of galloping inflation on wages and other outgoings. Numerous organisations have been coming to us to find them accommodation in the provinces. Every time there is a whole list of conditions to satisfy, and we have to come up with a variety of possible sites which fit the bill. It is applying the same technique we used to select urbanisation schemes for the Roskill Commission. It is a combined operation for us at Pall Mall employing a wide range of skills.

Take for instance when the Royal Life Boat Institution asked us to find them a site for a new headquarters to take the place of their premises in Grosvenor Gardens, Victoria. Apart from a head office building for a staff of 130, it was to include a depot where they could keep stores, carry out trials of equipment and execute repairs. The brief was for a site within two hours travel of London and one of the critical requirements was for ten feet of water in front of it at all states of the tide – not the easiest of assignments. Our search was limited to coastal and estuarial sites lying between Felixstowe and Weymouth plus the Bristol Channel.

The planners went to work and due to a fair amount of good fortune a satisfactory site was found; then the valuers valued and negotiated a purchase. This was followed by the building co-ordination/project management function which fell to our building surveying section. The RNLI's own marine engineers tidied up the frontage to get the sheet piling in for the depot site, but we negotiated with the Harbour Board to acquire the extra mud land that would be reclaimed in the process. Before they began the pile driving Bernard Holland had to schedule the condition of an old chemical factory opposite the site in which they operated delicate spring balances. This meant an exact record of every crack in existence before pile driving began – with photographs! – and why and when they had appeared.

We then, as co-ordinators, sat in on the panel which interviewed and appointed the architects. We started our proper building co-ordinator function by assisting the architects, quantity surveyors, engineers, heating and ventilating specialists and others to produce a workable design, and initiating construction. The building is now almost up. With any luck, by the time we celebrate our anniversary, it will be. Our agency section under David Chapman who joined us from Richard Ellis in 1973, disposed of the RNLI's lease of their Grosvenor Gardens headquarters which released funds to pay for the new office and depot at Poole in Dorset.

If you look out of the window now you'll see the town centre of Stevenage New Town. Some pretty impressive names on those office buildings, eh? When Christopher Jonas, Philip Jonas's son, joined us in 1967 after gaining experience and qualifying at Jones Lang Wootton, we began wondering how we could persuade 'the private sector' to subscribe money for the development of New Town schemes with which we were involved – and it is something we are still working on. It was all part of the plot which Christopher was hatching to bring the firm into the investment market. Although the principle has been adopted for one or two commercial developments of New Towns, our dreams of a complete private enterprise New Town has not yet been realised. But I can't see major financial institutions continuing much longer to put large sums of money on short term deposit when the country cries out for long term investment in New Cities, new homes and new industry.

'Property Shares Fall Further'. I really can't bring myself to read the financial pages of the newspapers these days, though of course for Christopher Jonas it has always been part of his job. Two years after he came to us we moved from the rebuilt Charles II Street to our present office at 18 Pall Mall and this gave him the extra room for the growing activities of our investment and agency section. He and Sandy Copland both became full partners in 1969, and indeed it was their arrival, together with the known prospect of being able to expand, which jolted us all into realising that we could not for ever stay cosily in the limited accommodation at Charles II Street where we overflowed not only into the building next door but another in Waterloo Place.

Continual regeneration is the secret. The injection of new blood which Sandy and Christopher represented had a welcome stimulating effect. In running a long-standing – and long-running – practice such as ours, it is more important than ever to be consciously on the watch for new ideas, new directions. The long run one has had in order to reach the present can constitute a rut from which it is difficult to escape because it has the attractions of being both familiar and comfortable. But at the end of it lies the setting sun, whereas after 250 years we see ourselves as always being where the sun is rising on new projects.

We have had a long relationship with Guardian Assurance and when they merged with Royal Exchange Assurance we were appointed advisory surveyors alongside Messrs Debenham, Tewson and Chinnocks.

The merger of the two companies coincided with their becoming keen buyers of investment property, and in 1969 we were appointed as consultants jointly with Debenhams of the newly formed Guardian Property Bond. Since then our relationship with this company has been strengthened by our being entrusted with the day-to-day management of part of their large portfolio.

This incursion into the property investment market is paying off very well – increased business, a wider clientele. We act as surveyors to Wyvern Property Unit Trust and, in 1972 were appointed consultants and managing agents by Samuel Montagu and Company to the property unit trust which they set up specifically for pension funds of local authorities.

Our investment clients regard property not as something to live in, manufacture in or cultivate, but as an item in an investment portfolio which they hope will earn them dividends and capital appreciation, just as any industrial or other shareholding. We advise clients where to put their money, the sort of return they should expect and the growth which is likely to come from different sorts of property. It takes Christopher and his staff all over the country making purchases from office buildings in London to industrial and shop property in Scotland.

We specialise in advising major institutions who seek to finance new development. Many good investments can be created by being in at the development finance stage. The participation of the chartered surveyor in Development Finance is a new and expanding side of the profession, and we at DJ are seeing to it that the advice we give on terms and conditions, and every other aspect of the increasingly sophisticated investment market, is second to none. We are gradually but surely introducing computerised techniques and laying the foundations of a service by which we aim to be able to advise clients in the role of consultant analysts and managers of the financial performance of property.

Seeing that collection of brightly coloured buildings over there illustrates the amount of progress of which this country is capable, if only everyone pulled together. You don't know what they are? We have just passed through Peterborough, another New Town, and the buildings are part of the new pumping station for the country's natural gas pipeline network. The surveyor has invariably been at the point of change as time has passed – buying the land for the very railway line which we are on today, referencing the land under which gas pipes run and advising on development strategy in new towns. It was because we saw another of these major changes coming that last September we despatched Christopher Armon-Jones, one of our Associates, to Aberdeen and asked him to look at the effect that all the drilling and production of oil from the North Sea would have on the land and property market in north east Scotland.

The reports which came back indicated that activity locally was tremendous and a ready market should be available for our services as Valuers, Planners, Building Surveyors, Letting Agents and Investment Advisers. He was keen that the firm should open a new office in Aberdeen and, having persuaded the partners to back him, DJ opened for business in Rubislaw Terrace on 2nd January this year – a nice gesture with which to start our 250th anniversary year. Property ranks quite small alongside the vast sums being invested offshore but as ever before it all needs most careful handling. Our first instructions in Aberdeen are proving how we are able to relieve the client of worrying over property matters thus leaving him to get on with the mainline of his own business.

The office locally provides a direct link with the long term investors for whom we act in London, and we see a major role to be played in introducing long term finance for the development which is so necessary in the area if the benefits to be reaped from the North Sea are to be realised. It is all very new, very exciting and gives to some of the young and keen members of the firm the opportunity to be on hand in true Driver style at another point of change in our lives.

Remember passing through Selby before we got to York? Wasn't that the town Drivers auctioned almost in its entirety for the Earl of Londesborough in 1905? Many of the buildings sold that day must still be standing – all of them I expect. I wonder what they'd bring to-day? I bet Guardian Royal Exchange wished they had put them in their portfolio in 1905! Particularly now I see in my paper that the Coal Board have applied for planning permission for an entirely new coal mine at Selby which they reckon will produce ten million tons a year by the mid nineteen-eighties. No one told his lordship about the possibility of *that*!

It is not only that new sections of the community are becoming landlords, but the role of landlord nowadays often becomes merged with that of tenant. In the inflation of 1974/5 the landlord has often only been receiving the return from the land which was fixed at the time it was leased, he has found rent reviews a cumbrous way of ensuring that his income increases with changes in money and property values. The landlord has therefore been looking favourably on meeting halfway the entrepreneur-developer who is his tenant, and coming to an arrangement whereby he gets a share of the annual income from the development. The hard line of tradition between land and buildings becomes blurred. The local authority which acquires land becomes the landlord and makes an arrangement with the development company, which has become the building tenant and submitted a development scheme which it subsequently builds. We are acting sometimes for the new landlord (the local council), sometimes for the new tenant (the developer). The object of the exercise is to enter into a partnership arrangement merging the function of landlord and tenant whereby the local authority gets a share out of the direct income and not just a ground rent related to the value of the land. Eric Real has been up to his eyes in this work.

The old divisions between surveyors labelled Landlords' Men and Tenants' Men have practically disappeared. Most of the younger firms tend to act mainly for developers perhaps. We like to think it is better to be, and to be known to be, in the whole market, to be available as consultants on both sides of the fence. Not at the same time of course! It enriches the advice you are able to give the one side, in our opinion, if you have had experience of being in the other camp. Not a very profound observation I agree, but it all boils down to integrity I suppose. Keeping your identity and not allowing yourself permanently to be in one man's pocket. Being professional. It is still the factor that matters. But whereas once integrity derived from the personality and record of the individual surveyor, and then from being known to be a member of the Institution, it is now the property of the individual firm.

As anyone who has read F. M. L. Thompson's excellent book *Chartered Surveyors, the Growth of a Profession* will know, the struggle to separate the activities of the genus 'chartered surveyor' from those of the many others who offered their services in a field open to all comers – the quantity surveyors, the auctioneers, the land agents, the architects and the rest – was a bitter one. If it had failed, further fragmentation of the Profession of the Land would have followed, benefiting neither client nor practitioner. It succeeded, but we at Drivers Jonas are aware how easily the process could be set in motion once again. For this reason to-day's partners are as assiduous as yesterday's in giving time and support to the Royal Institution of Chartered Surveyors and participating in what one might call the politics of the profession. Indeed, my father could be said, I hope without offence, to have given the office of Honorary Secretary which he held from nine years from 1963 to 1971, a degree of zestful attention of an unprecedented kind. For many years before becoming Honorary Secretary he was a member of the Council, a duty also performed by Ken Clemens and by Anthony Eden (who was President of the Land Agents Society in 1969, the year before it amalgamated with the RICS), and indeed myself and, more recently, Christopher Jonas. My father, Philip Jonas and Eric Real all served as chairmen of the North West London branch of the RICS. Philip Jonas was chairman of the RICS Junior Organisation in 1949, the year in which his father H. D. Jonas was Master of the Worshipful Company of Clothworkers, and his son, Christopher was Honorary Secretary of the Junior Organisation from 1969 to 1971 and Chairman in 1974/5. I was Honorary Secretary of the Junior Organisation from 1962 to 1964.

The corporate spirit of our own staff is no less important than that of the profession as a whole, and we have always felt it paramount that as our numbers grew we did not lose the personal touch – or with our clients either for that matter, but that's another thing. Soon after the war, the partners instituted an annual staff party which has been held every December for the past 28 years in the form of a dinner at which the senior partner briefly reviews the year's progress and each year a different member of the staff makes an irreverent reply in which by tradition the lampooning of partners is allowed full rein.

To celebrate our 225th anniversary in 1950 the partners held a dinner party at the Junior Carlton Club, as we have seen, to which they invited representatives of the older professional firms. A delightful toast to Drivers Jonas was proposed by Mr John Watson, the well-known member of the Lands Tribunal and lay magistrate. I was doing my national service as a seaman in the Royal Navy at the time. They kindly sent me an invitation and as luck would have it I managed to get leave of absence to attend.

My father's retirement at the end of May 1971 was marked by a dinner which the partners were privileged to give at Trinity House. It was attended by some 80 guests who included many distinguished clients and members of the surveying profession. The toast of the guest of honour was proposed in a witty speech by Sir Oliver Chesterton, who was President of the RICS in their centenary year of 1968. When Philip Jonas came to retire in August 1974 he did so in the knowledge that the

253

ninth generation was already in his place in the person of his son Christopher in whom runs the blood not only of the Drivers and Jonases but of another distinguished surveyor family, the Ellises of Farebrother Ellis, to which his mother belongs.

Do we find so much tradition and history embarrassing, a brake on progress? I don't think so. The fact that after the war we found ourselves with some ready-made clients of pre-war days perhaps led to a certain complacency, insofar as it was not so necessary for the firm to go out and find new business as it was for some of the younger firms. One of the disadvantages of being old is that it tends to breed conservatism, not that some judicious conservatism at the right time is any bad thing. It did however mean then that the firm was later in the field of post-war possibilities than those who entered it fresh, without tradition pointing them in any one direction, without prejudices as to the 'superiority' of rural over urban work. Their staff had little or no link with the twenties and thirties, and to them the eighteen-eighties and nineties were history, not files in the room next door of which the current number was still operative and in daily use.

We have shed our conservatism – and so have our clients. We, and they, had no alternative. Tax is now the shadow which hangs over every property, and fiscal considerations dominate every recommendation. I hope history will not accuse mankind of losing its humanity in the nineteen-seventies and causing decision-making to become a matter only of cold and mathematical calculation; but unless we are aware of the danger and take steps to avoid it, it is a judgement we will come to deserve. We may be heading in that direction.

In the short term however Durham is our destination, and it looks as if we are just about there. My mouth is dry with talking to you – yet how much have I left unsaid! and how much you will have to leave unwritten! No matter. A whole book could be written on Drivers Jonas To-day, and maybe someone will be doing just that in the year 2000 when we are 275 years old and all the land in Britain *will* have been nationalised and there is no private sector and public sector, and the increment value which Lloyd George objected going to the landlord 'who just happened to pick it up' without earning it will come to you and me, or rather our elected representatives our local council, who will build houses and hospitals and playing fields with the proceeds – and schools for the type of public education system they happen to be backing that year.

We all differ in welcoming or deploring the arrival of such a state of affairs. Some say it will put the teeth into planning, others that it will destroy Freedom with a capital F which they see as the right to own property. One thing however is certain; it will not come 'at a stroke' – even by 2000 probably. This seeming tide in the affairs of men on these islands is moving slowly, even if surely. If that is the way it is moving, we will move with it. We are equipped to assist the government of the day to implement such legislation; we are geared to advise owners upon every aspect of their involvement. We may have to shift our emphasis, but we shall not change our character. Enlightened advice to what we hope are enlightened clients is our stock-in-trade, and we aim to distribute it to all who seek it, with energy, alacrity and good humour, professional efficiency and an awareness of the times. We are paid to keep our minds on the job, and should they let us down we have underwritten them with every mechanical and electronic aid in the book – polaroid cameras whose pictures can be enlarged or reduced, and reproduced in neatly bound reports by our sophisticated photo-printing and litho section; moisture meters to test damp without opening up structures; cover meters to detect the depth of reinforcement bars in concrete; micrometers for measuring cracks and recording movement to a thousandth of an inch; pocket tape recorders and automatic typewriters; electronic computers which in seconds can calculate and print cash flows from whole portfolios of property and simulate the effect on income of projected capital value of a change rate of inflation, tax or rental growth. We are using the computers more and more to enable us to provide a near instant insurance valuation service for large groups of property, and for providing detailed risk analyses of property development schemes.

The mathematical power which this sort of machine provides gives a clear indication of a trend towards a more numerate profession. For us it is a platform on which we are making ready to move into the future, equipping ourselves to provide the answers to the questions which our clients will be putting to us in the nineteen-eighties.

Surveyors with a head office in the heart of London's West End (to say nothing of branches in Aberdeen, Milan and Southwark), equipped

255

with so sinister an array of electronic aids, may seem far removed, and not only in time, from nurseryman Samuel Driver clambering into the roof of All Saints to advise the haughty Malachi Hawtayne Esquire and other members of the Wandsworth Parochial Council on the replacement of the rafters as part of his duties as overseer. But in fact we have only gone full circle. For are not 'overseer' and 'surveyor' the same word? 'Supervisor' is a third. They all mean 'seeing over', and that is what we have been doing throughout the 250 years in which our clients have come to consult us on sale, purchase, valuation, management, compensation, improvement, development, investment. To paraphrase what you made Samuel Driver say on the first page, scratch a chartered surveyor in Westminster these days and you will find a man involved in some way in almost every aspect of contemporary life.

Here we are! To-day's destination – Durham. To report progress, eh? Oh well, that's not till tomorrow.

That's your tomorrow, he said. Before we reached the exit he turned to cross to another platform murmuring something about having to change conveyor belts, and disappeared in the crowd.

Author's Afterword

'We're celebrating our 250th anniversary in 1975; we haven't any archives to talk of; do what research you can and write a book on what could have happened.'

That was the brief and I followed it. So everything you have read has been written, not by those to whom it is ascribed, but by me. For there are no diaries, no journals, no letters (except the Brooks Estate and Credit Immobilier correspondence and Henry Jonas writing to Cissie Driver about his climbing), no memorandums, no minutes, no memoirs (except R. C. Driver's jottings in his private ledger). I invented them. I invented a few people too – and none of these appear in the index. The great majority of the people mentioned actually existed, including Thomas A. Jones the contents of whose 'Reminiscence' I have used in some form or other in its entirety, though not verbatim.

So the vehicle is fictitious; but the journey has substance. It is the ground the Drivers and Jonases travelled – and, at the end, which Drivers Jonas is still travelling. The passages which are pure romance are obvious; elsewhere there is a certain amount of conjecture but even this has a basis of fact; facsimile reproduction of actual documents show the narrative stepping on to solid rock, though absence of such must not be taken for lack of foundation in truth. But this is not a book for scholars. You are invited to take it all in your stride (which, if you are reading this, you have probably done already) and not worry too much about identifying the likely and the unlikely. But if you wish to play the detective you will find most of the clues in the bibliography.

Many more documents relating to the activities of the Drivers and the Jonases came to light in various parts of London and elsewhere during research than the partners knew about when they gave me the commission. But my digging was far from unaided, and I was given a head start by the spade work already undertaken by Mr Keith Jopp (who received material from Mr Robert Driver, son of Mr A. C. Driver, now living in retirement in Pembrokeshire, which was of great value), Mr Reginald Pound, and Mr G. R. Clark of the Crown Estate Commissioners who provided a list of Crown Estate Records referring to the Drivers which had been transferred to the Public Record Office. I am very grateful to these for pointing me in the right direction.

My thanks are due for the help given me by Miss Boast of the Southwark Room, Newington District Library, SE17: Dr Felix Hull, Kent County Archivist, Maidstone; Mr H. S. Cobb, Deputy Clerk of the Records, House of Lords, and his staff; Miss Elizabeth Stokes and Miss Joan Davison of the staff of the Royal Institution of Chartered Surveyors, and the staff of the library at Great George Street; Mr W. J. Smith, Head Archivist, and Mr A. R. Neate, Record Keeper, Greater London Record Office; Mr Guy Acloque of The Grosvenor Office; Dr F. H. W. Sheppard, General Editor, The Survey of London; Mr John North of the Library of the Religious Society of Friends, Euston Road; Miss Betty Masters, Deputy Keeper of the Records, Corporation of London; Miss Elizabeth Broome of *The Builder* library; Miss Janet Howell and Mr Roger Dowdell of Hastings Borough Council Solicitor's Department, and Miss Phyllis White, for information on the America Ground, Hastings; the staffs of the Guildhall Library, the British Library, the Historical MSS Commission, the Public Record Office Chancery Lane, British Transport Historical Records (PRO) Porchester Road, Wandsworth Public Library, Lambeth Public Library, Surrey Record Office.

For the post-World War 2 period there was plenty of real documentation to call upon, and in addition I am indebted to many partners and members of the staff of Drivers Jonas past and present for information and help in a number of ways, particularly Mr William Bishop and Mr Philip Jonas for a valuable account of their activities. My thanks are also due to Mrs Ainslie Johnston for all her help and the anonymous cataloguer of the Drivers Jonas documents in store at Boreham Wood.

H. B-K.

Chronological Table

1692   Samuel Driver 1 born (son of Charles Driver 1)
1699   Charles Driver 2 born (son of Charles Driver 1)
1719   Samuel Driver 1 marries Ann (?)
1720   Samuel Driver 2 born (son of SD 1)
1734   Samuel Driver 2 apprenticed to Tom Bincks
1741   Samuel Driver 1 dies
1754   Samuel Driver 2 marries Jane Purshouse
1755   Abraham Purshouse Driver 1 born (son of SD 2)
1758   William Driver born (son of SD 2)
1778   A. P. Driver 1 marries Ann Neale
1779   A. P. Driver 2 born (son of APD 1)
        Samuel Driver 2 dies
1783   Edward Driver born (son of APD 1)
1788   Charles Burrell Driver born (son of APD 1)
        William Driver marries Ann White
1789   Samuel White Driver born (son of WD)
1794   George Neale Driver born (son of APD 1)
1812   Charles Burrell Driver marries Ann Manning
1816   Robert Collier Driver born (son of CBD)
1819   William Driver dies
1821   Abraham Purshouse Driver 1 dies
1825   *100th Anniversary*
1850   George Neale Driver marries Mary Hutchinson
1852   Robert Collier Driver marries Maria Robson
        George Neale Driver becomes paralysed
        Edward Driver dies
        Charles Burrell Driver dies
1853   Charles Driver born (son of RCD)
1854   Maria 'Cissie' Driver born (daughter of RCD)
1855   George Neale Driver dies

1856	Robert Manning Driver born (son of RCD)
1857	James Hutchinson Driver (solicitor) born (son of RCD)
1860	Henry Jonas apprenticed to Charles Adams, surveyor
1863	Henry Jonas completes apprenticeship as surveyor and valuer
187?	Henry Jonas joins staff of Messrs Driver
1877	Arthur C. Driver born (son of Charles Driver)
1878	Henry Jonas becomes partner of Messrs Driver
	Henry Jonas marries Cissie Driver
1879	Harold Driver Jonas born (son of Henry Jonas and Cissie Driver)
1881	Robert Jonas born (son of Henry Jonas)
1888	Maria (Cissie) Jonas, née Driver, dies
1898	Robert Collier Driver dies
1905	Harold Driver Jonas marries Catherine Griffith
1906	Henry Jonas 2 born (son of Harold Driver Jonas)
1914	Philip Jonas born (son of Harold Driver Jonas)
1925	*200th Anniversary*
1928	Henry Jonas 1 dies
1935	Robert Manning Driver dies
1936	James Driver dies
1940	Philip Jonas becomes partner
1941	Christopher Jonas born (son of PGJ)
1943	Arthur Driver dies
1945	William Bishop becomes partner
1950	Harold Driver Jonas retires
1953	Harold Driver Jonas dies
1958	Robin Bishop becomes partner
1969	Christopher Jonas becomes partner
1971	William Bishop retires
1974	Philip Jonas retires
	Robin Bishop becomes Senior Partner
1975	*250th Anniversary*

Full Partners 1725–1975

(AND DATE OF THEIR PARTNERSHIP)

Samuel Driver 1	1725–41
Charles Driver	1725–?
Samuel Driver 2	1741–79
Abraham Purshouse Driver	1776–1821
William Driver	1779–1819
Edward Driver	1804–52
Samuel Driver 3	1806–57
George Neale Driver	1815–55
Robert Collier Driver	1837–98
N. A. Bowlen	1871–5
Charles Driver	1874–98
Robert Manning Driver	1877–1935
Henry Jonas	1878–1928
Arthur Charles Driver	1898–1943
Harold Driver Jonas	1900–50
Robert Collier Jonas	1902–1919
Philip Jonas MC FRICS	1940–74
William Bishop CBE FRICS	1945–71
Donald Whittaker FRICS	1948–58
Robin T. Bishop MA FRICS MRTPI	1958–
Eric R. Real FRICS	1958–
Anthony R. Eden FRICS	1962–75
Ken Clemens FRICS FRTPI	1965–
P. (Sandy) A. Copland BSC FRICS	1969–
Christopher W. Jonas FRICS	1969–
Bernard P. Holland BSC FRICS	1973–
Hugh M. Rayner FRICS	1973–
Rex Mercer FRICS FRTPI	1973–
David E. H. Chapman BSC ARICS	1974–

Offices 1725–1975

1725–1741	Samuel Driver at unknown address in Wandsworth
	Charles Driver at unknown address in Rotherhithe
1741–1816	Kent Street Road, Southwark
1816–1826	13 New Bridge Street, Blackfriars
1826–1850	8 Richmond Terrace, Parliament Street, Whitehall
1850–1863	5 Whitehall
1863–1898	4 Whitehall
1898–1919	23 Pall Mall
1919–1956	7 Charles Street (later renamed Charles II Street)
1956–1958	32 Hertford Street
1958–1969	7 Charles II Street
1969–	18 Pall Mall

Bibliography

F. M. L. Thompson, *Chartered Surveyors, The growth of a profession*, London: Routledge & Kegan Paul, 1968

John H. Harvey, *The Nurseries on Milne's Land-Use Map* [surveyed 1795–9; published 1800] Transactions of the London and Middlesex Archaeological Society, Vol 24, 1973

Ronald Webber, *Market Gardening*, Newton Abbot: David & Charles, 1972

Ronald Webber, 'London's Market Gardens', *History To-day*, pp. 871–8, December, 1973

Helen G. Nussey, *London Gardens in the Past*, London, 1939

John Abercrombie, *The Hot-house Gardiner on the General Culture of the Pine-apple and Method of Forcing Early Grapes, Peaches, Nectarines and other Choice Fruits*, Newington Butts, 1789

James Maddock, *The Florists Directory*, Walworth, 1792

Robert H. Jeffers, 'The Horticultural Trade: 1804–1954', *Journal of the Royal Horticultural Society*, vol. LXXIX, Part 2, November 1954

Wandsworth Notes & Queries, 'Wandsworth Vestry 1728–35', 'Beating the Bounds 1788', 'Highwaymen in 1734–8', London: Wandsworth and Putney Post Reprint, 1898

Gladys Taylor, *Old London Gardens*, London: Batsford, 1953

The Borough News Handbooks no 1 & no 2

Sherwood Ramsey, *Historic Battersea*, London, 1913

Lyson's Environs of London, vol I. Wandsworth, 1792, vol VI. Lambeth, 1811

Timb's Curiosities of Old London

Gideon Mantell, *History of Surrey* (E. W. Brayley, ed), Geological Section, London, 1841

Edward Boys Ellman, *Recollections of a Sussex Parson*, London, 1912

Batty Langley, *A Sure Method of Improving Estates by Plantations of Oak, Elm . . .*, London, 1728

Edward Laurence, *The Duty and Office of a Land-steward*, Dublin, 1731

Anon. *The Great Improvement of Commons that are enclosed for the advantage of the Lords of Manors, the Poor and the Publick*, 1732

John Cowper, *An Essay Proving that Inclosing Commons and Common-field Lands is contrary to the interest of the nation*, 1732

Nathaniel Kent, *Hints to Gentlemen of Landed Property*, London, 1775

Arthur Young, *Farmers Letters*, London, 1771

Anon. *An Enquiry*, London, 1781

Anon. *Observations of the Enquiry into the Advantages and Disadvantages of Enclosures*, London, 1781

Thomas Stone, *Suggestions for Rendering the Inclosure of Common Fields and Waste Lands a Source of Population and Riches*, 1787

T. Williams, *The Law of Auctions*, London, 1818

John Jackson, *The Auctioneer's Guide . . .* to which is added the Appraiser's Guide, 1823

A Detailed Prospectus of the Auction Mart instituted 1808, London, 1809

John White, *Some Account of the Proposed Improvements of the Western Part of London by the Formation of the Regent's Park, the New Street, the New Sewer*, London, 1815 (2nd ed)

M. F. Bond, 'Witnesses in Parliament, Some Historical Notes', *The Table* Vol XL, 1972, House of Lords Record Office

E. T. MacDermot, *History of the Great Western Railway*, Vol I 1833–63 London, 1927 (revised 1964)

John C. Bourne, *The History and Description of the Great Western Railway*, London: David Bogue, 1846 (David & Charles reprint)

Standing Orders of the Houses of Lords and Commons with regard to Railway Bills, London: James Bigg, 1836

A Civil Engineer, *Personal Recollections of English Engineers and the Introduction of the Railway System in the United Kingdom*, London, 1868

Edwin Chadwick, *Report on the Sanitary Condition of the Labouring Population of Great Britain*, London, 1842

James Woodforde, *The Diary of a Country Parson 1758–1802*, Oxford: University Press (The Worlds Classics) 1949

W. Wroth, *The London Pleasure Gardens of the 18th Century*, London, 1896

Survey of London
  Sir Howard Roberts and Walter H. Godfrey, General Editors
    Vol XXIII, South Bank and Vauxhall
    Vol XXV, St George's Fields

F. H. W. Sheppard, General Editor
Vol XXXVII, North Kensington

Maurice Beresford, *History on the Ground*, London: Lutterworth Press, 1957 (Milton Abbass]

Act of William IV Cap lxxv, 21 June 1836, for making a Railway from the London and Croydon Railway to Dover to be called the South-eastern Railway

Thomas Clarkson, *A Portraiture of Quakerism*, Vol 2, London, 1807

William C. Braithwaite, *The Second Period of Quakerism*, London: Macmillan 1921

William Diplock, *Hastings Past and Present*, 1855

J. Mainwaring Baines, *Historic Hastings*, Hastings 1955

T. W. Horsfield, *History and Antiquities of Sussex*, 'Hastings', p. 450, Lewes, 1835

Victoria History of Sussex, 'Hastings', vol 9

The Corporation of London, Its Origin, Constitution, Powers and Duties, Oxford: University Press, 1956 [Epping Forest, p. 181]

Maps and Plans in the Public Record Office, 1. British Isles c. 1410–1860. London: HMSO, 1967

Cluttons 1765–1965, Cluttons, (duplicated privately circulated)

David Wainwright, *Richard Ellis 1773–1973*, Richard Ellis/Hutchinson Benham, 1973

KENT COUNTY ARCHIVES, MAIDSTONE

Radnor MSS. U 270

Estate – Railway Papers

E 57/1875 Newspapers, prints of Bills, correspondence re South Eastern Railway Company's Bill 1875

E 58/1876 Report on extension from Sandgate to Folkestone

E 59 Circular letter to tenants re extension; replies; posters

E 61 Speeches of counsel re London Chatham & Dover Railway Bill

E 62 Correspondence re Bill

Knocker Collection U 55

B 35 West Peckham, 1838–42

B 40 Westwell 1832–41

Tufton MSS U 55

E 30 Railways 1835–83

Conyngham MSS U 438

E 74 Paper on SE Railway 1836–1903

Parliamentary Papers, Select Committee on Agricultural Distress (1833), V.Q. 11661 – Edward Driver. Session 29 Jan–29 Aug, Vol V, p. 555

Select Committee of House of Lords on Lands Taken by Railways (1845). Report 419; evidence by E. Driver – Q.267 (GWR 1834–5); Q.266–7 and 288 (S.E.Rly).

Report of the Select Committee of the House of Lords appointed to take into consideration the Practicability and the Expediency of establishing some Principle of Compensation to be made to the owners of Real Property whose lands may be compulsorily taken for the Construction of Public Railways. Session 1845

GREATER LONDON RECORD OFFICE AND LIBRARY, COUNTY HALL

Minutes of the Proceedings of the Metropolitan Board of Works, July–December 1875 [freeing of Thames bridges of tolls]
 MBW 1892 Charing Cross Footbridge
 MBW 1896 Lambeth
 MBW 1897 Vauxhall
 MBW 1898 Wandsworth
 MBW 1899 Waterloo
Report of the Metropolitan Board of Works, 1888

CORPORATION OF LONDON RECORD OFFICE, GUILDHALL

Affidavit by R. C. Driver, in Chancery 21 July 1875 between Commissioners of Sewers of the City of London, Plaintiffs v. William Bulkeley Glasse and others, Defendants [re Epping Forest]

PUBLIC RECORD OFFICE, (BRITISH TRANSPORT HISTORICAL RECORDS), PORCHESTER ROAD

File "Early Correspondence", A. 1834–43 GWR. 'Some early Bills of Cost Accounts and Demands made for Professional Services' . . . etc (Ref. HL. 1.16)

Crown Estate Papers

Crest 2/91	Burnham Abbey Estate 1756–1840
Crest 2/212	Bestwall Tithes 1791–1804
Crest 2/19	Cookham Manor; Inclosure 1814
Crest 2/16	Bray, Manor of; Inclosure 1808–14
Crest 2/15	Bray, Manor of; Projected Inclosure 1808–13
Crest 2/30	Ock and Murton, Hundred of, 1733–1859
Crest 35/341	Encroachment of Waste of Windsor Forest, 1810–12
Crest 2/742	Observations and Reports on Plans for improvement of Regents Park, 1811, 1813
Crest 2/746	Negotiations with Duke of Portland etc re laying out Regents Park, 1811–24
Crest 2/1736	Improvements, Regents Park; John Nash's Proposals, 1809–14*
Crest 39/10	Romford, A. P. Driver's survey 1797
Crest 39/37	Burnham Monastery Estate, survey, 1800
Crest 39/13	Valuation of Tithes, Bestwall, Dorset
Crest 2/1	Ampthill, Beds, Enclosure

DRIVERS JONAS ARCHIVES

Survey and Report upon the Scilly Islands . . . Taken by order of the Special Commissioners of his Majesty's Duchy of Cornwall by Edward Driver, 1829

'Reminiscence' of Thomas A. Jones (handwritten, undated)

Indenture re sale of premises to make a public highway from Kent Street to Walworth, December 30, 1780

Licence to build on land at Walworth, December 15, 1788

Preface to Edward Driver's Map of Manor of Lambeth, 1810

Probate of A. P. Driver's will, November 28, 1821

Articles of apprenticeship: C. B. Driver and his son R. C. Driver, February 1 1832

Correspondence re rent collection for estate of late Wm. Brooks, 1854–5

Probate of C. B. Driver's will, March 22, 1855

Paper headed 'Remarks on the valuation of mines'

Articles of clerkship: Samuel Jonas and his son Henry with Charles Frederick Adams, May 2 1860

* includes document headed 'Extract of Mr Nash's Report on the Progress of the Works in Marybone Park'

Statement of umpireship of C. F. Adams re straw and chaff at Foulmire, January 19, 1861

Correspondence between R. C. Driver and Credit Immobilier re purchase of Jefferey's Square, May 1864

Scale of Fees of Messrs Driver, 1866

Letter of Elihu Burritt to Samuel Jonas, April 28, 1868

Copy of magazine *Pump Court* with article on R. C. Driver as auctioneer, June 15, 1889

Deed of apprenticeship of Arthur C. Driver to Henry Jonas, January 30 1895

Papers re activities of the Ananias Club – Tommy Twigg, etc, 1897

Articles of apprenticeship: Henry Jonas, R. M. Driver, A. C. Driver and H. D. Jonas, April 27, 1905

Document of appointment of Drivers Jonas as agents for the Northern Estates of Greenwich Hospital, May 16, 1922

Auction Particulars 1809–1938

Business Index (10 volumes) 1861–1951

Robert C. Driver's Private Ledger 1853–1897 (in the keeping of Mr Philip Jonas)

Letter of Henry Jonas to Maria Driver from Switzerland

NEWSPAPERS AND PERIODICALS

The Times, July 14, 1909, page 9, column 5, report of the meeting of the Land Taxes Protest Committee

The Builder, April 30, 1898, obituary of R. C. Driver

The Journal of the Royal Institution of Chartered Surveyors, May 1898, obituary of R. C. Driver

Index